To the memory of Tara, third mate and
constant companion: for taking the dog
watch, for protecting us from pirates,
harbour thieves and rats

৪৪৪

To all our family and friends who knew
this bold and brave little Jack Russell

To all the people and their dogs who
have travelled this beautiful world
together.

Hubble & Hattie

The Hubble & Hattie imprint was launched in 2009 and is named in memory of two very special Westie sisters owned by Veloce's proprietors. Since the first book, many more have been added to the list, all with the same underlying objective: to be of real benefit to the species they cover, at the same time promoting compassion, understanding and respect between all animals (including human ones!). All Hubble & Hattie publications offer ethical, high quality content and presentation, plus great value for money.

More great books from Hubble & Hattie

Among the Wolves: Memoirs of a wolf handler (Shelbourne)

Animal Grief: How animals mourn (Alderton)

Babies, kids and dogs – creating a safe and harmonious relationship (Fallon & Davenport)

Because this is our home ... the story of a cat's progress (Bowes)

Camper vans, ex-pats & Spanish Hounds: from road trip to rescue – the strays of Spain (Coates & Morris)

Cat Speak: recognising & understanding behaviour (Rauth-Widmann)

Charlie – The dog who came in from the wild (Tenzin-Dolma)

Clever dog! Life lessons from the world's most successful animal (O'Meara)

Complete Dog Massage Manual, The – Gentle Dog Care (Robertson)

Detector Dog – a Talking Dogs Scentwork Manual (Mackinnon)

Dieting with my dog: one busy life, two full figures ... and unconditional love (Frezon)

Dinner with Rover: delicious, nutritious meals for you and your dog to share (Paton-Ayre)

Dog Cookies: healthy, allergen-free treat recipes for your dog (Schöps)

Dog-friendly Gardening: creating a safe haven for you and your dog (Bush)

Dog Games – stimulating play to entertain your dog and you (Blenski)

Dog Relax – relaxed dogs, relaxed owners (Pilguj)

Dog Speak: recognising & understanding behaviour (Blenski)

Dogs on Wheels: travelling with your canine companion (Mort)

Emergency First Aid for dogs: at home and away Revised Edition (Bucksch)

Exercising your puppy: a gentle & natural approach – Gentle Dog Care (Robertson & Pope)

For the love of Scout – promises to a small dog (Isn)

Fun and Games for Cats (Seidl)

Gods, ghosts, and black dogs – the fascinating folklore and mythology of dogs (Coren)

Helping minds meet – skills for a better life with your dog (Zulch & Mills)

Home alone and happy – essential life skills for preventing separation anxiety in dogs and puppies (Mallatratt)

Know Your Dog – The guide to a beautiful relationship (Birmelin)

Life skills for puppies – laying the foundation of a loving, lasting relationship (Zuch & Mills)

Living with an Older Dog – Gentle Dog Care (Alderton & Hall)

Miaow! Cats really are nicer than people! (Moore)

My cat has arthritis – but lives life to the full! (Carrick)

My dog has arthritis – but lives life to the full! (Carrick)

My dog has cruciate ligament injury – but lives life to the full! (Häusler & Friedrich)

My dog has epilepsy – but lives life to the full! (Carrick)

My dog has hip dysplasia – but lives life to the full! (Häusler & Friedrich)

My dog is blind – but lives life to the full! (Horsky)

My dog is deaf – but lives life to the full! (Willms)

My Dog, my Friend: heart-warming tales of canine companionship from celebrities and other extraordinary people (Gordon)

No walks? No worries! Maintaining wellbeing in dogs on restricted exercise (Ryan & Zulch)

Partners – Everyday working dogs being heroes every day (Walton)

Smellorama – nose games for dogs (Theby)

Swim to recovery: canine hydrotherapy healing – Gentle Dog Care (Wong)

A tale of two horses – a passion for free will teaching (Gregory)

Tara – the terrier who sailed around the world (Forrester)

The Truth about Wolves and Dogs: dispelling the myths of dog training (Shelbourne)

Unleashing the healing power of animals (Preece-Kelly)

Waggy Tails & Wheelchairs (Epp)

Walking the dog: motorway walks for drivers & dogs revised edition (Rees)

When man meets dog – what a difference a dog makes (Blazina)

Winston ... the dog who changed my life (Klute)

The quite very actual adventures of Worzel Wooface (Pickles)

Worzel Wooface – The quite very actual terribibble twos (Pickles)

You and Your Border Terrier – The Essential Guide (Alderton)

You and Your Cockapoo – The Essential Guide (Alderton)

Your dog and you – understanding the canine psyche (Garratt)

www.hubbleandhattie.com

For post publication news, updates and amendments relating to this book please visit www.hubbleandhattie.com/extras/ HH4880

First published July 2016 by Veloce Publishing Limited, Veloce House, Parkway Farm Business Park, Middle Farm Way, Poundbury, Dorchester, Dorset, DT1 3AR, England. Fax 01305 250479/email info@hubbleandhattie.com/web www.hubbleandhattie.com
ISBN: 978-1-845848-80-4 UPC: 6-36847-04880-8 © Rosemary & Robert Forrester & Veloce Publishing Ltd 2016. All rights reserved.
Readers with ideas for books about animals, or animal-related topics, are invited to write to the editorial director of Veloce Publishing at the above address. British Library Cataloguing in Publication Data – A catalogue record for this book is available from the British Library.
Typesetting, design and page make-up all by Veloce Publishing Ltd on Apple Mac. Printed in India by Replika Press.

Contents

~ Tara's journey across the oceans ~

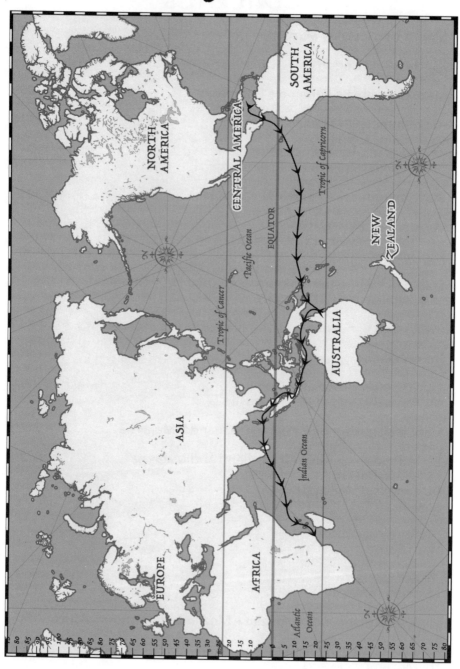

one

How it all began

This is the extraordinary story of a Jack Russell terrier, who sailed the oceans of the world with us, and who was more at home on a boat than on land.

A Jack Russell terrier? Not possible: not that sort of dog. Too lively, too independent, too much personality. Very true, but this bold little soul became a great sea dog, although I have to confess there were times when she felt seasick and miserable, and so did we, but it passed.

Now, I had better explain how Robert, my handsome husband, and I came to be on a boat in the first place.

We were living and working in Brazil in 1987 when Robert's older brother, Michael, died of cancer after a short illness. He was only 49. I can tell you that gave us both such a shock – and started us thinking. One day, out of the blue, Robert suddenly turned to me and said, "What are we doing, working so hard, when we mightn't even make it to 50?"

I glanced at him, and wondered what was coming next.

"I'm tired of all this. We're still young, let's go and look at the world now, and we'll work when we're older."

He had caught my attention.

"And how do you propose we should do this? Hitch-hike and walk, catch buses and trains?" I asked.

Now it was Robert's turn to look surprised. "Good Lord, no, we'll buy a boat and go sailing."

Now, I am sure the first thought that's popped into your heads is, 'Right, that all sounds like a great idea, but, er, how is this going to work in reality?'

Let me fill in a bit of background for you ...

80C8

Robert and I were in Brazil, running a small but successful tour business in Rio de Janeiro, and living in a high-rise apartment. We escaped at weekends to a rustic cottage on a nearby island, so life was comfortable.

We were, however, in Brazil because we had chosen to leave behind our life in Zimbabwe (formerly Rhodesia). Both of us came from farming families, growing up and leading an idyllic lifestyle in Zim, as all us ex-pats now fondly refer to it, surrounded by family and friends, cats and dogs, horses and cows, and, of course, the most wild and beautiful countryside, with well-stocked game parks and broad rivers; high mountain ranges and low, fertile valleys.

Robert and I met and married when I was 23 and Robert 27. We ran a tourist business in Harare (formerly Salisbury), and lived on a small farm some 20km away, where we grew maize and pyrethrum.

Life became complicated in 1973 with the advent of guerrilla warfare: tourists were shot and kidnapped, and we knew our business wouldn't survive this; so we sold it to a large tour operator before the going got too tough, and left for Brazil, by Landrover, in 1974. We had no children to think of; only ourselves.

In Brazil, there was always a cat or a dog, or a parrot, to keep us company. But now we were thinking of selling up and buying a boat, where, surely, an animal on board would mean extra responsibilities – quarantine problems, dealing with illness in the middle of nowhere, no vets, potential heartbreak if the animal fell overboard – the list was endless.

I pushed the thought right to the back of my mind and concentrated on what Robert was saying.

"Let's see if we can persuade Celso Antonio, our Brazilian business partner, to run the company for six months at a time while we go sailing. And then, when we come back, we can give him a break for six months."

I was quietly turning over in my mind the realisation that our only sailing experience was limited to a small boat we once used as a means to get to our island cottage, but as it took all day to get there, we had given it up for something faster – a power boat.

The idea, though, had been born and once we had made up our minds, there was no stopping us ...

෴

After much searching we found the ideal boat in Gibraltar: a previously-owned Oyster 435 ketch, strongly built and able to forgive our inexperience as sailors. For several years we lived on our yacht *Deusa*, crossing the Atlantic from Gibraltar to Barbados, then cruising the Caribbean and North American east coast.

Our next journey was to explore the Pacific, transiting via the Panama Canal. The motor needed an overhaul, and we decided to do this in Cartagena, Colombia, before continuing on our travels. The cost of the piston sleeves and other spares for our Volvo Penta motor were ridiculously expensive in Cartagena, however, and Robert decided it was cheaper to fly to Miami for the parts.

I was waiting for Robert at Cartagena airport on his return, and could see him through the glass partition in the Customs Hall, struggling with a large trolley of boxes, suitcases – and a basket.

"I wonder what's in the basket?" I said to myself, curious to know why he was carrying it so carefully. "Must be very fragile – maybe some crystal whisky glasses."

"Welcome back, the traveller!" I called, running to fling my arms around my tall husband as he emerged from officialdom, unscathed and with all the baggage. Living on a boat in such close proximity, through all the ups and downs of sea life, we missed each other very much when apart, and were always delighted to be reunited. "What have you got in that basket?"

"It's for you, I just had to bring you back something from Miami!" He laughed, giving me a big hug.

The basket felt wobbly ... crystal doesn't wobble. I rested the basket on one of the boxes of the trolley and carefully opened the lid. There, on a red-striped towel, stood a tiny, black-and-white puppy with surprised brown eyes. Not half as surprised as mine, though, I can tell you.

"Oh my goodness, a dog!" I cried, totally amazed, "You've brought me a little dog!"

I scooped her up and held her soft, furry body against my cheek. She stuck out her little pink tongue and licked me on the nose, her warm puppy breath smelling of milk and biscuits. It was love at first sight.

"Aren't you beautiful, you wriggly little thing, you. What's your name? Oh, Robert, what a crazy surprise! Where did you find her?"

"Let's get back to the boat and I'll tell you the whole story: it's quite a saga."

We called a taxi, loaded it up, and sped off to the boatyard with the new addition to our family wide awake and bright-eyed curled up in my lap, taking in all the new and strange surroundings.

Apparently, Robert had been sitting in our friends' house in Florida, paging through the *Miami Herald*, waiting for a phone call about the engine spares. An SPCA advert offering puppies to good homes caught his eye.

"That's it – I'll get a dog while I'm waiting. I do miss having an animal," he thought to himself and off he went to the SPCA. A dear little terrier-type bitch with a black patch over her eye won him over, and he paid for her 3-in-1 shots and de-worming, arranging to collect her in a few days' time.

"I've gone and got a dog, and she's going sailing with us," he told our friends, much to their astonishment. "Oh, wow!" they all gasped, "what an amazing thing to do!"

In typical spontaneous and generous American fashion, they organised a puppy shower party, with gifts of a soft basket, a string bag for taking towels and toys to the beach, a ball, food and water dishes, fancy collar and lead; in fact, more things than would fit in the suitcase.

On returning to the SPCA several days later, Robert was met by a teary-eyed assistant, who told him his puppy had been put down as she had had diarrhoea.

"You could've phoned me," he said, rather cross, "you'd no right to destroy her. Wasn't it my decision whether or not to take the dog?"

"I'm so sorry," said the distraught girl, "it's SPCA policy to euthanise animals showing signs of sickness, in case it spreads through the kennels. Your puppy got an upset tummy from the shots."

They gave him back his money, but it was a furious Robert who marched away without a dog. He now had a load of gifts from caring friends and no puppy to go with them. So he picked up the *Miami Herald* again, and this time looked in the 'Dogs for sale' column. There, in the middle of the page, was an advertisement for Jack Russell puppies, six weeks old and ready to leave their mother.

"Ah," he thought, "I must be meant to get a dog, because here is the answer to all the presents."

Talking about getting a dog is one thing, but to actually go out and find one is entirely a different matter. But once Robert has his mind set on something, he doesn't give up easily, so he was soon on his way to Palm Beach in the rental car.

A plump lady in slippers and curlers, a cigarette dangling from her fingers, welcomed him at the front door of her home, and invited him in to see the puppies, all yipping and falling about in their pen. One particular little bitch barked at Robert, running over to check his feet and friendly hand. She was bold and bright, and he immediately liked her positive attitude and pretty markings.

"I'll take this one," he said, picking up the wriggling, nibbling puppy. Little did he know just how bold and bright this little girl was going to be!

At that time Tara had no name; she was just 'the puppy.' And, as 'the puppy' she was bundled up in a little basket with a tiny teddy bear to keep her company. The teddy was from the mother's nest and smelt of her and all Tara's brothers and sisters, so was a comforter for the lonely nights ahead when she was in unfamiliar surroundings and missed her family. (The bear stayed with her for years until she tossed it overboard by accident.)

While still waiting for some Volvo parts to be delivered, Robert and Tara had a couple of days in which to spend quality time together. Robert took her to the club when he went to play tennis with friends; they went shopping, and sat around in the house watching TV. Tara soon got used to wearing a miniature harness and lead when she went out, and it must have been a very funny sight, this great big man with his tiny dog scampering along beside him.

With all the puppy shower gifts he needed to buy another suitcase, so, tucking Tara under his arm, he went looking for luggage. At a large department store he put her on the floor to sniff around while pulling suitcases off the rack. She needed to pee and, as the puddle spread across the floor, he looked at it with alarm, trying to swish it away under the luggage rack with his shoe, but, the more he swished, the more it spread in great, shiny sheets.

How can a puppy pee so much?, he marvelled. He spotted an assistant striding down the shop towards him, so, grabbing Tara and the case, he darted into the next aisle, pretending to be fascinated by fishing rods. The uniformed lady stopped at the puddle and looked around for a culprit. A mother and child strolled past and she glared at them accusingly. From then on Robert armed himself with a supply of paper napkins whenever he went out with his young companion!

At last the boat spares arrived and they could return to Colombia. Robert had all the correct papers, vaccines, shots and permits for Tara, and told staff at the airline check-in that the little dog was travelling on his lap.

"That's not possible," said the harassed airline representative, tired after a long day handling passengers, "go and speak to cargo at the end of these counters. The dog will have to travel in the hold."

"No way!" Robert glared at the weary man. "Animals die in the hold. You've heard the horror stories of pets frozen to death or suffocating from lack of oxygen?"

Tara looked mournfully at the fellow from the safety of Robert's strong arms, her big, brown eyes imploring him not to banish her to the belly of the aircraft. It was as if she knew things weren't going too well, and it was to do with her.

The airline man sighed, running his fingers through his short, stubby hair. He had dogs of his own at home, and felt sorry for her. "Very well then, I'll call the captain: he's the one to decide."

Eventually, the captain arrived, smart in his gold braid and blue blazer, and had a good look at the pesky passenger and his little puppy.

"Okay, the dog is very small," he said in his smooth, South American accent, "you travel with her on your lap, right at the back of the plane. You not let her go. Any pee-pee, any poo-poo, you clean up, Senhor!"

What a relief! The pair were soon settled in the aircraft, and Tara endeared herself to the air hostesses, who made a big fuss of both of them. During the flight they often came back to cuddle the little dog and bring Robert a whisky. One girl put the puppy on the floor to stretch her legs, and, seeing an opportunity to explore this strange place of exotic smells and many feet, Tara darted off under the seats, trailing her lead.

"Help! Help! The little dog's run away", screeched one of the girls in panic. "Call her back! Call her back!"

"I can't call her back", explained Robert, "she doesn't have a name yet. Go find her and watch out for the captain."

He said it was the funniest sight: all the air hostesses in their elegant jackets, scarves and tight skirts, crawling around on hands and knees, peering under the seats, calling "come, come, come, little dog," and no little dog to be seen. Passengers fidgeted and frowned as the search went on, wondering if there was a bomb scare. Aeroplanes are big, noisy places and Tara soon got scared, weaving her way back under the seats to the safety of Robert's familiar shoes.

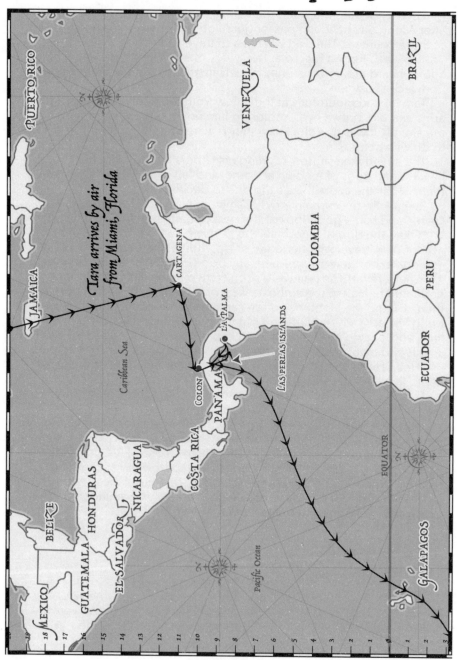

two

Colombia and Panama

Having a puppy on board is a bit like having a new baby in the house: we soon discovered that *everything* changes. A space is made for the new member of the family, and there is another, small life to care for, entertain and feed. Luckily, a good supply of designer dog food arrived with the luggage, and we were able to buy more of it in Cartagena. Our yacht was in the boatyard waiting for the parts to be installed in the motor.

Tara needed to go for a walk twice a day to exercise her little legs and answer calls of nature, and it was quite an operation to get her off and back on board. The wooden cradle that supported *Deusa* put our deck at least four metres above the concrete ground because of her two metre keel. It was bad enough climbing up and down a long and wobbly ladder on one's own, but a wriggling puppy under one arm made it was even more perilous. (Some of the worst accidents sailors suffer are when their boats are high and dry in yards, due to risky ladders, bad scaffolding, or stumbling on a length of rope to pitch head first onto the hard concrete below.)

The friendly Colombian yard folk enjoyed playing with our puppy when she descended from her lofty perch, picking her up with their greasy, paint-stained hands, and rubbing their prickly chins on her smooth, black face. She loved it, returning the attention with slobbery kisses.

All puppies like to chew and nibble on things, and, in this respect, there was some very dubious stuff for her to try out on the filthy yard floor: blobs of black muck, muddy water, oily rags, scrapings of anti-fouling paint; discarded food. What a temptation for a young dog, sticking her pink tongue into everything lying around the boatyard. We rushed her out of there as quickly as possible to play on a strip of grass nearby, where she could scamper after a ball like a little clockwork toy, and roll in the sunshine, exposing her pale tummy to the sky. After a couple of days, however, we noticed that said tummy was covered in angry red spots, and her eyes were swollen and watery. She was scratching like mad as if she had an allergy - later, I saw a worker spraying herbicide on a patch of weeds, which must have been what caused her terrible discomfort. We gave up walking on that piece of grass.

TARA

How did Tara get her name? Well, we wrote a long list of possibilities to suit this happy little soul, with her black-and-tan face and white-flagged forehead, one of which was Ara, a star present in the night sky when she was born. But when we tried calling 'Ara! Ara! Ara!' it just didn't sound right. Adding a T made it much more distinct, and so,with much ceremony, a big hug and a sprinkling of water, she was named Tara, and soon got to know her name, pricking up her floppy little ears, rushing to greet us whenever we called her.

We didn't realise it at the time, but, when we booked into the boatyard, we found ourselves located in quite a notorious area of Cartagena.

"Don't walk out of the gates," warned several of the workers, "there's some bad guys around here."

"Why's that?" I asked, "the people we've met seem very nice."

"Oh no, you must be careful," the yard manager shook his head, "this is where the rich folk come to buy drugs. You'll see them in their fancy cars, driving down the street outside the yard. You can buy a gram of cocaine for $2 and a crystal of crack for 50 cents. Marijuana is available by the bundle!"

Robert once lost his way walking to a hardware shop, and ended up in the slum backing onto the yard. People were most interested in him, thinking he was a prospective client, calling "Hey, amigo, you want to buy something? Let me show you what I've got." The expensive cars were certainly there, cruising this scruffy part of town with its dirt roads and open sewers.

Because of the local criminal presence, two large, fierce dogs were released each night into the yard to guard it, which meant that, living on board, we couldn't get off the boat, even if we wanted to pee. We resorted to using a couple of empty, 2-litre coke bottles, which became the best solution for daytime as well, because there was just one toilet in our corner of the boatyard, without a seat, and used by at least twenty workers. Luckily, Tara never met the guard dogs as they would have snapped her up in one gulp. She was taken down for her last pee before they were let out at 10pm, and the first pee of the morning at 6am when they were locked up again. Tara was very good, she could go all night – unlike us!

Quite often the police came round to the boatyard, checking registration numbers on the power boats, climbing up ladders to run their hands over the hull, feeling if the numbers were sanded out and others applied. They told us that the drug trade was very profitable, and some owners sank their boats in the bay after a particularly good run to conceal the evidence.

Finally, after twelve difficult days, *Deusa* went back in the water with her newly-repaired engine, and we were able to motor out to the anchorage, heaving a huge sigh of relief to be free of the yard.

One morning, I was chatting on the VHF radio with a friend, Tara playing beside me in the cockpit, when she tumbled off the seat onto the cockpit floor (known as a 'sole' in a boat). She yelped, and I saw her back leg was caught in the cockpit drain.

"Help! Help!" I called to Robert, who was working down below. "Quick, Tara's fallen and hurt her leg."

He rushed up on deck, scooped her up and checked her right hind leg, which seemed to be all right. However, she limped when she walked, so we decided to take her to a vet in town just to make sure. This was only her second ride in a car, and even though her leg must have been hurting, she sat very still on my lap, enchanted by the view as we passed by. This little dog hardly ever cried out in pain during all her long life with us, even when we knew she was suffering. She was incredibly brave and stoic, and if anything was wrong, all she would do was give a warning nip, as if to say "Be careful, that hurts."

Dr Ingrid, the swarthy, round-faced vet, listened as I explained in my halting Spanish how Tara had fallen and jammed her leg in the cockpit drain. She took an x-ray, saw there was a green stick fracture, and bound it up in a plaster cast, with instructions to bring Tara back in twenty days. Poor Tara: what a miserable thing to happen to a puppy.

Now we had to be careful that the plaster didn't get wet, especially as Tara loved to participate in any action that involved water! Jack Russells aren't known to be water dogs, but Tara certainly had the mindset of a Labrador in this respect, and plunged into all puddles, streams, washing bowls and the sea whenever she got the chance. Laundry was no exception, and when I had a tub full of suds on the back deck she was right there, pulling out the shirts as fast as I put them in.

"Hey, Tara, little dog, put those clothes back! They're not clean yet; we have to leave them to soak." She pricked up her ears and cocked her head to one side, a shirt collar seized in her small, sharp teeth. You'd think she really understood what I was saying.

"Good dog, let go," I commanded, grabbing the rest of the wet shirt, but this had now become a game, and she backed off, taking a better grip on the dripping garment, growling ferociously in her puppy voice, and shaking her head, as if to say "It's mine, it's mine, *you* let go!"

Of course, I won by picking her up and prising open her locked jaws. You could see her thinking, "Just you wait, I'll grow bigger and stronger, and then we'll see who wins the laundry war!"

Some days later we noticed the plaster cast was slowly working its way down Tara's leg like a loose boot. I hoped it wasn't from getting wet in the long grass when we went walking, or playing in puddles when my back was turned, so I took her back to Dr Ingrid's surgery. Unfortunately, she was away that day, so I spoke to her assistant, who agreed something was wrong. They disappeared with Tara into a back room. When I heard her yelping in pain I rushed to rescue her, but was barred at the door. Finally, she appeared from the depths of the surgery with a nice new, white plaster, looking very unhappy.

"Oh my poor dog, what have they done to you? Why were you crying, you're such a brave girl, you never cry!" I cradled her in my arms and carried her to the waiting taxi. This time she was not so enthused about the car ride, lying silently in my lap with her eyes half-closed.

The vet told us the cast should stay on for at least four weeks, by which time we should have transited the Panama Canal and would have to look for a vet in Panama City to remove the plaster.

ജാരു

Our return to Panama was a bumpy, three-day passage, with strong winds and rough seas. Not a good introduction to sailing life for the newest crew member, who was not only coping with a heaving boat, but a sore and plastered leg as well. We kept Tara down below in her cosy bed, and only brought her on deck when nature called. Unfortunately, she developed diarrhoea, which meant even more visits to the foredeck, where she had to keep her balance and we had to ensure that the plaster did not get wet from the waves splashing onto the deck.

It was at times like these that Tara must have wished she was still with her mother, and we wondered about the wisdom of having a dog on board. One thing about these frequent visits to the foredeck was that Tara soon learnt to pee and poo on command. In our later travels by car and train, all we had to say was "Pee pee, Tara!" and she would oblige. Neat trick! Robert told me he chose a bitch instead of a dog because a dog cocks his leg: quite a balancing act in a rough sea!

One day I was playing with Tara on the yacht club lawn in Colon harbour in Panama, waiting to transit the canal, when I noticed something funny about her skin. Robert strolled past and I called him over. "Have a look at this. Tara's coming out in red bumps all around her neck and by her plaster." "I see what you mean" he said, stroking Tara's little head as she gazed up at him with trusting eyes. "Let's see if we can find a vet here in Colon; this looks quite bad."

Being sailors, we have many medical challenges while at sea and on remote islands, so we carry a lot of reference material, including a couple of wonderful books called *Where there is no doctor* and *Where there is no dentist*. Someone needs to write *Where there is no vet*!

Omar Lorenzo, the burly Panamanian vet who mainly dealt with large animals, came on board, and said it could be lice, recommending a very poisonous injection of Lindane (normally used for sheep; perhaps he wasn't used to dealing with dogs). Robert and I looked at each other in horror, decided that this was far too violent a remedy for such a small animal, and began asking around amongst our sailing friends for other solutions.

Someone knew a vet called Sandy, single-handing her boat, *L'il Bit*, in the Rio Dulce area of Guatamala. She came up on a regular SSB (Single Side Band) radio schedule, the yachting community's way of keeping in touch by long distance. We called her and explained Tara's troubles, as well as the rather evil smell coming from the plaster cast.

The radio crackled and spluttered and we couldn't at first hear what she was saying, but finally the words came through the static.

"Cut off the plaster immediately" she advised, "something's gone wrong under the cast, and that's causing the infection. If I'm right – and I'm pretty sure I am – put her on a course of broad spectrum antibiotics for at least ten days and then call me back."

We kept a good medical supply on board and had the antibiotics Sandy recommended. Having both lived on farms in Africa, we knew that human medication can be used for animals in the correct dosage.

With great difficulty, and holding down a wriggling nipping dog, we snipped away at the solid plaster, little by little revealing a rotting, smelly leg, oozing pus, and with a nasty cut on one side. Sandy was right, and we also realised why Tara had been yelping in the vet's rooms in Cartagena. They had cut her leg with the saw when removing the original cast, never admitted to it, and placed a new cast over the wound. Now, she was covered in sores from this septic cut. Poor little dog, she was very unhappy, and so were we. The antibiotics worked, thank goodness, and, combined with swimming in the sea every day, the sores and her leg soon began to heal, and Tara was once again the cheerful little soul we had grown to love so much.

⁎⁎⁎

Tara and I met several yachtfolk walking their dogs as we enjoyed our twice-daily romp on the yacht club lawns. One girl, with a blue-eyed Husky, told me the most remarkable story. They were sailing along the Panama coast, about seven miles offshore on a dark and windy night, when they realised that their beloved dog was no longer on board. In dismay, they turned around their boat, back-tracking on their course, desperately searching the black waters with a powerful spotlight, but in the wind and the rain, there was no chance of spotting their dog. Arriving at the next anchorage, they sent out desperate messages to sailing friends, spoke to locals and hired a car, driving back along the shoreline, speaking to villagers just in case a strange, blue-eyed dog had been found. They were quite sure that their dog had drowned, in reality: seven miles to shore on a pitch black night is a very long way, after all.

The couple cruised the Panama area for several months, not hurrying through the canal, like most of us. Some time later they were telling the sad story of their lost pet to local residents, when one of them looked surprised. "Wait a minute," he said, "we know an equally strange story of a blue-eyed dog turning up on a farm, half-starved, thin as a rake, with matted hair full of burrs; obviously a family pet; quite friendly. The owners of the farm fed him and then started asking around amongst the foreign community, but no-one had lost a dog. You know how it is amongst foreigners, there are not that many of us, and these stories get passed around. This could be your dog!"

Well, you can just imagine the incredible hope these people felt as their friend started to make phone calls, track down the farmer, and determine whether the dog was still there. Amazingly, he was, and they were reunited with their beautiful Husky. I looked at this handsome dog with great respect: what an incredible animal he was to survive that swim, find a home, and finally meet up with his owners again.

three

Panama Canal

Transiting the Panama Canal is a great adventure. So much paperwork to complete: measure the boat, arrange for friends, relatives – anyone! – to help with the line handling, book the boat for a transit day, see who would be rafted alongside, arrange for a pilot to guide us through. Line handling was a most important task, and without four able-bodied people on board, besides Robert as captain, we would not be allowed to transit. We had to have two handlers at the bow and two at the stern to help guide *Deusa* into and out of each lock, via heavy ropes attached fore and aft of the boat.

A lot of the documentation was completed at the canal offices, and meant a taxi ride into town, to which Tara was invited, much to her joy. Off we went, papers under one arm and our little dog under the other, all dressed up in her smart red harness and matching lead. Looking so cute, and being such a lively little animal, everyone wanted to cuddle her, particularly the ladies, so it was never a problem taking her into offices or restaurants.

Our niece and nephew, Didi and Greg, arrived from California to be line handlers, laden with lots of American treats and a case of wine. Our other line handlers were Panamanian friends, Joe Wolff, and his partner, Anna. Big Joe – in his dark glasses, baseball cap, gold watch, and droopy moustache – had been a canal pilot, and now drove tug boats in the harbour. Having done the transit many times on yachts, he was an excellent person to have aboard, as was the glamorous Anna, an administrator in the Panama Canal Authority office.

The journey through the canal from the start of the lock gates on the Atlantic side to the finish of the lock gates on the Pacific side is 48 miles, with the lock gates taking up 1.9 miles of this distance. It is possible to make both sets of locks in a day with the very early start necessary to cover the mileage, and a fast yacht could make it all the way through. However, we thought it would be much more fun to spend the night in the man-made Gatun Lake that linked the two sets of locks.

On the day of the transit we waited, jittery and tense, in the anchorage for the pilot to come on board, beady-eyed Tara keeping a sharp lookout from her favourite perch on the life raft atop the cabin roof. This essential piece of *Deusa's* equipment was our security in case we should do something drastic, such as sink in mid-ocean. It sat in a very accessible place, and all we had to do was toss it overboard, and a rip cord attached to *Deusa* would pop it open into an eight-man raft with provisions, water, fish hooks, flares, pencil and paper (as if one wanted to make notes while shipwrecked), compass, and other survival essentials.

If anyone came too near *Deusa*, Tara would leap from the life raft onto the deck, sounding the alarm that we were being invaded. It didn't matter if it was friend or foe, it was still an invasion as far as she was concerned. Other people in the anchorage found it quite bothersome to be near a barking dog, but for us it was an excellent early warning system that we were about to have visitors, welcome or not.

After some delay and a few urgent phone calls, the pilot boat came alongside and dropped off an immaculately-dressed Panamanian. Sr Roger, in his bright white uniform and shiny black shoes, was ready to guide us on our intrepid journey through one of the most amazing feats of engineering of the last century. In theory, all captains of yachts and ships transiting the canal have to relinquish their authority to the Canal Pilot, who guides their vessel through the canal, but, in reality, Robert always remained at the helm, and Roger sat beside him, giving instructions.

No-one thought to introduce Tara to the pilot as we lifted the anchor and got under way, and, feeling that she was being ignored, she decided to make her presence known. Climbing down from her perch, she crept along the deck, heading for Roger's white-socked foot as it rested comfortably on the cockpit sole under the table. He was explaining to Robert how we would enter the first lock and possibly raft up with another yacht behind a large Panamax container ship. Just as he reached a crucial point in the briefing, he let out a yelp of surprise and lunged for his leg.

"What's happening?" said Robert, looking around for approaching danger, then spotted Tara sneaking away. She had taken an instant dislike to the pilot with his strange-accented English and bulging briefcase of canal paperwork, so had nipped him in the ankle. Tiny, needle-sharp puppy teeth can bring tears to a grown man's eyes. And Roger was not amused.

There were many apologies, soothing words, offers of strong coffee – perhaps a tot of rum? – and Tara was whisked away to be contained by a crew member. With so much going on she hated to be restrained, so wriggled and kicked to get free and join in the fun.

We were all allocated points of control. Greg and I were on the aft deck of *Deusa* to handle the stern lines, and Joe and Anna were on the foredeck to take the bow lines, tossed to us from the canal line handlers standing high on the pathways of the lock.

"I'll take care of Tara!" Didi volunteered, keeping Robert and the pilot company under the shade of the awning, our small dog held firmly in her lap.

Four lengths of strong rope were needed on board, each measuring a hundred feet in length. These went from *Deusa* up to the line handlers on shore. The only way they could pick up our heavy rope was to throw down a thin line with a 'monkey's paw' knot at the end, which we tied to our ropes and the shore people hauled them up. In the effort to get it all correct, not miss the tossed line, be good deckhands and look efficient, we overlooked the one crew member who really liked to catch a ball!

Roger instructed Robert to motor ahead slowly until he was into the first lock, whose open gates were like welcoming arms to embrace us and send us on our way. The shore line handlers looked tiny as they waited, twelve metres above us, on the high walls, the lines curled in their hands ready to throw down to us.

As the 'monkey's paw' soared through the air, this was just too much for Tara, and she wriggled free of Didi, rushing to the bow with a yap of delight, tripping up Anna, who was waiting to make the catch. As Anna stumbled and fell, Joe leapt for Tara and floored her with a rugby tackle. By now both Joe and Anna were in a heap on the foredeck with a flattened dog under them, so missed catching their lines. The handlers on the wall frantically gathered up the lines to throw again. Robert kept *Deusa* moving forward slowly as the pilot shouted to Joe and Anna.

"Hey, you two, stop messing about with that stupid dog and get those ropes ashore: time is running out."

Roger, understandably, didn't much care for Tara, and his ankle was still stinging from her painful nip. Didi rushed forward to grab Tara and carried her away in disgrace to spend the rest of the passage below decks, until we got through the three locks to Gatun Lake, at that time the largest man-made lake in the world; its locks the most massive concrete structures ever built.

Yachts are tied together to transit the locks but, as there was no other yacht scheduled to transit with us, we were on our own behind a massive Panamax container ship called *Bright State*. Each lock was just 33 metres wide by 320 metres long, and Panamax ships were made specifically for the canal, and didn't exceed certain measurements. We'd been warned that when these monsters started their motors to move forward, we would get hurled about, and alarming stories circulated the anchorage of yachts being smashed against the sides of the lock because of big-ship backwash. The big ships had their own line handlers: heavy tractor 'mules' weighing 55 tons, which ran on tracks on the walls to guide the ships through the locks.

The great lock gates towering above us slowly closed, and, little-by-little, our view of the open bay and twinkling sea disappeared, leaving us in a huge, high-sided bath with our enormous companion. We could hardly believe that the gates were being powered by just two 40hp motors, which had been operating for the last eighty years!

The first lock began filling with fresh water from the lake, gravity-fed through great, six metre-wide pipes embedded in the 19 metre-thick walls. Up and up we rose, until we spotted our land line handlers nearby, no longer distant stick figures, standing on the canal path. The fill was incredibly fast, taking just ten minutes. In the opposite canal water was flowing out, and a huge red ship slowly sank from view as if it was being carried into the underworld by invisible demons.

"Now you must start your engine, Captain Robert" said Pilot Roger, "and watch out for the wash from *Bright State*.

Roger was a very cool guy, who soon took off his fancy pilot's uniform and made himself comfortable in a T-shirt and shorts, accepting a cup of tea and some cake.

A tense shiver ran through *Deusa's* crew, and those who were standing sat down on the deck in case they were tossed overboard by the swirl. Just as well they did, because we were soon thrashing about like a fish on the hook. How scary it was as we plunged from side to side, skimming the rough walls of the canal. Just one snapped line and we would plunge bow first into the hard concrete. Tara could hear the noise and feel the movement, and added her canine comments by barking hysterically, running round and round the saloon, leaping on and off the sofa, hoping to spin herself out on deck. Getting very hot with all this excitement she threw herself into her water bowl on the galley floor, sloshing water everywhere.

Once again we carried out this procedure for the second lock, motoring in behind *Bright State,* waiting for the lock gates to close behind us so that water could flow in and lift us to the third step. All-in-all the three lock gates at Gatun raised us by 26 metres to join the Gatun Lake. The locks are all operated by gravity, and an amazing 52 million gallons of fresh water is used each time a ship transits the Panama Canal. No wonder they had to build such a very big dam across the Chagres river, creating Gatun Lake.

With a collective sigh of relief we passed through the last lock, and motored quietly into the lake and our anchorage at Gamboa, where we would spend the night. I gave Robert a great big hug, and we all cheered our pilot. The banished Tara was liberated, and we enjoyed the scenery of dense jungle and small islands we passed, even spotting a sloth hanging in a nearby tree. We were more than ready to celebrate with some good Californian wine, and congratulate each other on getting through unscathed, unlike several of our yachting friends whose boats had nasty scars to prove that things can go very wrong.

ഇരുള

I had a lovely little, hand-carved wooden canoe, a 'cayuco' from Guatamala, which was only a couple of metres long, with just enough room for one person, and which we stowed on the foredeck. This was my favourite means of transport whenever we got to an anchorage. A really interesting, jungly island of tall trees near the anchorage beckoned, and, launching the canoe, I happily paddled away with binoculars slung round my neck.

Gliding quietly along the island I heard bird calls and the rustle of leaves as something slithered or scuttled away in the thick undergrowth. The evening light on the calm waters turned pewter and gold, the spiky twigs of the trees stark against the fading sky. Into this quiet reverie dropped another sound: a snuffling, puffing, panting behind me. Turning carefully in the canoe, I saw a small triangular shape cutting a ripple through the water; there, swimming valiantly to catch up, was Tara.

She must have watched me climb down the stern ladder into

the canoe and silently paddle away. Sometimes she was invited to come along, but this time she was told to stay, and may have toppled overboard, leaning far out to catch sight of me as I disappeared into the twilight. No-one saw her go, heard the splash or missed her boisterous presence. They all thought she was exhausted by the day's activities and was curled up asleep in a corner.

The lake was full of alligators and small dogs make tasty snacks, so I quickly hauled her, dripping wet, into the canoe, scolding her thoroughly for following me. She was so pleased with herself that the cross words skimmed over her head.

"I made it! I made it!"' she seemed to say as she leapt from side to side with yips of joy, scattering bright beads of water from her wet coat. Forgetting about bird-watching I had intended to do, I did my best to keep the canoe upright and my binoculars dry, as well as prevent Tara plunging off the canoe in her excitement. Great entertainment was had by all the boats in the anchorage, who watched my dog's determined efforts to capsize the canoe.

Early next morning a new pilot, Wilbur, joined us for the three descending lock gates, and once again Tara was banished below. Thank goodness that, in all the time Tara lived on board, she never figured out how to climb the companionway stairs leading from the saloon to the cockpit, which gave us a fair amount of control over her movements. With Customs and Immigration authorities coming on board at every new island, this was quite important, and she would bark herself hoarse while they sat in the cockpit, unmolested, going through our papers. Of course, we could never pretend there wasn't a dog on board ...

☙ЄӠ

So, here we were, about to leave the Atlantic and cross into the Pacific: goodbye to one ocean and hello to another. Now we had to motor through the narrow, eight-and-a-half mile channel of Gaillard Cut, hewn through solid rock and shale: an artificial valley cutting through the continental divide of Panama, which was considered an amazing engineering feat because it was so tough to dig. Time and again landslides thwarted the workers drilling through rock to lay dynamite, and prevented bulldozers from removing the rubble. Opinion at the time was that the canal would never be completed because of the Gaillard Cut (now known as the Culebra Cut). However, the Americans who had taken over from the French and were now constructing the canal, persisted, as it would make an incredible difference to their shipping routes. Even though it was 500 feet wide, we worried about being a Panamax sandwich if two big ships crossed paths in this restricted area.

The final set of three locks that would step us down into the Pacific lay just beyond Gaillard Cut, starting with the Pedro Miguel Lock that stood 26 metres above sea level, which lowered us by nine metres in order to enter Miraflores Lake, and the next two sets of locks a short distance away. Miraflores could vary in height from sea level because of the great difference in the Pacific Ocean's tides. An extremely high tide meant a drop of only thirteen metres, whilst an extremely low tide meant a twenty metre drop to join the Pacific Ocean in Panama Bay.

Somehow, the decent was not quite as traumatic as the ascent, maybe because we knew what was going to happen, and could be better prepared for any drama. On the descending locks the controllers let the yachts go in front of the big ships in case one broke down, stranding the yachts in the lock. This time, we were tied up with another yacht, our friend Scott on *Inl*, with several solid fenders between our two boats preventing the boats rubbing against each other. (We did all this preparation in the anchorage before heading for Pedro Miguel, our first descending lock.)

Now we couldn't see the lock gates closing behind us, but could watch the gates ahead of us as they slowly grew taller and taller, and we went down and down, as if descending in a lift, with the diminishing water gurgling out around us. Finally, the great, rusty brown-streaked gates eased open to reveal a stretch of smooth water leading to the next lock – Miraflores.

On the ascent to Miraflores we were thrown about a lot more, and the line handlers really had to work at their stations. The descent was much more gentle, although, at one point in the Miraflores lock, Joe wasn't paying attention to his line, and *Deusa* swerved to starboard (right) like a frisky young horse. *Inl*, securely tied on our starboard side, was very vulnerable for a moment, and Scott's eyes grew as round as saucers as he saw his little ship heading for the concrete. Thank goodness a loud shout soon got Joe's attention, and we straightened up again, much to everyone's relief.

Wilbur, a much more serious pilot, didn't strip off to casual gear, and kept on giving commands with a whistle to his lips. Not quite Robert's style – he's more used to blowing the whistle himself! However, Wilbur did endear himself by complimenting him on the competent handling of his yacht.

Moorings at the Balboa Yacht Club were available for yachts to use when waiting to enter the locks, and those that had just come through from the Atlantic, and were now preparing to sail out into the Pacific. For me, as an avid amateur port captain, it was just the best place for ship-watching. A steady stream came and went through the canal – big ones and small ones; even the *QEII* – and we had a ringside view. As the moorings were so close to the canal traffic we weren't allowed to use our dinghies, so the yacht club supplied a taxi service to get us to and from our boats. A bit slow and a bit irregular, but at least it was transport.

ಬಂಥ

Joe and Anna offered to take us on a tour of Panama City, which was founded in 1519, and is full of history and tales of buccaneers such as Francis Drake and Henry Morgan, in search of the Spanish gold. For several centuries, trade routes had existed across the Panama Isthmus, one of which was the Camino Real (the Royal Way) linking Portobelo town on the Atlantic side with Panama City on the Pacific coast.

TARA

"I'll pick you all up tomorrow and we'll make a day of it. We'll show you around." said Joe as they got off *Deusa* and headed ashore.

"Can Tara come, too?" I asked and was given a nod by Joe. We felt sorry for her being alone on board, and hadn't yet rigged up a safety net around the deck to prevent her falling in, or trying to follow us. She was very easy to carry, well-behaved under most circumstances, and everyone loved her.

Fabulous murals lined the walls inside the administration building where Anna worked. They were painted by William B Van Ingen, completed in 1915, and covered about a thousand square feet of wall space. Originally created in New York, the murals were shipped to Panama in several panels, and depicted the construction of the canal in all its stages. It was a hot day, and Tara soon found a fountain to dive into – she had no fear of water and was already showing an inclination of being a great swimmer. The rest of us cooled down with ice creams, and she enjoyed one, too, carefully licked from a hand-held cone. Dogs love sweet things, and this little dog was no exception, always willing to try what we were enjoying, gazing up at us with pleading eyes and ears pricked.

We spent a wonderful day with Joe and Anna, visiting both 'Old Panama' – as the ancient ruins of the first city are called – and 'New Panama,' with its high-rise buildings and fancy restaurants. They dropped us back at the marina in the evening, where we made plans for the following day.

"I must take advantage of the washing machines tomorrow," I commented to Robert as we climbed on board *Deusa* with Tara, having taken a water taxi from the Balboa Yacht Club. "The clothes are piling up, and I may as well do sheets and pillowcases as well; get it all done before we leave."

The next morning we called the water taxi service and headed ashore with a big bag of laundry for me, and an excited Jack Russell for Robert to walk in the club grounds.

"You're going to take much longer than me," said Robert, walking off with Tara. "We'll find our own way back to the boat. See you later."

Robert had a funny story to tell me when I got back with my load of wet and washed clothes. He had been returning to *Deusa* after taking Tara for her promised walk when he saw an irate woman carrying a large bundle of laundry, marching towards him.

"I wonder if she met Rosemary in the laundry room?" thought Robert, "I don't recognize her, but she obviously knows who I am as she's coming straight for me with a fierce look on her face!"

Dropping the pile of washing at Robert's feet, the woman shook her finger in his face.

"Don't you ever, ever think you can change your shirt more than once a day!" she growled, retrieving her bundle and stalking off.

Robert stood there, amazed and dumbfounded, not having a clue who she was, but imagining I had been gossiping with her in the laundry. I had not, and we never saw her again, but the point was made. Laundry on a boat is a continual challenge of water, weather, time and space, and this lady was obviously fed up. A man changing shirts whenever he fancied in this hot and sweaty Panamanian weather was simply not on. Before we set off for the Galapagos Islands and French Polynesia, there was a lot of provisioning to be done, and, from Balboa Yacht Club, with its long walk on the jetty and equally long wait for the water taxi, this wasn't easy. Robert and our friend, Scott, had gone into Panama town looking for boat parts when they made a very interesting discovery. Right downtown near the banking and residential centre of El Pontilla, a new marina - Clube de Yacht y Pesca - was being built by the Intercontinental Hotel.

"Hey, Robert" said Scott, "let's see if we can bring the boats around and anchor here: it's so much closer to the shops and supermarkets."

The pair approached the imposing gates of the marina to be immediately turned away by the officious uniformed guard. It was a private club, and they were not allowed inside the hallowed ground. At that moment, a young fellow turned up, speaking English with a Spanish accent, and was delighted to meet the two yachties, introducing himself as Miguel.

"My dad is a commodore of the club," he said " I'm sure he'll let you stay here for a few days. I'll go and call him."

His father thought it would lend a bit of class to have yachts anchored in the basin, and said we were welcome. However, some of the snobbier club members complained that we were polluting the water in their pristine pool. We weren't the culprits: we saw human waste and sanitary products floating past us every day, and discovered two large, open drains discharging raw sewage into the marina basin. Walking along the seawall, we found a whole lot more, discharging directly onto the beach. Disgusting, and no place to take a dog walking or swimming, so Tara had to be content with short walks around the edge of the basin. Being in a town was always frustrating for her, so we invented games to play on board to use up some of her boundless energy. She was still a young dog, of course, and needed lots of exercise.

However nasty and smelly the yacht basin was - and we couldn't escape the smell by staying below - it was still very convenient for shopping. Scott's girlfriend, Debi, and I made many trips to the nearby supermarkets, carrying loads of purchases to our boats by taxi and dinghy. Provisioning of a boat is hard work, firstly to get the stuff on deck, and then down below to store in all the nooks and crannies, lockers and drawers, securely packed away so that nothing could come free and roll around. Most importantly, it was essential to ensure that nothing could fall into the bilges (the bottom of the boat) and block the bilge pump. Lots of things to consider; lists to be made, my useful and diligent assistant, Tara, 'helping' by chewing pencils and tearing up notebooks.

ಶುಲ೫

Friends often asked us where Tara slept. When she was very young and small, she would curl up at the foot of our bed in the aft cabin, wedged into a corner, but as she grew and took up more space, we made a place for her on the platform behind our bed. Two aft-opening portholes gave a good airflow through the cabin, and this was one of Tara's favourite look-out points, her white toes dangling over the ledge; bright eyes following all the movement in the bay. We always closed these portholes if Tara was below when we left the boat, as she could have wriggled out to follow us. This was her night bed, or 'confined down below' bed.

Then she had her day bed, the puppy shower bed she arrived with from America. This didn't last long, however, as it was soft, and deliciously chewable, so was soon replaced with a handsome Panamanian reed basket, lined with a blanket. The new bed sat on a ledge by the cockpit hatch under the dodger (a spray and wind shelter), and was a snug spot out of the rain and sun.

And toys? All dogs have toys, but Tara was quite possessive with hers, and didn't really like us to join in a game with them. The only thing we played together with was a tennis ball that I threw from the aft cabin, through the corridor, past the galley and saloon, and into the forepeak, giving her around thirty six feet on a straight run. Not much, but enough. She would thunder after the ball, snatch it up, race back to me, leap across the bed and proceed to chew it up. She'd hand it over after a while, all wet and soggy, to be tossed through the boat again.

Tara was almost catlike in some of her games. We had a nice, thick bedcover, which I'd wriggle my fingers under, pretending to be a mouse. She'd leap and pounce with great joy, digging like crazy, trying to find a tunnel under the bedclothes, snapping and grabbing with her sharp teeth. At times the game got too rough, and I had to stop it before the cover – or my hands! – were ripped apart. Tara had so much energy it was hard to keep her exercised when we were at sea, but, like us, some exercise was provided by keeping our balance against the constant movement of the boat.

As Tara grew older she didn't like being cuddled as she had when a puppy. Her strong and independent nature made her a wonderful and entertaining companion, always ready for an outing, a swim, a walk along the beach, but, please, no cuddles!

ಬಿೃಲ

All of the yachts transiting the Panama Canal helped each other as line handlers, and Debi, Scott and I were now going to help our friends, Ken and Paddy, bring their boat *Imago* through the locks to Balboa Yacht Club. Transiting the canal was a great adventure and I did it three times, returning by train all along the lake and the locks, to help the next boat. *Imago* had the Russian boat *Raroia,* with Sven and Annette on board, tied alongside, as they only had an electric motor powered by solar panels, and couldn't make it through the locks on their own. *Raroia* was only twenty-six feet long and home-made, very environmentally-friendly, and so close to the water it was possible to sit in the cockpit and dabble one's fingers in the sea. Too close for me, but ideal for Tara – she could leap into the water with the greatest of ease!

Robert remained on *Deusa* at Flamingo Island, caring for Tara and

Mobay the cat on *Inl,* anchored close by. We would be gone for 48 hours, and it was a safe anchorage where the Panamanian coastguard kept impounded yachts; they slept on board each night, so Robert was in good company.

With *Imago* safely through the canal, we regrouped in the Flamingo anchorage and planned our next passage, poring over the charts.

"Come over for a drink" said Paddy on the VHF radio, "and bring Tara with you; we'll introduce her to Dudley."

It sounded like a good idea. Tara needed to do some socializing, and what better moment to meet this big, black-and-white cat, mascot of *Imago*. We arrived alongside in our dinghy, Tara leaping about, all out of breath and excited, dressed in her harness and lead. She had begun to scrabble onto *Imago's* decks when she was met by a fierce, golden-eyed stare. A sharp swat of a large, prickly cat paw sent Tara spinning back into the dinghy with a yelp of shock and surprise. Dudley stalked off in indignation, his tail in the air, and Tara looked most bewildered, beads of blood spotting her nose.

"Oh dear" I said to Paddy, "perhaps we'd better start again without Tara: we'll take her back to *Deusa*."

But Paddy insisted we come on board with our dog, and we sat in the cockpit, while the cat sat in a huff down below. They never made friends, those two, even though we travelled many thousands of miles in each other's company. Tara saw all cats as enemies from that day on, and nothing could convince her otherwise.

four

The Darien

Our plan was to visit the Darien area of Panama, where many ethnic Indian tribes lived along the rivers of this impenetrable swamp. No road exists between North and South America because of the Darien, and we three boats thought it would be an interesting place to explore: a good adventure - something different.

We stopped for a while in the Las Perlas islands off the Panamanian coast, enjoying the cold, clear water and good fishing we had missed for so many weeks whilst getting through the canal. Now, Tara could scamper to her heart's content along the rocks, chasing crabs and startling seabirds. She liked to play for longer than we did, and it became a battle to get her back to the boat. We tried all sorts of tricks - tasty titbits in our pockets, calling her to catch a crab, inviting her for a swim - so that we could grab her and return to *Deusa*. She soon wised up to this, though, and headed off in the opposite direction as we called, helplessly watching her white tail bobbing off into the distance.

"What are we going to do?" Robert asked me. "It's such a shame to keep her on a lead when there are miles of beach for her to run on, but if she won't come back we're going to lose her. Some islander will eventually pick her up and carry her home to his kids."

"Well, if they can catch her, that is - we certainly can't! We'll just have to hope she'll get tired and hungry and eventually come back to the dinghy. Meanwhile, we may as well bring a good book and a glass of wine and wait!"

Robert laughed. This little dog never got tired; never got bored. Like a clockwork toy she chugged on through the day.

෨෬

The Darien - 11,800 square kilometres of swampland and forest - was a very different experience, with its murky waters, thick mud, and jungle. Our first stop was at the village of Punta Alegre, where we had to anchor at least a mile offshore because of the shallow water. Soon, three canoes headed out to visit us, with offers of rides up the Mague river to visit Indian communities. We did some fierce bargaining, and eventually agreed to go with Carlos in the biggest canoe, a golden-brown Panamanian in a floppy straw hat and grubby T-shirt, who offered the best price, and would pick us up at 6am the next morning.

Meanwhile, it was the last day of carnival at Punta Alegre, and we were invited ashore to meet the villagers and watch a beauty pageant of the local lovelies. Liking the idea, we set off in two dinghies, clutching our dog, to see what the village had to offer. Guiding our dinghies along a tiny channel through black mud to the sticky beach, we were soon surrounded by scores of little kids, laughing and shouting. This was just too much for Tara, who barked hysterically. I don't know who was more alarmed, the kids or the dog, but they all ran away! We muffled Tara and clambered out, dragging our dinghies through the disgusting, smelly gloop, much to the amusement of the watching crowd.

A pretty brown girl in a scarlet T-shirt and green shorts came and introduced herself. "Hi, I'm Kenya" she said, extending her hand in welcome, "I look after foreigners when they come to our village because I learnt English at school. Let me show you around. The government recently built a school and a clinic for us, and things are much better now."

We wandered around the neatly-painted homes and gardens full of flowers. Kenya was very knowledgeable about the plants and trees, taking great pride in explaining the various medicinal cures they offered. A crowd trailed along behind us, and some horribly diseased and mangy dogs snapped and snarled in the background, so Tara remained firmly tucked under my arm, though struggling desperately to get down and join the fray. Did she know she was a dog? Once or twice she met dogs when out walking on the lawn in the Colon Marina, but otherwise had only people for company.

"The judging of the beauty queen is going to take forever" said Scott, who did not fancy wading back to the dinghies in the dark. We were all sitting in the local bar, enjoying a beer and chatting to the people who had gathered around to look at the 'gringos.'

"You're right," Robert agreed, "this is no place to get stuck – the tide's in at the moment, but who knows how long this pageant is going to take?"

Time is not too important in Panama, and what was originally planned for 5pm might not happen until 8. We made our apologies and said we had to catch the high water back to our boats. We had also left Ken guarding the fleet, and even though he probably didn't miss us, if we had not returned by the time it was dark, he might have wondered where we were.

ഇരുഇരു

The next morning we were up at 6am, ready and waiting for Carlos to carry us up-river, raincoats in hand, picnic basket packed, and cameras in plastic bags.

"Tara," I said, crouching down to her level, "this is not a trip for you: it's a long way, so please be a good dog, stay on board, guard the ship, and don't bark when we leave. Uncle Ken will come and visit you as he's staying on *Imago* with Dudley."

TARA

Tara looked at me in disgust – who cared about that beastly cat!

She looked so forlorn as I tucked her up in the back cabin, feeling very guilty about leaving her. She didn't understand why she couldn't play with mangy dogs and chase village chickens.

What a good day we had, visiting the people of Mogue. The big, brown river was lined with tall mangroves buttressed by great roots, and the frothing water from our passing canoe washed through trees unconfined by banks. The ride took about 45 minutes and, as the waterway narrowed, we began to see land plants and small ferns on muddy verges. Finally, we arrived at a landing with a sign announcing 'Mogue Community – Virgin Paradise – this way,' convincing us we weren't the first visitors! A well-trodden path led through thin jungle into a clearing of huts balancing precariously on stilts. It all looked so harmonious and peaceful, so we were shocked to meet two men carrying AK machine guns. Our guide said they were the local police force, but it was a bit too much fire power for our little group! Did they think we were drug traffickers? Of course, the Darien was well known for drug-running from Colombia to Panama, and further north.

Soon, the ladies appeared at the central market place, carrying brightly-coloured woven baskets, plates and pots. Many of the women were bare-breasted, a sarong knotted around their waists and naked babies slung on their hips The baskets were beautiful: tightly woven and dyed with colours of the forest and the earth. The men wore modern-style shorts and had plastic sandals on their feet. Some of the small, naked children were painted in black dye right up to their mouths – to ward off evil spirits, we were told.

Robert got bored with all the bartering and wandered off, landing up in the chief's house.

"Hey, I'm over here," he called as he saw us strolling past, "the chief is inviting us into his home. Climb up the pole."

A single pole with steps hacked into it, and a decorative figurehead carved at the top, lay against the side of the house built on stilts. When visitors are welcome the notches are on top, so one can climb up. If the residents of the house want privacy, they turn the pole so that the notches face downwards. What a neat way of preventing unwanted guests!

Once we had all gathered around the chief's table, a speaker began to explain what the meeting was for. We understood Spanish, so translated for the others. The chief, Sr Leonardo, was the supreme leader of the indigenous people of the Darien, and also a herbalist and botanist, recognised by the Panamanian government. What a handsome brown man he was, square-faced and square-bodied, with bright, penetrating eyes. He told us that healing has three parts: herbal, spiritual and 'secret.' He used the word 'secret' but we wondered if he meant 'mystical,' or was it a secret, not for strangers! He spoke of his wishes for his people and how he hoped to develop tourism to his village. They were in the middle of a healing session when we arrived, and at the back of the platform a sheet hung from the rafters, concealing a person lying on a bench.

"This man is very sick, the doctors have given up on him, and now he comes to me. The doctors can cure some things – they can fix a broken arm, pull out a tooth, sew on a severed thumb – but sickness of the spirit world, that is different. We have always maintained our ancient traditions, and I'm teaching my assistants so we can maintain our ways in this changing world."

"Thank you, Sr Leonardo," responded Robert, "we are all very honoured to be guests in your house today. The world is becoming more and more aware of the healing herbs of the forest, and how necessary it is to preserve them."

The big man smiled and waved as we bade him farewell. The tide was about to turn, and we needed to catch the full river before the water ran out ... and it runs out fast in this great, swampy land.

Robert had spent some twenty minutes with the chief before we arrived, and had learned that they only grew enough food for the village, and took from the sea sufficient only for themselves, and not selling to others. They felt that as long as they had this policy, nature would always provide for them and never let them down. No-one had a better house than his neighbour as they didn't want envy and quarrelling in the community.

Back on board we regaled Ken with our adventures, petted our animals, and showed off our purchases. Then it was time to plan the next move, on up to La Palma, the capital of the Darien, at the mouth of the Tuira River that runs into San Miguel bay. We were all nervous about this part of the journey as the tide can race up to six knots (about 6.5mph) through a narrow gap called 'the cut' – or so we'd been told. When a current moves this fast through a restricted area, it's hard to control the boat, and one hopes and prays that nothing goes wrong, like engine failure or a steering cable break. And there was another good reason for being worried: a large ferro-cement yacht with four adults and three children on board had struck rocks just outside the cut, holing the hull, and very nearly sinking.

The next morning found us anxiously hanging around, waiting for slack high tide to make a run through the gap.

"The more we wait the more nervous I'm getting." I remarked to Robert, clutching Tara so tightly that she squeaked, "Just because we've got the best chart and the deepest keel we're responsible for leading the way. What if we get it wrong?"

"Oh, nonsense, Rosemary, you always worry about things unnecessarily, we'll be fine. We've got a powerful motor, a good depth sounder, and me at the helm." laughed Robert, and thumped the deck next to him, "This is a good, strong ship; she always looks after us."

It was true. We'd had some scary moments in the Caribbean, survived a hurricane, had close shaves with jagged reefs; made some bad decisions, but *Deusa* saw us safely through.

Tara and I sat in the cockpit, my eyes glued to the depth finder, an instrument that showed the depth of water under our keel. Tara had indicated that I should not hold her so tightly, please, so now I just had my arm around her – much more for my comfort than hers. In her dog world she had no fear or sense of danger. Robert stood, white-knuckled, at the helm, feeling his way ever so cautiously through the murky water. It was only a short passage of 200 metres or so, but it seemed we were hours getting through: we heaved a sigh of relief as we turned the corner and saw the little town of La Palma snug along the riverbank ahead of us.

"We're through, we've made it," we called *Inl* and *Imago* on the VHF, "the depth was never less than four metres under the keel."

The yellow ferro-cement boat was lying in the bay, and soon its dinghy was heading our way to show us the best spot to anchor. Later, we all went ashore to meet them in the local bar, and discovered that they were two families sailing together. They had met twenty years ago, and had been friends ever since, sailing together for the last four years. Their misadventure of hitting the rock sounded horrific: it was a miracle that they saved their boat. Somehow, they got it to the beach by La Palma where it sank into two metres of thick mud, which blocked up the holes so that they could pump out the water and begin repairs.

La Palma had one main street, its many little shops selling dried goods and canned food. Several bars, a couple of restaurants and a hotel was the sum total of the town. Every building was on stilts over the water because of the great variance in tides. Landing at low tide was absolutely revolting; a thick layer of slimy black mud overlaying the shingles and broken glass. Very slippery, too, so one wrong step could spell disaster. It was imperative that we wore shoes to protect our feet. Sandals were no good: they were pulled off in the sticky mud! We had to rinse our shoes, our own feet, and Tara's feet before we stepped back on board after a visit ashore – a messy and protracted business.

Once again eager local lads offered to take us in their motorized canoes to visit the Wounaan people in the village of Bocas de Lara, about an hour and a half journey upriver, and for this we chose a young black Panamanian called Julio because we liked his friendly attitude and quick smile.

"First, we must buy gasoline," he explained as we climbed into his canoe, loaded with all our gear. "My cousin sells fuel over there in that green house." He waved a hand at the opposite bank where several brightly-painted houses leaned over the water on their long, stilt legs.

Julio edged the canoe up to the landing and fuel came jiggling down in five litre jugs tied to a rope. A little cloth bag was attached for the money, paid to the lady standing on the wooden balcony above us, who winched up the empty cans and the cash, clattering and bashing against the flimsy wall of the house. Now we were all set for our trip; this time travelling a much broader river and only coming close to the muddy banks when we cut corners and rounded curves. After quite a long journey the village appeared ahead of us, much more structured than the previous one we had been to, with zinc roof huts and electricity from a nearby generator. Open-plan houses lined each side of a broad, grassy path leading to the communal meeting place, where women gathered to show us their crafts.

Once again we were offered beautiful baskets, little bags, woven vases, intricately chiselled tagua nuts, and carved cocobola wood. They showed us how the raffia strands were dyed in different coloured earth, soaking for 24 hours. Some of the brightest yellows were achieved by boiling the raffia after it had been soaked in mud. The ladies wove the baskets to a certain point and then the men finished them, though why, we never discovered.

Exploring the Darien for such a short time was like cracking open a door just a fraction for a glimpse into another world. Unfortunately, we'll never know much about the ethnic people we meet, their cultures and beliefs, in our fleeting encounters with them.

At the village it was clouding over, and fingers of mist twined amongst the tall mangroves along the water's edge, giving the impression of a very ancient land. Hazy mountains appeared to shimmer in the distance – but were they mountains or clouds ...?

ജഇ

The journey back down river was uneventful, until, that is, the boat's engine began hesitating and spluttering.

"Oh dear," said Julio in Spanish, bending down to shake the fuel tank "it looks like we're running out of gasoline."

We didn't believe him for one minute: we had bought nine gallons of fuel from his cousin back in La Palma, and were accustomed to operating outboard motors, so knew their usual consumption. However, it was hardly the moment to argue as we sat rocking quietly in the ripples of our passage.

"Not to worry," Julio announced with a big grin, "I have a friend who lives close by. I'm sure I can borrow some gasoline from him. Just give me some money!" He got out and dragged the canoe up the squashy mud bank, disappearing into the dense green wall of foliage.

"You know what I think," said Ken, as we contemplated our fate in the middle of the Darien jungle, "I think Julio sold a couple of gallons to those villagers back there to make an extra buck, and this is all planned. How come we break down right by his friend's house?"

We decided there were two possible plans of action. Take the backrests off the seats and use them to paddle on down to La Palma on the falling tide, or sit and wait for Julio to come back. The popular vote was to stay where we were, Then Paddy, the ever-vigilant botanist, spotted a snail shell on the river bank.

"Oh, I'd love to have that shell," Paddy mused aloud, and Scott, the gallant Scott, volunteered to fetch it for her. Much to our delight and hilarity he disappeared up to his knees in the thick, oozing, black mud, gas bubbles rising to the surface with loud plops of sulphuric air. He could hardly keep his balance as he extricated one black leg after another to clamber up the bank, egged on by us singing "Mud, mud, glorious mud," a well-known song by Flanders and Swan. Scott seized the shell and struggled back to the boat, proudly presenting it to a delighted Paddy. We spent a good hour cleaning him up, which helped pass the time until Julio returned with the promised fuel.

TARA

The motor started first pull and we cruised on down-river, running out of fuel again as we drew up to *Imago* for Ken and Paddy to get on board. Ken gave Julio another gallon of fuel to get Scott and Debi to *Inl* and ourselves back to *Deusa*.

∞∞

Sitting on deck with Tara, I noticed a dilapidated rice mill on the shore opposite us, and wondered if I could buy some wholegrain rice, rather than the white, polished stuff sold in the shops. It was definitely worth a try, so Tara and I set out in the dinghy at high tide to talk to the miller. Tara liked to ride on the bow of the dinghy, her toes digging into the rubber inflatable buoyancy pontoons to keep her balance. When visiting people she wore her harness and lead, as she would bound off into the bush the moment we hit the beach – or mud, in this case.

When I told the miller, an older man with a nut-brown face and grizzled beard, what I wanted, he didn't think he was hearing me correctly above the din of the mill. Who, in their right minds, wanted to eat unpolished rice with half the husk still on? Foreigners were a strange lot, obviously, and he humoured me with a kilo of untreated rice. Then I saw the rice bran lying in a bin.

"What will you do with that, Senor?" I asked pointing at the bran.

"That's for the pigs and chickens," he replied. I explained that I made bread, and a little rice bran as a substitute for wheat bran might be good. I even promised him a loaf if it turned out well. That convinced him and I got a bagful.

The bread gave off a very peculiar smell whilst baking, and Robert and I wondered about pesticides in the growing and storage of rice. Here I was trying to get the pure and natural thing and all I might be doing was poison us both! It certainly was strange bread, and crunchy to chew. Maybe the bran was floor sweepings with a sprinkling of fine sand, as that's what it seemed like.

I took a small loaf to the miller's family, hoping I wasn't going to poison them as well. The miller's wife, Thelma, a big, motherly sort in a floral apron, cut off large chunks, slathered them in generous dollops of margarine, and handed these around to her kids, who dipped them in their coffee before taking a bite. They were far too polite to say that it was anything but delicious!

But the rice, that was something else. Rice was part of our staple diet on board as it was easy to store, and we and Tara ate it with fish. It was really tough-going, chewing through the rice husks, and Tara turned up her nose, only picking out the fish bits. So much for healthy eating ...

∞∞

It was time for us to return to the Balboa Yacht Club in Panama City, and meet up with Margi and Gerard Moss, some wonderfully adventurous friends, who were flying their single engine Brazilian plane to the four corners of the Americas. We thought they were landing at the airstrips furthest north, south, east and west of the Americas, when, in fact, they had to get to these points by foot, boat, dog sled or helicopter. By the time they visited us in Panama, the pair had visited one of their destinations – Froward Rock in the Magellan Straits of Chile. Margi and Gerard had written a book about their previous travels around the world in their plane, and we had it on board, often checking on their experiences as we sailed some of their route, particularly through the Pacific islands. Their mode of travel was so fast compared to ours. They visited the Darien, San Blas and Perlas islands in three days – it took us more than a month, going the long way round on water.

Gerard kept fit swimming each day, and he had brought his very special designer go-faster, slim-fit goggles for maximum eye protection and speed through the water.

"Where are my goggles?" he called to Margi as they were descending the stern ladder for a dip in the sea.

"What do they look like?"I asked Margi as I cast my eye across the deck.

"Oh, you can't miss them: they're bright yellow; you must've seen Gerard wearing them yesterday."

The search was on for the goggles, which Tara participated in with great enthusiasm and waggy tail. We couldn't find the goggles anywhere, however, until we shook out Tara's bed in the cockpit. Lo and behold, there were the goggles, neatly trimmed of their hi-tech fittings, with a few bites out of the strap for good measure. Gerard was not amused, and we had a serious talk with Tara about eating other people's possessions being a bad idea, with no food value, to boot.

೩०೧೪

Living with a dog in such close circumstances was an unusual experience. We found every puppy tooth that fell out; every whisker shed, and were aware at all times of the moods of this little animal with whom we shared our limited space. A lot of the time she lived on the same level as our heads, unlike most land dogs, who meet their owners at knee level. When we sat in the cockpit she would settle in her basket on the shelf behind us, together with the navigational equipment and a container for bits and pieces. From here, she surveyed the stern of *Deusa*, and would leap over us with a rush to defend the boat if anyone arrived in a dinghy at the back ladder. As her basket was on my side, I was the one who got flattened in the stampede, often having a drink or a book knocked out of my hand in the process.

If she wanted to watch the bow of *Deusa* Tara would sit on the life raft facing forward, from where she could watch the coming and going of other boats, fisher-folk, swimmers, birds, and the dreaded jet skis. If there was a sound in the night when she was in her basket behind our bed, she would leap up and gallop across our sleeping bodies, dashing into the saloon to see what was going on. Even though this was quite a nuisance at times, we always had a good night's sleep, knowing that Tara would react to any noise or movement on the boat.

five

Out into the Pacific – Galapagos

Time was slipping by, and we needed to begin our long journey to the Galapagos Islands off the coast of Ecuador, catching the good winds and currents to head out into the Pacific Ocean. We arranged with our friends, Debi and Scott, on *Inl* and Ken and Paddy on *Imago*, to keep in touch by radio twice a day during the passage, taking down all our GPS positions as we were all travelling in the same direction, heading for the Galapagos Islands, where we hoped to meet up again (each boat sailed at a different speed so we wouldn't necessarily arrive on the same day). Scott and Debi left two days before us, and *Imago* one day, so we were quite spread out. We calculated that it would take us a week to get to the Galapagos but *Inl* and *Imago* could take a little longer.

I had dreaded heading out into the Pacific for many years, putting off going to Panama for as long as possible! Surprisingly, I now felt quite confident about this next leg of our journey, and, although we lingered in Central America, enjoying Belize and the Yucatan Peninsula of Mexico for a couple of years, I knew that sooner or later Robert would want to move on.

I'm not very brave, and get extremely anxious before an ocean passage: my imagination running away with me as I think of all the terrifying things that could happen. Storms, huge waves rolling us over; high winds; hitting sunken containers on dark nights; Tara falling overboard, and, even worse, God forbid, Robert falling overboard, when I'd be all alone on the yacht. It was for this reason that we made sure we could both run *Deusa* on our own without the other, if, say, ill-health, a broken arm or leg, or some disability immobilized one crew member. We would often practise pretending to be on our own, and this was particularly good for me in building confidence.

When we first started looking for a yacht we would visit brokers, sometimes having to wait a while in their reception room until someone was available to speak with us. Glossy yachting magazines were spread invitingly on glass-topped tables, and I would page through them to see what useful hints I could pick up - how to pickle vegetables, how to preserve butter, how to wash your hair in salt water. Invariably, I would come across an article written by some hardy sailor who had survived 47 days in a life raft, or who had run his yacht onto a coral reef and watched it break up before his eyes. There were so many tales of doom and gloom that I soon stopped looking at the magazines, because I knew I would be put off this grand adventure before we even started.

⧣⧢

A calm, early morning sunrise of glowing pink and gold welcomed us as we motored out, leaving behind the Perlas Islands of Panama. I gave a sigh of relief: I was getting butterflies in my tummy for nothing. How peaceful the sea; how gentle the breeze. Not for long the peace and quiet, however, which vanished as the wind filled in from the stern, gusting up to 35 knots (about 40mph), making for a very uncomfortable ride. "Oh, damn," I mused, "just when I thought this would be a good passage, I'm now going to get seasick and scared."

The auto pilot couldn't handle the downwind sailing and short sharp waves, so we had to hand-steer, making the first night quite miserable. I felt depressed at the thought of several days all dressed up in my wet gear and safety harness, trying to keep my balance as *Deusa* tossed and rolled in the rough sea. Tara stayed below, looking quite ill, sprawled on the settee, wedged amongst the cushions, and only invited out now and then for a quick pee or poo.

Robert, on the other hand, looked well and happy: his eyes sparkled, and he was delighted to be out in the open ocean again, the helm in his strong hands.

The fishing line was out, and we soon caught a seven kilo dorado, which meant several fish dinners. It was one thing to catch the fish, but another thing entirely to gut it on the heaving back deck. Robert caught it; I cleaned it! After filleting the fish, it was essential to wash away the blood before it soaked into the teak deck, and I dipped a bucket into the sea as it frothed past the hull, holding on like mad to the knotted rope ripping through my hands. What one had to do for dinner!

It was very reassuring having friends to speak with on the radio as we made the crossing; to know there were other yachts out there on the endless horizon of wide ocean. With the passing days we fell into a routine of watches and meals, sleeping and waking, one of us always up and about. At night we'd try for six hours per watch, giving the one off duty a fair amount of time to sleep. Robert, being a night owl, went from 1900 to 0100, and I, the day person, got the sunrise, taking over at 0100 and going until 0700. Initially, I battled to stay awake on my watches, then couldn't sleep when it was my turn to relax, but eventually exhaustion took over and we slid into a rhythm.

My tiredness led to some strange hallucinations which weren't induced by seasick pills. The cockpit winches – used to control the sails – turned into rabbits, with long, floppy ears, the companionway down into the saloon became covered in tartan cloth, and once I spent considerable time talking to someone I didn't know, who was sitting in the cockpit with me.

On calm nights I could do all sorts of things, such as sewing, wood carving and cooking; reading and writing was still beyond me, because of my tendency to seasickness. However, my feeling of seasickness was due to an inner ear imbalance, and thankfully never affected my stomach, so the smell of food was not a problem. It was fun to cook at leisure, as I had time to bake bread and cakes, and it helped to pass the long night as well, popping below to check on the oven. Unless he had to work on the motor or fix something in the bilges, Robert didn't get seasick, so he was able to read, work on the computer, or listen through earphones to book tapes when he was on watch. One way of controlling seasickness was to take the helm and steer the boat; another was to use pressure bracelets on the wrists, and – the most unusual one of all – a dab of Vicks Vaporub in the belly button, sealed over with a plaster!

During the day we weren't so formal with our watches, both up and about for meals and a chat. If it wasn't too rough, Tara was also on deck to stretch her legs; most of the time on her lead because we still had no safety net around the deck, and the boat was often heeled over at an angle of up to 20-25 degrees. One of Tara's great passions were dolphins leaping and playing around the bow. She'd hear their sonic sounds and longed to join them in the water, yapping her head off as she strained at her harness. The dolphins were not frightened of this noisy land animal, however, often cruising close by to look at her. She heard them at night – even down below in the cabin – and would sound off in a frenzy of barking as their high-pitched squeaks echoed through the hull.

For many of the days there was very little wind which gave us an opportunity to try out the various sails we had, such as the spinnaker and the mizzen staysail. The mizzen staysail – used in light winds – was a pretty, blue-striped sail that was easy to handle, and slotted into the gap between the main and mizzen mast. The spinnaker was much more of a challenge, being such a large, balloon-like sail, and we were worried about using it. However, with some careful planning we got it up and flew it for a while, admiring its lovely shades of blue as it billowed out over *Deusa's* bow. But we had an assistant we didn't bargain for. Tara barked incessantly at all the action, and tried to grab the flapping sails. Even when the jib – a strong triangular sail running from the bow to the top of the main mast – began fluttering, she went off into hysterics, and it was like having a third pair of eyes on board, watching for the slightest wind change. It was always useful to be warned so we could trim the sails and make sure we were getting maximum power from the wind.

ଛଔଔ

During this passage we nearly lost Tara overboard. As it was a calm day, for once, she was off her lead, enjoying the sunshine by the aft cabin hatch. Tara wandered over to our dinghy, stowed on davits at the stern, to have a look at it, jumping into it with one smooth leap from the aft deck. As she was quite accustomed to travelling in the dinghy, she didn't think twice about jumping in when she saw the little boat so invitingly close.

I was sitting in the cockpit with my binoculars looking for seabirds, and Robert was down below at the chart table, studying the GPS and marking our position. Glancing around, I saw Tara teetering on the edge of the dinghy, the smooth Pacific Ocean flowing beneath her. What a scary sight: my heart nearly stopped and my mouth went dry. The boat had only to roll slightly and Tara would lose her balance and plunge into the sea below. We were moving along quite gently, but to stop and turn around would take some time, and we could easily lose sight of her in the vast ocean. One exercise we learned for 'man overboard' was to throw floating objects such as deck cushions, buoys, and life jackets, into the sea at regular intervals, laying a path back to where the person or dog had gone overboard. I dared not startle her by calling her name, or walking towards her.

Many thoughts flashed through my mind. This little dog had been with us now for quite a while, and was part of the family. We were devoted to her and she to us. If Tara slipped and fell overboard, part of us would go, too. Would we find her in the deep and rippling ocean, with her tiny head only just above the surface, paddling frantically to catch us up as we slowed the boat and turned around? What if we couldn't see her as she struggled through the water? What if we never found her and she drowned, or, worse still, was mauled by a shark and died an agonizing death?

"Robert," I called softly, leaning over into the companionway so Tara couldn't hear me, "come up here quickly. See if you can get Tara off the dinghy without startling her."

Robert appeared in the companionway looking horrified, and approached Tara very slowly, talking quietly to her all the time.

"What are you doing, you silly thing? There's an awful lot of water out there; how are we going to pull you out of the sea if you fall in?"

Tara looked extremely pleased with herself, her pink tongue lolling out, her eyes sparkling in delight at her daring. She had no fear – or no imagination! Luckily, she didn't slip as Robert crept towards her, speaking constantly, then grabbed up the bundle of black and white, wriggling, happy dog and carried her back to the cockpit, where we fastened her onto her lead. Only then did we heave a sigh of relief and I went below to make us a cup of tea to calm our shaken nerves.

Living on board since she was six weeks old, Tara soon learnt to use the port side (left side) foredeck as her toilet. Being a very clean little dog, she always asked to be brought up on deck if nature called. Now, with longer ocean passages, and the possibility of rough weather, it was too dangerous for her to visit her favourite pee-place unattended. Thank goodness we had taught her to pee and poo on command at a very early age when she first joined us, as all we had to do was snap on her collar, and, holding tight to the lead, place her on deck just outside the cockpit. Even in the pouring rain or with salty spray across the deck, she would relieve herself, then shoot back into the safety of the cockpit to be rubbed down with a dry towel. This saved a lot of worry, and the command worked equally well when visiting friends on land with her.

ဆာလ

"Come on Robert, wake up! Come and look at this, I can see land! It's for real, not just a cloud on the horizon."

TARA

Robert was not amused at my waking him, as he'd only got his head down after 2am, and now it was early dawn. His attitude was that the land wouldn't go away, and, in fact, was getting closer and closer.

I was overjoyed, though, and felt that the Captain should share in this miracle, especially as he was also the navigator. It had been a week since we left the Perlas Islands, and now we were sailing into Wreck Bay in San Cristobal Island, one of the major islands in the group of eighteen large islands and three small islands that make up the Galapagos archipelago. Our calculation of a seven-day journey had been very accurate, and obviously *Inl's* estimate of nine days and *Imago's* of eight days had been equally good, as we all arrived within six hours of each other, which was quite remarkable, considering we'd travelled 1012 nautical miles (2024 kilometres).

We were all so pleased with our successful passages that we celebrated with a nice, cold bottle of Chilean wine, compliments of our good fridge! What a thrill to see land after days at sea, the same thrill that has delighted sailors for centuries. The feeling of achievement, the satisfaction of correct navigation, meeting up with friends again: all were part of the sailing adventure. The great joy of making landfall made up for all my misgivings and fears, and, in some way, made the arrival at new destinations so much more intense.

What luxury to sleep at anchor; to snuggle up in bed together, Tara safe in her basket on the platform behind us. No night watches, no tightrope walking on dinghies, no storms and dark seas, just secure in harbour.

During the first night we heard the bleating of sheep mixed with the distinctive bark of sea lions. How strange, we thought, the townsfolk must have herds of them for wool and mutton. But in the early morning light we saw that the 'sheep' were baby sea lions, all along the rocky shore, bleating for their mothers to come and feed them. The sea lions were quite unperturbed by human presence, basking in the sunshine on black rocks by the houses, sprawled out on fishing boats, and swimming amongst anchored yachts.

We arrived the day before my birthday – March 18 – so there was good excuse for further celebrations. Robert brought me tea in bed, made breakfast, and even washed up plates and mugs all day. Paddy and Ken gave me a paperweight of shells in pale blue fibreglass, made by them and very beautiful. They also gave me a pair of knitting needles and some string, as well as two knitted washcloths. Was this a hint for me to get busy making my own kitchen towels? They were the most industrious couple, always making lovely things as presents for friends.

The Galapagos Islands are magical, as everyone knows, but pets have to be kept on board, and are not allowed to set paw on any beach. However, if Tara didn't get to see all of the fascinating creatures of the Galapagos, some of them came to visit her – particularly the sea lions. Swimming around *Deusa*, diving under the hull to pop up at the bow or stern, splashing about and calling to each other in the squeaks and grunts of sea lion speak.

Tara was beside herself, frantically trying to keep track of them, racing to the bow – bark! bark! bark! – then tearing back to the stern – bark! bark! bark! – and skidding to a stop just before she shot off the aft deck, narrowly avoiding joining her aquatic friends. You'd think by the end of the day she'd be hoarse and exhausted, but these tough little terriers are very hard to wear out.

One big, old sea lion heaved himself into our dinghy, tied at *Deusa's* stern. Tara nearly went berserk, and would've hurled herself at the large, bristly beast if we hadn't grabbed her in time. She got a lot of exercise on board in Galapagos.

The anchorages weren't very large, and she soon drove everyone – including us – crazy with her constant barking, so we often sent her down to the saloon for a bit of peace and quiet. By now, we were recognised as the blue-hulled ketch with the noisy dog, and yachts didn't anchor too close by. Of course, this had its advantages as it meant we didn't get tangled in other peoples' anchor chains, as so often happens in a crowded harbour.

Tara stayed down below on *Deusa* while we explored the various beaches of the Galapagos Islands. The seals, the sea lions, the saltwater iguanas, and the booby birds were all so tame and unconcerned by our presence. We walked for miles along the rocky shores and beaches, sometimes hiring a vehicle and driver with friends, so that we could adventure inland for a change of scenery.

⁝

From San Cristobal we moved on to Santa Cruz Island where we visited the Charles Darwin Institute. Francisco, a local Ecuadorian guide, showed us around. "We incubate and rear the tortoises here," he explained as we leaned over the edge of the pen to look at the tiny little shapes, "and once they get to a certain size we restock the islands. Come and look at the big ones over here."

In another pen huge tortoises lumbered slowly around looking for food. "These guys can weigh up to 250 kilos and live for 150 years." he explained, pointing to one particularly massive animal. "Did you know that, in years gone by, sailors used to call in at the Galapagos Islands to cut wood and capture these tortoises for meat. They'd leave them on their backs in the holds of the ships, where they'd survive for up to a year."

Poor tortoises, did they feed them or give them water when they were held prisoner? I wondered.

It was here on the Galapagos Islands that Charles Darwin observed all the varieties of Finch in their various habitats, and began thinking about evolution. He gathered a lot of material on his travels on the *Beagle,* and later wrote his book, *The Origin of Species.*

Our time on the islands was not all play; we had to restock with food and diesel. The food was fine; the diesel was a messy operation. We three boats all helped each other, first carrying jerry cans of diesel to fill up one yacht, then moving on to the next. Because of a world rally stopping in the Galapagos, the price of everything, including diesel, more than doubled, and our first offer was US$3 a litre; we rolled our eyes in horror. Finally, after much research and friendly persuasion by Ken, Robert and Sven, they were able to buy it at US$1 a litre, transport it in jerry cans in an open truck to the dinghies, and finally onto the waiting boats.

This operation took a couple of days, and we had to be very careful not to spill any fuel in the harbour or on our decks: there were substantial fines for polluting the water in this nature reserve. Tara was kept out of the way as she always got diesel on her paws, leaving oily prints as she scurried down the companionway stairs and leapt onto our bed (washing bedclothes was a major operation).

Our East German friends, Sven and Annette, arrived on their boat, *Raroia,* and told us a horror story of what happened to them as they arrived at San Cristobal Island. Five miles out of Academy Bay, they were drifting along under sail with very little wind on a dark night when, suddenly, they saw a ship coming straight at them out of the blackness. Immediately they tried calling it on Channel 16, the VHF radio channel for general communication, but got no answer. They then turned their powerful spotlight onto their sails, illuminating them brightly, but the big ship kept coming.

Annette was terrified, and thought the ship would ram them, as Sven tried to steer Raroia out of the way. The great big, three-masted schooner scraped all along their side, knocking off a wind generator and punching a hole in the solar panel. They were lucky to survive. Raroia was so small, and the 120-foot, steel-hulled schooner didn't feel a thing. Sven sent up a bright red flare, and the schooner finally got on the radio to ask if they were all right. When Scott confirmed they were still afloat, but had sustained damage to the wind generator and solar panels, the big boat continued on its way. They limped into Academy Bay and made a report to the Port Captain.

"Ah yes," said the Port Captain, a swarthy, sweaty man, "this kind of thing happens all the time with the schooners and fishing boats. They turn on the auto pilot and don't bother to keep a watch."

Sven had a battle to get compensation for the damage, and discovered that the owner of the schooner and the Port Captain were friends! Waiting for a new wind generator and solar panels to be imported from the mainland was not a problem for Sven and Annette, as, luckily, there was a lot of work to be done on the rally boats, and Sven was an excellent mechanic and electronic engineer, so much in demand in this respect.

The rally boat crews were very stuck-up and unfriendly, and we independent sailors rather looked down on them travelling all huddled together. Debi had an amusing conversation with one of them, who told her it was much safer to travel in a group, and how it was so helpful as all the paperwork was done for them. At a cost, of course.

"And would you believe it," said the girl in her designer yachting clothes, "we even get ten days in Galapagos: more than most people."

"Oh, really," responded Debi with much satisfaction, "we were offered ninety days but only have time for a month." We had faxed the

Ecuardorian embassy for permission to visit Galapagos while still in Panama, and because of this future planning, got extended visas, so could enjoy our visit without worrying about leaving in a hurry.

The rally was happening in Panama at the same time as we were there, though we didn't meet any of the entrants; only heard about them afterwards. They were invited to an elegant party at the British Ambassador's house as the rally organiser was British, and well-known for the various rallies he ran in the Caribbean. As well as the wealthy yacht owners the rowdy young crew members were also at this party, full of drink and high spirits.

"Hey guys," one of the lads called to his mates "our organiser looks awfully hot in that formal attire, let's cool him off!"

Grabbing the wine glass from his hand they tossed him, dinner jacket and all, into the pool, much to the shocked amazement of all the guests.

A true diplomat, the Ambassador rose to the occasion, and, setting aside his glass on a nearby table, removed his jacket and jumped into the pool to join the floundering organiser, announcing to his dinner guests that it was a good evening for a dip.

The next day the Panamanian English newspaper enjoyed reporting that the rally organiser had 'laundered money' in the Ambassador's pool: cheques for the next leg of the journey had been in his pocket, and so got soaking wet.

᠅

The last island to visit before we made the long journey to the Marquesa Islands in French Polynesia, some 3000 miles away, was Santa Maria, and Post Office Bay, where the sailing ships of yore used to drop off and pick up mail from an old wooden barrel, delivering it all over the world. We later checked the barrel, and found lots of letters in it, so added a couple of our own.

Deusa's hull was growing long, green 'hair,' which we couldn't believe, as she had been treated with anti-fouling paint in Cartagena just six months previously. The other two boats, *Imago* and *Inl*, were just as bad, and we wondered if it was during our trip to the Darien that we picked up some foul sort of weed. We borrowed a wander-lead from Ken – a most useful piece of equipment consisting of a long tube which we could attach to one of our dive tanks with a mask on the other end – so that Robert could dive under *Deusa* with a constant air supply, to scrape off all sorts of muck.

If sea lions had been fun, Tara thought that Robert doing this was even better sport, and she leapt up and down with excitement, nearly falling off the deck in her efforts to see what he was doing. This little dog did everything with such dedication and single-mindedness; nothing diverted her from the task at hand. Eventually, of course, she fell in by-mistake-on-purpose, and swam round and round, peering into the water to catch a glimpse of Robert under the hull. Now and then a finned foot surfaced as he kicked himself forward to another patch of weed, and Tara bit into this with great delight, trying to wrench it free.

TARA

All too soon it was time to sail on towards French Polynesia, and Tara now had a new occupation: scanning the wide ocean on the lookout for any sea creatures large enough to bark at. Dolphins were prime candidates, and playing around our bow wave filled this role very well. It was one thing to be at anchor and think 'how amusing' as we watched our dog chase around the deck, pulling her out of the sea if she fell in, but it was quite another matter under way, with the large genoa sail poled out and the main sail tied back with a preventer. If Tara was to fall overboard, it would take time to turn the yacht around and go back to rescue her. We had already experienced a bad scare with her leaping into the dinghy and balancing on the edge, so kept a very careful watch for dolphins, tying her up or banishing her below decks before she spotted them. Her sharp ears enabled her to pick up their sonic sounds long before they broke surface at the bow, however, and the only way we knew that dolphins were with us at night was when Tara became very excited, begging to go up on deck to stare into the dark sea.

—Marquesas ~ Polynesia ~ Samoas—

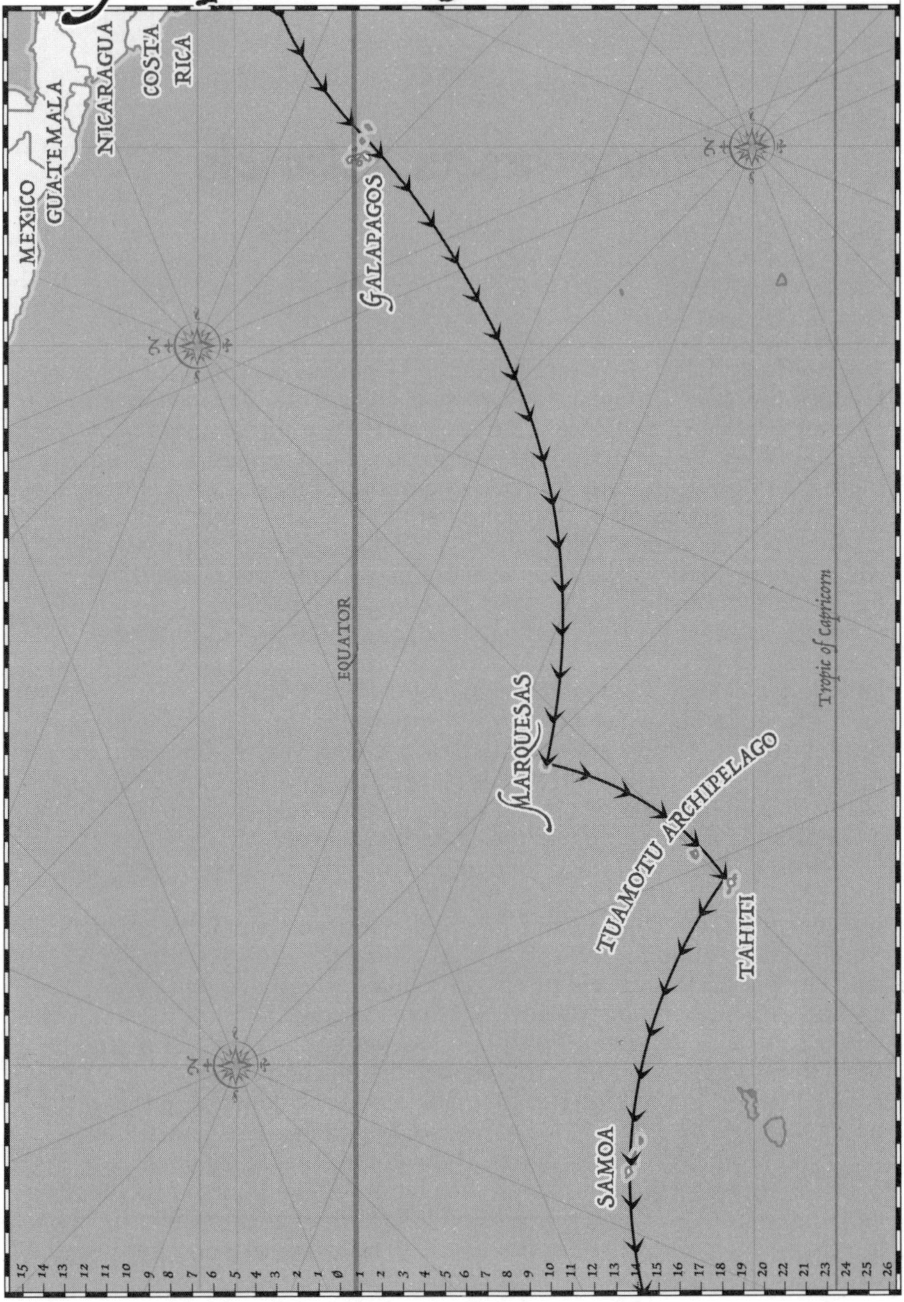

six

Marquesas Islands

It was wonderful to make landfall in the Marquesas (a group of volcanic islands in French Polynesia, an overseas collectivity of France in the southern Pacific Ocean) after 23 days at sea; the longest single passage of our journey. We all three enjoyed going ashore to stretch our legs, meet the people, and buy fruit and vegetables. Tara was on a lead to prevent her running off and sticking her nose where it didn't belong.

One day, we were strolling along a quiet beach near a farmhouse, when Tara suddenly jerked the lead out of my hand and dashed into a thick clump of bushes just beyond the sand. Wild cackling and squawks promptly assailed my horrified ears and, out of the greenery, flew a desperate white chicken, barely airborne, hotly pursued by a delighted little dog, a clump of tail feathers clamped in her teeth.

"Help, help, Tara's got a chicken!" I shouted to Robert, who was some distance away, rushing after hen and dog as they vanished around the back of the farmhouse. With all this racket going on, the lady of the house appeared in the doorway, wiping her floured hands on her apron, and gazing in astonishment at the unfolding scene.

"Pardon, Madame" I gasped in my limited French as I tore past, "le petit chien ..." but then I was lost for words.

Meanwhile, the chicken and Tara had made a circuit of the house, and were coming round for the second lap. Flinging myself at the trailing lead I managed to stop the merry-go-round and retrieve one very excited dog. Robert had, by now, arrived, and saw that the situation was under control as far as capturing our dog was concerned, but waited to see if there was going to be trouble with the chicken owner.

We needed to apologise to Madame, and find out if her bird was badly hurt. The poor thing had vanished, and there were only a few scattered tail feathers as evidence of the crime. Thankfully, Tara's lack of experience as a hunter had left the chicken shaken but in one piece, and, fortunately, Madame brushed off the incident as yet one more crazy foreigner who couldn't speak French. With relief we watched her broad back disappear into the house to continue baking.

ΣΟΩ

We often came across great, bare expanses of exposed coral at low tide, and let Tara run free to explore on her own. Rock pools were totally fascinating to her, and she'd plunge in to seize a crab or small fish, dabbling with her front paws in the shallow depressions, sometimes dipping her entire head under water. She never caught anything – the fish saw her coming from a long way off!

Once she realised the liberty of being off the lead, she took off for miles and miles, until she was only a small, black-and-white dot on the horizon. Her wandering off in this way was an ongoing problem, and the final solution was to find a small, uninhabited island or atoll where Tara could run free, and we could reclaim her when it was time to go back to *Deusa*.

&OCR&

Some of the anchorages we used when provisioning the boat, or meeting up with friends, were really bad, and Atuona, on the island of Hiva Oa, was one such. The town was two miles from the bay and easy to reach; cars and trucks gave us lifts to stock up at the supermarket and buy diesel at the gas station.

Sitting on *Imago* in Atuona bay one day, we noticed *Deusa* getting dangerously close to another boat.

"Look at our boat," I said to Paddy as we sipped tea in her cockpit, "she's getting awfully near that rusty old sloop: she's drifting closer and closer."

"You'd better go and do something about it, quickly," said Paddy putting down her mug and getting up to lend us a hand with the dinghy.

The next minute *Deusa* had knocked into the old boat. Robert and I leapt into the dinghy and rushed over to discover that the stern anchor line had been cut, and our yacht was drifting. Fortunately, we had a spare anchor, so, with the help of friends, set it to prevent any more damage. But this wasn't the end of our problems. There was a storm warning, so we decided to move away from this bad anchorage to somewhere more secure.

After we lifted our bow anchor, I tried to pick up the marker buoy to our stern anchor with a boat hook, but it pulled out of my hands and wrapped around our propeller, stalling the engine. This was a bad situation, so we dropped the bow anchor again, hoping it would hold.

By now, several dinghies had come to our rescue, trying to fend off *Deusa* from other boats.

"Pass me a knife" said Ken, "I'm going to cut the rope from around the propeller."

Robert ran to get him a knife, and Ken jumped into the filthy harbour water after tying his dinghy to our stern. Seeing Ken plunge into the water was just too much for Tara, and she leapt off the deck after him, to lend a helping paw. Now we had to rescue the dog as well as the boat, but luckily a passing dinghy grabbed her, throwing her onto *Imago's* deck to be taken care of by Paddy. This dog needed to participate in everything, and couldn't understand why she wasn't always welcome!

Thankfully, with many hands helping us we resolved the tricky situation, and were able to move to a safer location. We always found the yachting fraternity wonderful people, ready to help at a moment's notice.

∞∞

What makes a Jack Russell terrier a keen fisherdog? When she joined us on *Deusa* at six weeks old, all of Tara's natural instincts to kill rats or chase foxes down holes became channelled toward a marine existence. What was there to hunt along the beach but scuttling crabs and little silver fish? Tara dedicated her time to running up and down in the shallows, pouncing and snapping at the shadows and shapes that darted and dashed in the clear water.

Lemon sharks liked to hang around the anchored boats, waiting for tasty morsels chucked overboard when cleaning freshly-caught fish on the back deck. These sharks were bold and curious; not afraid of swimmers, especially if they were spearing fish, and would even swim by the shore to check out anything new. They were not dangerous, but the word 'shark' inevitably conjured up an image of *Jaws*, and we were respectful of their presence.

Tara loved the freedom of the beach, and I enjoyed looking for shells while she played in the water. One day, I was some distance away from her when I saw a lemon shark heading in her direction. There was no use calling as she never liked to be interrupted in her fishing.

I started running back, imagining the shark gliding up to seize her by a slim white leg or black nose as she stuck it underwater. I could now see the shark in the shallows, its fin sticking out of the water as it edged in for a closer look at the strange creature prancing about. Not a very big shark – maybe a metre at the most – but certainly big enough to have a go at Tara. With a pounding heart I ran as fast as I could, hoping to frighten off the big fish as I splashed into the water.

By this time, Tara had also seen the shark and, being the fearless soul that she was, pounced at it with a yelp of delight: finally, this was the big one! The shark was startled by the bold, boisterous attack, and fled into the safety of deeper water. Phew, that was a lucky escape! After that scare, I decided that Tara and I would keep closer company ...

This was easier said than done, however, as Tara would often scamper away amongst the coconut palms following enticing smells, poking her nose into fallen fronds and dark holes dug by land crabs. Sooner or later she was going to have a confrontation with a crab. Either the crab would get her by the nose or she would grab it by the shell. You had to admire the courage of a crab as it waved its claws at the dog snipping and snapping around its head.

One particular crab must have been older and wiser than some of the others, because, as Tara lowered her head for a bite, it seized her nose in a vice-like grip. Off she went, howling through the forest, wildly shaking her head to try and dislodge this terrible thing. When I finally caught up with the rampage through the woods, the crab was nowhere to be seen, and Tara was nursing her wounded nose. It was a lesson well learned, and since then she was more respectful of crabs.

Once we were out of shark-infested waters Tara loved to snorkel with us, as the coral reef was often close inshore near a beach. She'd swim with us for a while, then, growing bored, head ashore for a run along the sand to stretch her legs in the sunshine. Every now and then she'd swim out again for a visit, and, feeling tired, climb onto Robert's back for a rest, sticking her nose into his air tube, snorting loudly to let him know she'd arrived. Of course, Robert nearly had a heart attack the first time this happened, thinking some sharp-clawed monster had grabbed him, and surfacing with a curse, throwing Tara off his back! She found this very amusing, swimming around him in circles with a great big grin on her face.

As a security measure we always towed the dinghy with us when swimming, so that we could drop her into it, if needs be, and continue snorkelling, while she stood on the bow gazing into the clear water. Once she'd caught her breath, she'd leap off with a great splash, giving the dinghy-tower yet another fright.

At anchor, Tara liked to sit in the dinghy when it was tied behind *Deusa*, hanging over the back of the little boat, trying to catch the fish swimming around the stern. She'd get so carried away, craning her neck further and further over the edge, that, finally, she'd topple into the water, much to her surprise. Luckily, we were nearby when this first happened, and realised we would have to do something about it if we didn't want to spend hours watching our dog amuse herself staring into the water, looking for tiny fish. So we taught Tara how to climb back into the dinghy when the outboard motor was in the 'down' position with the propeller in the water. She was able to climb onto the fins on each side of the propeller, and, using her front legs, heave herself up and over the back of the dinghy to land in a tangle at the bottom of the small boat.

You might wonder how we taught her this very clever trick. Well, initially, we would swim with her around the dinghy, and place her back legs on the fins and her front legs on the back of the dinghy, pushing her up and over the edge with a hand on her round, black-and-white backside. Once she got used to this, Robert would sit in the dinghy calling her while I stayed in the water and helped her get into position to haul herself out to safety. It was surprising how quickly she learnt, and very soon we didn't have to do a thing but sit in the dinghy and call her when she was in the water.

Eventually, we were quite confident to leave her swimming behind the dinghy for as long as she liked, and get out of the water when she was tired. Of course, we were on board watching because she was never allowed to go swimming without our permission, and never allowed to jump directly from *Deusa's* deck into the sea. She was always invited into the dinghy by one of us, and only when we said the word 'go' would she launch herself into the water with a great splash. She would stand, legs trembling and ears pricked, waiting for the magic word, hardly able to contain herself, but she was becoming remarkably obedient for a Jack Russell terrier.

Sometimes we forgot about the Tara rescue system, and pulled the motor up into towing position, which took the propeller out of the water and meant Tara couldn't reach the fins to haul herself out. So, as an added precaution, we taught her to cling to the ladder on *Deusa's* stern until someone rescued her.

Once again we swam with her, and showed her how she could hook her front legs over the middle rung of the ladder that was just in the water, and rest her back legs on the lowest rung, which meant she could catch her breath if she was tired. She soon understood and came to the stern of the boat to hang on until she had rested, or needed bringing up on deck by one of us. Sometimes, Robert swam around *Deusa* with a brush, scrubbing along the waterline, taking off the algae growth and barnacles that stuck to the hull and slowed us down. Tara thought this wonderful sport, paddling along beside him, trying to grab the brush, nipping at his feet, swimming up to the bow and back, taking the occasional breather on the ladder, then rejoining him in his work. She was devoted to Robert ,and accompanied him whenever she could.

I taught her to look for him, and started this game when we went ashore. Keeping her with me, I would let Robert walk ahead some distance to hide behind a boulder or a tree. Releasing Tara, I'd say, "Where's Robert? Find Robert, Tara."

Off she'd go, racing up the beach to where Robert had disappeared. Even if we were strolling down the beach some distance apart and she was with me, as soon as I said "Where's Robert?" off she ran to him. It was a very endearing trick but she never learnt "Where's Rosemary?" She thought that was a silly question.

⊱⊰

Like most sailors we fished while under way, and there was always a line or two trolling off the stern, hoping to hook supper. Tara, being the constant fisherdog, (fisherbitch doesn't sound so good), used to sit with her ears pricked inquisitively, watching Robert with great interest as he got out the tackle box and set up the rig. When we got a strike, she was the first to arrive at the whirring reel to help bring in the fish. Help was not the right word, really; hinder is more appropriate, and we had to restrain her while we brought the fish aboard and killed it with a shot of cheap rum in the gills. The rum suffocated the fish very quickly and cleanly as compared to beating it over the head with a hammer, splattering blood all over the deck. An over-excited dog and a flapping fish with hooks and line in a jumble was a bad combination.

Once the fish was hanging by its tail on the back deck, we let Tara go, and if there was even a tiny thread of life still in the fish, Tara bit and mauled it. But as soon as the life spark was gone, she stood guard over it fiercely. Robert was allowed to touch the fish but when it came time for me to gut and fillet it, there was a terrible scene. Snarling and growling, ears flattened, eyes flashing, she dared me to come one step closer. I felt nervous and unsure of where I stood with her at times like these, when my jolly companion of many swims and many walks was preparing to tear me to pieces! Tara had very sharp, very white teeth and large canines and I believed she would bite me if I took hold of the fish. It was the strangest behaviour and very distressing. Did she see me as a fellow dog, and this was her meal, not to be shared? Or was it pack hierarchy, and she thought me lower in rank? However, before we had had her spayed and she came on heat, I was the object of her desire; she wouldn't leave me alone and became quite bothersome for ten days or so, as long as the heat lasted, which I suppose means I must have been another dog to Tara! I asked friends with dogs on board if they experienced any of these behavioural patterns, but no-one had an answer for me.

The best way to lure Tara away from the fish was to pretend there were dolphins around, and, as she ran forward to look, I'd seize the fish, slap it onto the carving board, and slice it up. Having gained possession of the prize, I was now in control, and she lost all interest, just as if it had never crossed her mind to have a fish-fight. It was a very unusual and sometimes unsettling experience living at close quarters with such a determined little animal.

৪৩৫৪

Our next stop in the Marquesas was the bay of Anaho on Nuka Hiva island. It was a rough and bouncy day, with twenty knots of wind, and, as we drew close to the island, the sea became more and more agitated. The beauty and power of these tall, volcanic islands, with their finger rocks and strange sculptures carved by centuries of wind and rain, was stunning. Just as we turned the northern corner, about two miles from Anaho Bay, our big genoa headsail ripped with an almighty explosion, giving the three of us a huge fright, with Tara barking and Robert and I shouting to each other over the noise of the torn and thrashing sail.

"Grab Tara," he yelled over the noise, "she's going to get hurt if she tries to bite the flapping sail." I seized the frantic dog and shoved her down below. Then we looked at the damage.

A great, gaping blue hole punctured the space where a moment ago there had been a stretched white sail, pulling us along at five knots.

"We're going to have to get this down: it'll break something the way it's flying about in the wind," shouted Robert, starting to haul in the frenzied sail with the roller furling winch. Normally, the sail furled away very neatly around the forestay on the bow of the boat, part of the rigging that supported the main mast, but this time pieces stuck out everywhere from the forestay, like an untidy maypole, billowing in the wind.

It was a sorry-looking *Deusa* that limped into Anaho Bay to be met by a number of friends rushing to our rescue before we even dropped anchor. Mike, Karen and Falcon from *Beau Soleil*, Ralph from *Onça* and John from *Jump Up* converged on us, and proceeded to haul down the torn sail, whilst we stood by, feeling helpless. John even brought his bosun's chair (used by sailors to work on masts and rigging), as he knew it would be impossible to unravel the mess without being hauled up the mast to reach across to the forestay where the sail was caught up. They were all having such fun, telling each other what to do, that we decided the best thing was not to interfere, and watched with interest instead. Tara remained down below, complaining loudly, running round and round on the settee, hoping to spin herself up the companionway steps to add to the confusion.

This was the calmest anchorage since Panama, and what a relief to be still for a change. On shore, an enterprising Polynesian family grew vegetables to sell to the yachts. They had created quite a large patch of lettuce, cabbage, green peppers, carrots, chives, parsley, bok choy, green beans – you can imagine what a wonderful surprise this was for us vegetable-starved sailors! Louise, the elegant, black-haired, golden-skinned Polynesian lady of the family, had a captive market: this was the first green stuff we had seen since leaving Galapagos over a month ago.

The torn sail was taken to the beach and laid out under the palm trees so that we could study the extent of the damage. Mike and Karen came to give us advice, as Karen used to work in a sail loft, and Mike had sailed all his life and knew about sail repair. As the sail was already twelve years old they felt it had come to the end of its useful life, but suggested we convert it into a light staysail which fitted in behind the roller-furling genoa sail, onto an inner forestay; another part of the rigging supporting the main mast. This was a good idea as it gave us an extra sail which was lighter and larger than our heavy-duty staysail that we used only in stronger winds.

While we took on this task, Tara joined us to romp and play in the long grass around the coconut palms, dashing down to the sea every now and then to freshen up.

"It's so peaceful here," I said to Robert, as we measured and cut a new sail in the shade of the trees. At that moment there was a yelp of excitement from our dog. She had flushed some chickens from under a bush and went tearing off after a brown hen that took flight in alarm.

"Tara! Tara!" I shouted, rushing after her. Bellowing her name had, as usual, no effect whatsoever, so I waited to see if she would return. And return she did – the brown hen in her mouth – trotting straight to the dinghy, very pleased with herself, and waited for a lift back to the boat with her prize.

"You bad dog!" I scolded her, "Give me that chicken immediately. You've no idea what trouble you've caused."

I fell upon her, she dropped the bird, who hobbled away, minus a few feathers and her dignity.

"Who should I speak to about the chicken?" I asked the two Polynesians sitting on a nearby log, but they merely laughed and shrugged their shoulders. I felt quite relieved, because if Tara had killed the bird we would have had to pay a fortune in compensation. Karen told me if that if this had happened in Tonga, the owner would have been furious, and we would have had to flee for our lives!

৪০উৎ

Correspondence was difficult to manage while sailing, so we had arranged for fax messages to be sent to us at an hotel in Taiohae Bay, just a couple of hours away. Once our sail repairs were done, we sailed around to this bay, and Tara and I walked up the hill to the hotel, where we were met by a young German Shepherd dog who pounced on Tara and nipped her playfully. Tara yelped and was about to retaliate so I picked her up, but that didn't stop the puppy enthusiastically leaping up all over us, taking a chomp at whatever part of Tara was dangling down.

"Go away, you bloody dog" I swore. Unfortunately, the hotel owner heard me, and came charging down on us in a fury.

"Don't speak to my dog like that, this is his place: how dare you tell him what to do!"

Come to think of it, she was right, he was in his territory and we were intruders. I needed to know about fax messages, so tried to look humble and apologetic as I held my irate and struggling terrier. There were no messages for us after all that, and it was the last time I climbed the hill with Tara in tow.

೮೦೮೪

My feet had been bothering me since the Galapagos Islands - they were cracked, red and itchy - and I needed to visit a doctor as I wasn't able to cure the problem with any remedies we had on board. They drove me mad. Whenever we went ashore and walked on the beach, the grains of sand would rub into the sores, and the salt water would sting. I couldn't decide whether I was better off wearing shoes to keep the sand out, or to go barefoot and put up with the pain. The sand got into the shoes in any case, and acted like sandpaper, so whatever I did was a miserable situation.

I was also worried about visiting other boats in case my feet were infectious. It was always polite boat etiquette not to wear shoes on board, but anyone looking at my feet wouldn't want me on board in any case. And, of course, anyone visiting our boat would be worried they'd catch what I had. Socializing was one of the joys of meeting friends in anchorages, and I got most upset about my predicament, snapping unnecessarily at Robert and neglecting Tara when she needed a walk or a cuddle. Luckily, Robert could do all this while I sat and brooded about my poor feet.

I discovered there was a doctor in the nearby village, so off I went to visit him.

"Hmmm, yes, let me see," he said, a French flavour to his English, looking at my unhappy feet and consulting his medical books.

"You've got syphilis; your feet have got bumps and blisters just like these pictures. Have a look!" He thrust the fat tome into my hands. I looked at the photos of swollen feet with suppurating sores and raw flesh, and decided this was definitely NOT what I had.

"There's no way I've got syphilis," I spluttered indignantly, "that's not the right diagnosis: you've got to come up with something better than that."

We eventually came to the conclusion that it was an allergy, and that Vaseline would help the cracking skin, which meant I had to wear socks

51

on board and even in bed, so that I didn't walk Vaseline into the carpets or the deck, or mark the sheets. I suppose it helped a bit, and kept the skin supple, but it still wasn't the answer, and I only discovered much later when I went to see a doctor in Fiji that I had tinea pedis - a form of athlete's foot - and was finally given the right medication.

Back on board *Deusa* we were discussing the progress of the day when the VHF radio crackled to life.

"*Deusa, Deusa*, this is *Onça*, why don't you come over for a sundowner?"

"What a good idea," we replied, and jumped into the dinghy with our drinks in a cooler box (when visiting other yachts, everyone took their own alcohol or soft drinks).

We were sitting comfortably in the cockpit when a nearby yacht began to signal frantically at us, pointing to the water by *Onça's* hull. We couldn't figure out what they were trying to tell us, so leaned over the side of the boat, to see Tara's little head bobbing along, swimming down the side of the boat with her beady eyes on our dinghy. She must have fallen in when barking at a passing canoe, or, hearing our voices, jumped in to come and join the party.

She was now so fearless of water that it became a worry she would come looking for us if left alone on board. However, she was intelligent enough to learn that 'No!' meant 'No!' and we had several sessions of leaving her on deck, taking the dinghy, and motoring away, telling her to stay. We would go and hide behind a nearby boat and watch what she would do. As soon as we were out of sight, she'd jump in and swim after us. We would then pick her up, tell her she was a bad dog, and put her back on deck, repeating the operation. It only took two sessions of being unceremoniously dumped back on *Deusa* for her never to follow us again.

In fact, Tara was developing quite a vocabulary, and understood words such as 'down' to jump below into the saloon; 'dinghy ride' when she would run onto the back deck and look longingly at the dinghy; 'walk'; 'swim'; 'stay,' which she and I would practice on the beach; 'sit,' which was often the first part of stay; 'dinner' when she came running to see what was in her bowl; 'where's Robert'; 'pee-pee'; 'bed,' and 'dolphins,' as well as many other words.

One warm summer evening all of us on the anchorage were invited ashore for an ethnic dinner and show by a friendly Polynesian couple called Etienne and Yvonne. They lived right near the beach, their bamboo and thatch home fringed by tall palm trees, and a large clearing in front of the house was swept clean for parties. Trestle tables ringed the arena attractively decorated with palm fronds, banana leaves, and hibiscus flowers. As we arrived and pulled our dinghies up the beach, young girls of the family welcomed us ashore, decorated us with necklaces of fresh flowers, and led us to the tables. We were served a typically Polynesian meal of breadfruit, goat stew, and pawpaw, piled high on large platters.

The breadfruit is a tall and handsome tree with fat leaves and rough, football-sized fruits that form part of the islanders' staple diet. One way of preparation is 'poi-poi': fermented breadfruit buried in the ground and left to rot, then dug up and mixed with fresh breadfruit into a thick, sour, tongue-tingling porridge (an acquired taste!). Burying the fruit was one way of preserving it in times of abundance, and it could be stored underground for months. Also on the table was boiled and finely-mashed breadfruit that tasted like blancmange, fried breadfruit that tasted like potato chips, and baked breadfruit that tasted of nothing in particular!

During the meal, Robert leant over and whispered "I can't eat this stuff, it's disgusting!"

"Oh, come on, just give it a try," I whispered back, "this is a really ethnic meal and a lot of effort has gone into preparing it. If you were really hungry you'd think it was delicious!" But I had to agree with him: it was not delicious at all! We waited until the dancing began, then put our plates on the ground, where a large, bony dog gobbled down the food.

The dancing was terrific: a group of young girls dressed in brightly-coloured pareos (sarongs) were led by a transvestite, and put on an artistic and elegant performance of cultural themes, with flowers woven into their long, black hair, slender brown arms and supple bodies swaying to the music.

We were told that boys are often brought up as girls - 'mahus' - in the Polynesian culture, to help the women with housework and cooking. The mahus are totally accepted and respected in their society, and are generally homosexual, though some do marry and have children of their own. In olden times they were often the shamans and visionaries of their people.

"Etienne," I asked in English, "are any of your children married?"

"Oh, no, none of them!" he replied, laughing and slapping his broad brown thigh, "Young people make love for pleasure, and when a child comes along and they have no means to care for it, the grandparents rear the baby in their own household with love and joy."

"In fact", he went on to explain "a woman has greater value as a marriage partner if she has already had some children to prove she is a good breeder!"

seven

French Polynesia

Tara was welcome on many of the yachts to which we were invited for drinks or dinner, which meant she wasn't shut down below on *Deusa*, feeling all alone and deserted. One evening, we were all over at *Dragonder* having a party, celebrating the birthday of the owners' young son. It was a great boat for a get-together, with ample wooden decks and space for adults to sit and children to play. The deck was crowded, and Tara ran around excitedly, greeting everyone and enjoying the cuddles and pats she received.

Jean-Marie, *Dragonder's* delightful French owner, wandered off to look for another bottle of wine up in the bow of the boat, which was unlit, and in the dark stepped on something squishy. Thinking his child had dropped a piece of fruit on the deck, he bent down to pick it up, but it didn't feel like fruit at all and stuck to his fingers. So he gave his fingers a quick sniff.

"Merde!" he exclaimed out loud, and we all looked round to see what had happened. "Your little dog, she has shitted on my deck, I have stepped in it, and now it is on my hand!"

Tara had relieved herself on the foredeck, just where she would go if she was back on *Deusa*. Jean Marie was not amused, and it was a long time before Tara was invited back as a result.

⊗⃝⊗

We continued to have trouble getting our dog to come with us when we left the beach to return to *Deusa*. Initially, we asked friends to call her, and she would come galloping to them, when she was grabbed and handed over. But she soon got wise to this and, in the end, wouldn't come to anyone. She was growing more and more self-confident and loved to explore the wonderful world she found herself in – the intriguing smells, the strange sights – and further and further she ran, never turning back, never tiring. Eventually, Robert took over dog control, and she was kept on a long line which gave her some liberty, but which meant we could always reel in our errant Jack Russell.

While we were at anchor amongst the islands, we'd go spear fishing on the neighbouring reefs, and I'd accompany Robert, snorkelling near the dinghy which we anchored in a patch of sand amongst the corals.

With this mode of fishing it was essential to get the fish out of the water and into the dinghy as soon as possible because of the ever-vigilant sharks waiting for any opportunity to snatch a quick meal. Cruising along quietly in the sunshine, admiring the dappled reef and colourful fish, I noticed that the dinghy was drifting into the shallows as the tide slowly receded.

By now, Robert had swum some distance from me, so I thought it a good idea to move the dinghy closer in case he speared a fish. Picking up the anchor, I dangled it below me and towed the dinghy, looking for a deeper sandy patch. Suddenly, out of the corner of my eye, I spotted a white-tipped shark, about one-and-a-half metres long, leisurely swimming towards me with a flick of its long tail. I had read about how to scare sharks, so I shouted into my mask "go away! go away!" and shook the little anchor menacingly.

To my absolute horror, the shark kept coming straight at me, opening its sinister shark mouth to take a snap at the anchor tines dangling a couple of metres below. The shock of the shark jerking at the anchor was so great that I flew out of the water and into the dinghy in one fluid motion, flopping onto the hard fibreglass floor with the anchor clanking in behind me. I lay sprawled for a while in the bottom of the little boat, with my head spinning and my heart thumping, until I calmed down. It wasn't a very big shark, but it was extremely bold, and too close for comfort. After that I stayed in the dinghy and paddled towards Robert who, by now, was sitting on a rock with a speared fish.

Seeing me coming towards him, Robert slipped into the water, holding the fish over his head.

"No, no!" I shouted as loud as I could, "get out of the water, there's a shark around here and it's hungry. It's already tried to eat the dinghy anchor."

Whether Robert heard me or saw my wildly waving arms, he got the message, and climbed back onto the rock to wait for me to paddle over. I didn't see the shark again: I think we both got such a fright that we shot off in opposite directions.

Finally, we got back to *Deusa* with two nice snapper for dinner, and our next door neighbour, Annette, on *Affinity*, asked us over for a drink. Annette liked dogs and invited Tara as well, who was very pleased as we hadn't taken her with us on this particular fishing excursion, precisely because of sharks.

"You're such a lucky dog," I said, picking her up and giving her a hug, "people love you to visit their boats so they can get their dog-fix."

This was certainly true: many of our friends really missed their animals they left behind when they took up the cruising life. An animal on board had complications, but the pleasure of having a dog or cat companion far outweighed the negatives in our view, by. We even met people with parrots, monkeys, and – once – a goose!

Tara raced around this bigger boat with great glee, peering in through all the hatches, leaping into the cockpit and out again. The cockpit was in the stern of the boat, and she was used to our centre cockpit with a lot of deck behind it. During one particularly enthusiastic leap, she bounded out of the cockpit onto what she imagined would be a solid aft deck, but there was only deep blue ocean ... The result was hilarious. She tried to backtrack in midair, her eyes as big as saucers and her mouth open in shock. Splash! – she was in the water, surfacing, with a lot of coughing and spluttering. Once we'd hauled her back on deck she found the whole episode a huge joke, and was soon running around again, shaking sea water all over us.

𝕏

We moved on to the island of Moorea, an easy sail of seventeen nautical miles, to our destination in Cook's Bay. The island was quite beautiful, with great jagged peaks, deep bays, and well-protected anchorages. People told us to walk up to the Belvedere, a 7km hike on a paved road to a spectacular view looking over Cook's and Opoahua Bays. What a good idea, we thought, exercise for us and Tara. Armed with a bottle of water, a camera, video and binoculars, the three of us set out through a cool, leafy teak and chestnut forest, dark green ferns spreading out under the trees and spilling onto the road. Every now and then we came to a sunlit pineapple plantation in a clearing, tended by smiling, waving people and barking dogs. Tara was on her lead so all she could do was bark return insults at the top of her voice.

On the way a notice board pointed out an archaeological site of tumbled, moss-covered stones, where once priests and warriors ruled through fear and superstition. The ancient temples and sacrificial altars were felled by the forces of nature that wrapped them in trailing creepers and strangling trees.

Finally, we broke out into dazzling sunshine on the crest of the hill, and there, way below us, lay *Deusa*, peacefully at anchor, swaying with the light, offshore breeze. It certainly was a spectacular view of the two bays divided by the ridge of rocky mountains, and we sat and gazed for a while, sharing the water with Tara, puffing and panting beside us.

The warm sun made us drowsy and we really didn't feel like walking back down again, so I went over to a family who had arrived in an open truck, children tumbling out of the back to run in the long grass.

"Bonjour, Madame," I tried in my awful French "est possible un 'lift' por moi, mon mari ,e le petit chien?"

"But, of course, my dear," responded this lovely, round, smiley lady in a voluminous floral dress, holding a bright red sunshade, "we won't be up here long, and you can jump in the back with the kids and the aunties – there's lots of room."

I was so relieved she spoke English, I could have hugged her.

Soon, the crowd had seen enough of the view and waved us over to climb aboard, and, squeezing in amongst the excited children, we trundled back down the hill. Two of the ladies sitting in the back cracked open a bottle of beer and offered to share it with us.

Feeling emboldened by my success at finding an English speaker I tried these two golden-brown women.

"Where are you from; do you live around here?"

Luckily, the older lady, wrapped in a gaily-coloured pareo and clutching a woven basket, was able to speak some English.

"Me from Papeete – cette jeune fille, ma niece, Ile de Austral. We take ferry, visit la famille, have le piquenique." She pointed to the bulging basket, smiling and showing us three breadfruit and a large tin of corned beef.

"You," she pointed at Robert, me and Tara, "you piquenique avec nous – la plage?"

I looked at Robert. He had spotted the breadfruit in the basket, and his memory of dinner the other evening loomed large in his mind. Looking horrified, he frantically shook his head behind the good lady's back.

"Merci beaucoup, Madame, you are so kind," I replied, "but we must get back to our bateau."

Climbing off the truck and waving our new friends goodbye, we walked back to our dinghy tied by the jetty. There, we found a young couple sitting on the planks, dangling their feet in the water. They were not as brown as the Polynesians, and we wondered if they were tourists. Always interested to know about people, I started a conversation.

"Hello, my name is Rosemary. This is my husband, Robert and our little dog, Tara. Do you live around here – we come from that blue yacht you can see anchored over there."

"My name is Marie, and no, we do not live here," said the girl, speaking English with a sexy French accent, "Louis and I are teachers, out here on a four-year contract."

"Oh, fabulous!" I exclaimed with my usual enthusiasm, "what a wonderful experience to work with these charming people and learn about their ancient culture."

But Marie was not impressed.

"What culture? These people have no culture! The only culture they have is what they learned in the last two hundred years from the French colonizers. Before that they were savages and cannibals."

We were very taken aback by her words, never expecting a response like that from teachers – and such a bitter response, said with such venom. She spoke good English, so there was no mistaking her meaning.

"We can't wait to leave these backward islands, and we've already put in a request for another posting. We've made no friends with the local people; they just don't want to know us. They're more friendly with the tourists than with us who live here. We always see tourists visiting their homes – we've never once been invited."

And with an attitude like that who would want to invite them, I thought to myself. We were going to ask them over to *Deusa*, but after that conversation decided against it.

ഇൻഈ

It was only a short sail to the next island, Raiatea, where we had heard of an anthropologist – Bill – who was running tours to an archaeological site called Marae Taputapuatea, one of the largest and best-preserved sites in Polynesia. We soon found Bill in his little shop in the local village, and booked a tour with him for the following day.

Sunburnt and stooped, with a floppy bush hat on his head, a stick in his hand, and stout walking boots, Bill looked every bit the part of intrepid explorer. As we walked with him, people called out greetings, and children ran up to say hello as he fished in his pocket for a handful of sweets.

"I've lived here for many years," said Bill, "I'm very fond of the islanders, and teach the kids English in the little school down the road." He waved his stick towards a low, thatched building squatting amongst tall palm trees.

"The French government look after the people very well. They get free housing for those who can't afford a house, financial help for each child in the family, free schooling, clinic, hospital and dentist."

Looking around we had to agree with him. People looked happy and contented, though they would certainly need subsidies. French Polynesia was one of the most expensive places we had visited. Friends said that the local folk, besides vegetables and pineapples, grew a particularly strong brand of marijuana with a good market value that helped earn extra cash.

Of course, this was illegal, but the authorities turned a blind eye, and maybe enjoyed a joint themselves now and then. Occasionally, we were offered a packet, but visitors had to be a lot more cautious. Police sometimes arranged a 'sting' to catch unwary tourists, and then make them pay hefty fines in order not to go to jail. I asked Bill what he thought about marijuana.

"You know, it's a lot less harmful than alcohol. People get very aggressive with drink, beat each other up, slice open skulls with those long coconut knives; get very sick. Dope doesn't do that, just makes you relax and laugh, and chill out with friends."

Bill loaded us into his old Kombi van and we set off for the volcanic basin below Mt Temehani, where the ruins were.

"Do you see all this land?" asked Bill, waving an arm at the lush greenness all around us.

"The French government has opened it up for settlement, but no-one wants to come here. They say the spirits of the dead live in the mountain until they reincarnate. I don't blame them – who wants a haunted house?! Did you notice in the village we've just left, that all the gardens have croton bushes, with pretty variegated leaves? It's said they ward off spirits so everyone plants crotons."

I glanced through the rear window and looked again at the brightly-coloured bushes, painted in green and gold; red and yellow. They didn't appear to have flowers, just brilliant elongated leaves with stripes and blotches, whirls and dots.

"And another thing," continued Bill as we bumped along a dirt track, "don't think, as a foreigner with some spare cash, that you can buy a property wherever you like. Polynesians have rights to the land if they, or a parent, ever lived on it. I'll give you an example. An international hotel complex bought a prime piece of land on a beach near here. They had started building when an islander declared that their grandmother once had a little hut on the shore. End of building project. The land belongs to that family forever, and today you can see the abandoned foundations of the five-star hotel that never was."

We finally arrived at the ruins scattered along the seafront, once a great religious centre of eastern Polynesia dating back to 1000AD. Voyagers from all over the Pacific gathered here for human sacrifices to the gods, to share knowledge and navigational skills. Restoration had started in 1994, and there was hope of declaring it a World Heritage Site. We closed our eyes and listened to the wind rustling in the palm fronds, and the sea burbling on the shore, imagining all the high chiefs in their ceremonial dress arriving in great canoes from across the bay.

On our way back to *Deusa* Bill told us how his wife had died some time ago, and he now lived alone. He was thrilled when his only son came to visit a couple of years ago, but it was a shortlived joy as he dropped dead from a massive heart attack the day after he arrived.

Bill looked down at his weather-beaten hands and cracked fingernails.

"The villagers all came to the funeral. They gathered me into their hearts and I never feel alone anymore."

৪০০৪

We needed to check out of the Society Islands at Bora Bora, but, before leaving Moorea, I had to do some provisioning. Another yacht gave me a lift into town, towing our dinghy behind it. We planned that Robert and Tara on *Deusa* would head slowly for the pass through the reef, and I would catch up in the dinghy once I had finished the shopping.

I must have taken too long with the shopping, or Robert was drifting faster than he realised, because the ebbing tide was rushing out, carrying *Deusa* with it. I jumped into the dinghy with all my parcels, and roared off after my fast-vanishing home, but there was no direct route. Reefs kept on shelving up to just below the water, with little waves breaking in places: I'd lift the motor, paddling furiously with an oar to scrape over the sharp coral until I found deep water again. Luckily, the dinghy had a solid fibreglass hull otherwise I could not have risked a puncture on a rubber floor.

"This is ridiculous," I thought, "I'm never going to catch up, and soon Robert's going to be through the pass. He won't leave me behind, but I hope the dinghy's got enough fuel to get there."

The wind was getting up and spray slopped over my shopping bags as the dinghy bounced through the choppy sea. I arrived, dripping wet, twenty minutes later at *Deusa's* stern, and all Robert could say was, "Why did it take you so long?" Typical man: I won't repeat what I said in reply!

eight

The Samoas

The wind was beckoning us on towards American Samoa as we said goodbye to all our friends in the anchorage, did some more provisioning from the little shops on Bora Bora, and stowed everything away for the passage. Whether we travelled one mile or 1000 miles it was the same routine – nothing could be left lying around. Robert had his charts out on the nav table and I had prepared a meal before we set out. This leg of the journey would be 900 nautical miles.

Once we were away from the anchorage, Robert sat on the aft deck and prepared his fishing lines, one on each side. Soon, one of the reels was whirring out. We grabbed Tara and started to bring in the leaping, struggling fish. But this one was lucky: it shook the lure out of its mouth and got away. Releasing Tara, we put out the line again and settled down to a day of gentle sailing. Next minute, the line buzzed again, Tara leapt to her feet and we all rushed to the aft deck.

Flapping and flopping in the water was a desperate brown Booby, a bird about the size of a domestic chicken but with a slimmer body. The bird had swooped down on the lure, hoping for a fish, and the barbed hook was firmly wedged in its beak. We hove to in order to stop our forward motion, and once again tied up Tara, barking and complaining loudly. Carefully reeling in the struggling bird, we managed to dislodge the hook. We carefully laid the alive but exhausted bird in the dinghy to recover, leaving Tara tied up until it had recovered sufficiently to fly away, some twenty minutes later. No sooner had Robert reset the fishing lines than we caught *another* bird, but this time the poor thing drowned before we could get it on deck. After this sad occurrence, we set a different lure, which didn't skip along the surface, attracting fishing birds.

We were eight days at sea, and the time wasn't without drama. Our beautiful new staysail, that we had so carefully made from the old jib, split right down a seam with a loud ripping noise. What a dismaying sight, but as the wind had strengthened we didn't need it, so stowed it away to be repaired in calmer weather.

Then the mainsail haulout line snapped, leaving the sail to flap wildly in the wind until we got it under control, and Robert replaced the line. What next?, we asked ourselves, thinking of how things usually went wrong in multiples of three. Sure enough, when we had to use the motor in a head wind, it started to stagger and choke.

"Oh, no," groaned Robert, "I hate fixing the motor in a rough sea – please find me a seasick pill. This is going to be a horrid job."

I knew he was right. There's nothing worse than being on your hands and knees in the engine compartment, the warm smell of diesel wafting nauseatingly around your head, as the boat rocks and rolls in the swell. Luckily for Robert, it was only a clogged fuel filter, and a new one soon had the motor running sweetly again.

What a huge relief to arrive in American Samoa and sail into the sheltered waters of Pago Pago harbour! We looked for the Customs and Immigration wharf but couldn't see anything remotely official-looking. Then yacht *Imago* – which was at anchor – pointed out a dilapidated little strip of concrete where two yachts were tied up.

Thank goodness there was a fresh water hose on land, with which we washed down our salty decks, our salty selves, our salty dog, and topped up the water tanks. One of the boats had called the diesel truck, and we all purchased good, cheap, American diesel without having to jerry jug it out to the anchorage.

Eventually, the officials arrived in their smart navy and gold braid uniforms, and stood around on the jetty, not bothering to clamber across the yachts waiting for check-in. Robert took our documents to them and, as they didn't ask if we had any animals on board, Robert didn't volunteer any information in this respect. Later, a particularly daring official made the effort to check a boat tied alongside us, and, as he stepped across *Deusa*, Tara, lurking down below, spotted him, and barked loudly.

"Aaaagh!" squawked the unsuspecting official, leaping in the air with fright. "You've got a dog on board. Have you declared it?"

Robert was very quick-witted.

"This dog was born in America, Officer. I bought her in America, and she doesn't need declaring!"

"Oh, right," said the official, not knowing how to respond to Robert's quick response.

Having cleared in, our options were to tie onto a mooring buoy with several other yachts, or to anchor. Anchoring was not a good idea as the bay was very polluted, and had three huge hurricane chains across the entire muddy bottom to prevent boats dragging. It was safer to use a mooring, though bad luck on our neighbours, who would have to put up with a Jack Russell yapping at them all the time. As it was, our friends on *Imago* were tied up with two terriers on one side, and some dubious English people on the other. It would have been fun to tie up on the other side of her for a stereo terrier symphony!

Ken and Paddy invited us out to the Pago Pago Yacht Club for an evening drink, and to meet all the people of the yachting section who had been participating in the mini Pacific Games. We were tired from our journey, so not the best time to go out, and, as total strangers amongst a jolly crowd of drunks, the more we regretted being there. We couldn't wait to leave, and Ken said we would have to walk back to our boats as all buses stop after dark.

However, there were buses for the Games people, and Ken spotted one, waving it down. Stepping across a dark patch by a tree to get on board, he suddenly disappeared with a cry and a thump. We didn't realise it but the dark patch was an open sewer, and we couldn't see where Ken was in the blackness of no street lighting.

"Ken! Ken! Where are you?" we all shouted in total panic, standing very still in case we fell down something dreadful as well.

"Can you see anything, Paddy, can you hear anything?" we called to her in the dark, cursing ourselves for not bringing a torch.

"I can hear him," called Paddy, "he's over here and is conscious because he's talking. Come and help me get him out of this hole!"

Amazingly Ken had no broken bones, and was able to clamber out of the deep hole, with only some bad scrapes to his arms and legs, though he did look a sight, covered in dubious dirt, and smelling quite horrible. The bus driver had waited for us during all of this, and we eventually got back to the anchorage very shaken; particularly Ken. Accidents can so easily happen in faraway places, and even though we had health insurance, medical facilities and skills could be questionable, accompanied by potentially huge hospital bills.

Luckily, Ken's wounds healed well, due to Paddy's care and vigilance. It didn't bear to think about what sort of nasty infection might come from an open sewer ...

ഇൻ

At the mouth of the bay was a tall mountain called The Rainmaker, which, true to its name, it really was. It rained for days and days, and we were all prisoners on board. It was getting too much, so one wet day we decided to take Tara for a walk, despite the weather. Robert was designated dog handler, and I strolled beside them. As we were ambling along by the village houses, Tara spotted her favourite sport, chickens, and made a rush for them. Robert was not paying attention, and the lead slipped out of his hand in a flash.

Off went Tara, yap, yap, yap, and off went the chickens, flap, flap, flap, up behind the house and into a whole pack of cur dogs. It was the funniest sight, this big man running after Tara, shouting her name, the entire melee disappearing from sight. The local dogs scattered with wide, frightened eyes as Tara bowled past them, closely followed by a large and angry Robert. Luckily, Tara's lead snagged on a tree root and Robert was able to gather up his wayward hound, casually strolling back to the main road as if nothing had happened. Looking back, we saw several dogs peering boggle-eyed round the side of the house. A large lady in hair curlers had come to the front door, and was looking up and down the street, hands on her ample hips, trying to identify the source of the rumpus.

ഇൻ

Some of the chores we have to do in harbour when we arrive is to catch up on mundane things such as laundry, the repair of computers, health issues, sending faxes, etc. Unless you've lived on a boat with piles of dirty and often damp laundry, you can't imagine what a delight it is to find a laundromat with eight machines and eight dryers. With a lot of washing to be done - sheets, towels, clothes - this is very good news. Then, as both our Toshiba computers had crashed and needed help, much to his delight, Robert found a computer shop. He had become more and more proficient at software repair as time went by and we had no outside help, and, in the end, was even able to help fellow yachties with the knowledge he had acquired on our travels.

My feet were still bothering me. I had tried everything: lifting the carpets in the boat in case the fibre was irritating them, keeping them out of sea water, trying different creams - but nothing worked. The doctor in the Marquesa Islands said it was an allergy, and the doctor in Papeete thought I should take anti-fungus pills. The pills cost US$55.00 so I didn't buy them. Now, in Pago Pago, I paid my US$2 and stood in line at the clinic for yet another opinion. This doctor also said it was a fungal infection, and gave me some cream and pills at a far better price than the doctor in the French islands. While at the clinic I saw some of the most overweight women I have ever seen, and wondered why these Polynesians were so gross: I discovered why, later ...

A tour around the huge tuna canning factory near our anchorage was being offered, so my good friend Paddy and I signed up. The factory was surprisingly clean, considering the terrible smells that wafted from it, choking everyone in the vicinity. Lines and lines of people stood at conveyor belts pulling the skins off steamed tuna, and packing the flesh into large cans. The amazing thing about this place was the singing - Samoan songs of wonderful melodies rising above the roar and hiss of the gigantic steamers and pressure cookers. Theatrical in impact, it was a scene from some grand opera, with the huge pipes, spouting steam vents, clanging trolleys laden with fish carcases, bright lights and a chorus of voices, rising up and up.

The people working in the factory were mostly from Western Samoa as no American Samoan would do anything as menial as clean fish for US$3.50 an hour. The Western Samoans were delighted to work for this wage: back home, salaries were very bad, and there were not many jobs, in any case.

On our tour we were shown the employees' clinic. The walls were covered in charts of very overweight women and warnings of diabetes II.

"You will see," said our guide, pointing to the charts, "that our Samoan ladies are very strongly built. Part of that is genetic. Weight is carried on the hips and thighs, but not on the upper body."

We nodded our heads in agreement: we'd all seen some massive people while walking in the village.

"The problem is American fast foods imported to our island. It tastes good but is very bad for us, and we are abandoning our traditional diet of fish and yams. Now you see the ladies putting on weight everywhere, upper body and arms, and they are getting all sorts of health problems."

Robert and I enjoyed a fast food snack now and then, but, really, our shipboard diets were very good as we primarily ate fresh fish with rice and what vegetables we could buy in the markets. People often asked if we got tired of eating fish, but there are so many ways to prepare it: roasted, baked, stewed, pickled, and even raw as 'sashimi' with wasabi mustard.

ଗଠଙ

Some cats have no respect for small dogs. We were preparing to leave for Western Samoa, provisioning the boat and taking on water from the crumbling Customs dock, and Tara was tied up on deck while we carried packages of food from the supermarket taxi. Our backs were turned when a local tabby cat strolled onto our boat, sitting down just out of reach of Tara to take a bath, licking a paw and leisurely passing it behind her ears. The cat was a comedian with no fear of dogs, and Tara nearly strangled herself straining to get at the nonchalant feline, shrieking insults at the intruder, her eyes popping out of her head with effort and affront. The cat took absolutely no notice, and continued to wash.

Scrambling back on board to stop the racket, I picked up the cat and politely asked her to leave! She was a plump kitty; no doubt was well cared for by the tuna factory a short stroll away.

Later in the day, once our provisions were safely stowed away, we cast off from the decrepit jetty and sailed away into the sunset for an overnight passage to Western Samoa, just 75 nautical miles away. (A nautical mile is a little longer than a land mile; equivalent to 1.1508 land miles. Speed through water is measured in knots per hour, which is relates to nautical miles.)

ଗଠଙ

The town of Apia in Western Samoa was quite different to Pago Pago in American Samoa, and boasted decent sidewalks, paved streets, nice shops and lovely artisan work, such as war clubs (once used for fights amongst the various tribes), talking staffs for chiefs to hold while addressing a meeting, wooden ceremonial drums, and tapa cloth, made from the bark of the mulberry tree, soaked in water and beaten flat with wooden mallets. Yachts don't have much room for storage, so we were careful what we bought as souvenirs. Here, we were told that Tara could most definitely NOT come ashore, so she stayed patiently on board while we explored this new island.

A treasure trove of fresh fruits and vegetables greeted us at the open market: rows and rows of glowing produce on low stands, the owners sitting on woven grass mats behind. All around were yams and taro (a starchy root rather like a potato), breadfruit and bananas, raw cocoa beans, lettuce, cabbage, tomatoes, carrots, and sea cucumber intestines. The sea cucumber is really an animal – so-named because of its resemblance to that vegetable – which are harvested and dried for medicinal purposes as well as eaten as a delicacy, as we discovered. We weren't too keen on them, but delighted in everything else.

From Paddy I learnt how to preserve fruits, vegetables, fish and chicken, much like our grandparents used to do, using a pressure cooker and special preserving jars.

Robert Louis Stevenson lived in Western Samoa at his 162-hectare home 'Vailima,' meaning five waters, and named after the streams that ran across his property. The local people called him 'Tusitala' – the teller of tales – but he didn't live amongst them for very long, because, five years after he arrived, he died of a fatal brain haemorrhage whilst helping his wife, Fanny Osborne, prepare dinner. He was only 44 years old, but had been plagued by ill health for a large part of his life. We visited his home and climbed the steep trail cut by 200 sorrowful Samoans as they carried his body to its final resting place looking over the sea, just below the summit of Mt Vaea. The Samoans loved him, and would often come to him with their problems.

Stevenson wrote his own requiem, and here it was, engraved on his tomb, the wind rustling and sighing through the trees the peaceful backdrop.

> Under the wide and starry sky,
> Dig the grave and let me lie.
> Glad did I live and gladly die,
> And I laid me down with a will.
>
> This be the verse you grave for me:
> Here he lies where he longed to be;
> Home is the sailor, home from the sea,
> And the hunter home from the hill.

There was something so hauntingly poignant in the words we read as we stood high on the windswept hill looking down on the distant ocean: they brought tears to my eyes and a lump to my throat, as I thought of beloved family members and friends no longer with us.

ഇന്‍ഇ

One day Ken and Paddy, Robert and I hired a little jeep to explore, and we all agreed that we had never seen such a beautifully kept island in all our travels. Each village took pride in the appearance of its garden lawns, with neatly planted bushes, creepers and flowers growing in a profusion of colours amongst clipped and brushed grass. The road wound through village after village, and each was as immaculate as the next with their open fales (meeting places), and many, many churches. We were told the Samoans took easily to Christianity, and made very good evangelists, travelling through the Pacific, converting other islanders.

It was getting toward sunset when we noticed a lot of men dressed in white shirts and pink lave-laves (skirts) walking along the road. Later, it was explained that these were untitled men (young males who had not yet entered the hierarchy of chiefdom, and did not have the title of chief, mayor or orator), who ensured that everyone was in their home ready for the evening prayers (Sa) held each day at sunset. Some villages started at 6pm; others at 6.30pm, and a curfew was rigidly adhered to. If one was on the main road it was okay to continue driving slowly, but on a side road one had to stop for at least twenty minutes.

While in Western Samoa we met a charming Australian family: Peter, Cathy, and their three children. Peter was a marine biologist who worked for the Australian government, restocking the reefs with giant clams on the island of Savai'i. They took us on a visit around the island in their jeep, and Peter stopped to see the local chief, Ullu, a solid, fine-looking man in his early fifties. Peter had been stocking some nearby ponds with tilapia fish, and wanted to ask the chief how the experiment was going.

Just as we were about to leave, the gong rang for the 6pm curfew of Sa, so that meant we had to stay right where we were. Naturally, the chief invited us all in to his fale for prayers. It was an open-plan room with rolled up pandanu mats for walls, that could be lowered in case of inclement weather. More rolled up mats lay along the edge of the cement floor, and must have been for sleeping on. We sat cross-legged on the mats in a semi-circle with the chief one side, his wife, Anita, on the other, and their slim, brown daughter, Fui-Fui, by us. The prayers began with chanting in a beautiful melodious harmony, and then Ullu and his wife got on to all fours, and he started to speak, with his wife responding now and then. Finally, the prayers ended with another chant.

Ullu sat back and addressed us in Samoan whilst his wife translated for us in good English.

"Welcome to my home," he said, his deep voice rumbling from somewhere inside his broad chest. We all nodded and said 'thank you.'

"Your friend, Peter, who has brought you here today, has helped our village very much. He has given us two new aluminium boats with motors so we can go fishing. He has brought us nets and ropes and cement for building houses. The Australian government is very good."

Peter smiled and looked embarrassed. Anita brought us cool glasses of lemonade, then continued to translate for Ullu.

"It is getting late; the sun will soon be gone. Stay with me and my family in our house tonight. There are enough sleeping mats for everyone, and Anita will prepare dinner for us."

I thought this was a wonderful idea, and a great experience to spend the night in a Samoan home, but Robert didn't look too happy at the prospect of lying on a thin mat on a hard cement floor in a communal family room. There was also Tara to think about: she would be very sad to spend the night alone.

"Thank you so much, Chief Ullu," said Peter, "It is very kind of you, but we really must be getting back, and Cathy is expecting me. My friends have to look after their boats out in the bay."

Back at Peter and Cathy's house a big bowl of ava (a slightly sedative drink made from the crushed roots of the kava plant, and the traditional drink of Western Samoa) was waiting for us. We all took a glass of this new beverage. It tasted bitter with a thin, earthy flavour, numbing the tongue and giving a feeling of well-being. Apparently, this was a ceremonial drink throughout the Pacific, and Cathy told us that we would come across it in all the islands we visited.

"Let's go out for a meal," proposed Cathy, always the party-animal, "there's a live band and dinner at a hotel just down the road from here."

We decided that Tara would be alright if we did this, as she was on deck and not shut down below. If there was chicken on the menu we would bring her back a piece as a treat – a change from the fish and rice diet.

So we all jumped into the jeep and soon found the loud music and colourful crowd in their sarongs and lave-laves. Dinner was dished out of great, black cooking pots – a scoop of curried chicken neck; a dollop of rice and three bananas – all piled onto a breadfruit leaf lying in a woven coconut palm basket. What a brilliant idea: no washing up, and a totally disposable biodegradable plate. We ate the gooey chicken curry with our fingers: there wasn't even a table to sit at, so we had to balance the palm basket in one hand and dip our fingers into the mush with the other – quite a messy challenge, but very tasty.

"Now, here's how it works at Samoan parties," explained Cathy, "women are fair game, and you either dance with your partner all night, or be prepared to be asked by all sorts of people."

We listened with interest.

"If you refuse someone," she continued, "you must refuse all requests, otherwise you will cause terrible offence to the refused man, if you then accept someone else."

I seized the opportunity to ask Robert for the next dance. And the next, and the next. He soon got bored of this game, however, and we went back for a drink at the bar.

Cathy grabbed my arm, "Come, let's dance!"

"What?" I said in shocked surprise, "women dancing together?"

"Why not?" she said, dragging me onto the floor with Robert looking on, bemused.

A Samoan woman in a festive sarong joined in, and the three of us danced together. When the music stopped we went back to join our group. To my horror, a little weasel of a man arrived and asked Robert and the group if he could dance with me! They all nodded happily before I could open my mouth, so off I went for a waltz with a guy who came up to my armpits. As soon as the dance was over I rushed back to Robert, but, guess what? – the next time there was a slow dance weasel-man was back again, bowing humbly and asking everyone if he could dance with me. I pretended not to notice him but he would not go away, so Cathy told him in Samoan that I was tired and he finally left.

"It's you who wanted to go to a Samoan party;" said Robert with a broad grin, "serves you right for wanting to get to know the locals!"
He has a great sense of humour and is often amused at my ethnic adventures, observing quietly on the sidelines, and pulling my leg when he gets the chance.

Tara was overjoyed to see us when we arrived back on board that night, smelling faintly of curry and carrying a doggy bag for her.

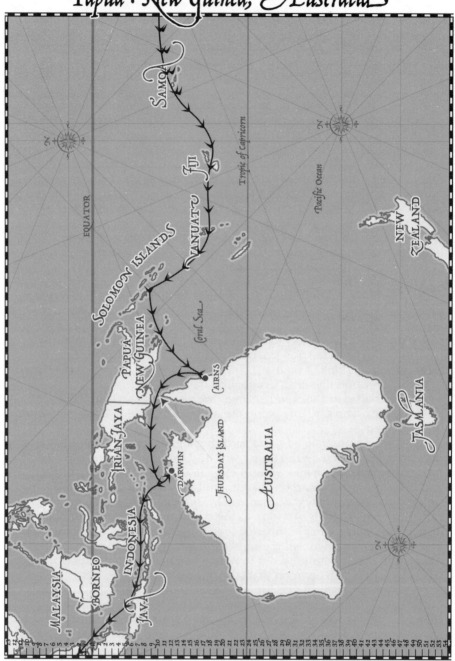

nine

Fiji and Vanuatu

Our long sail to Fiji was going to take us at least a week, so we broke our journey after three days, stopping at the Tongan island of Niuatoputapu ('New potatoes' for those of us who couldn't pronounce it) for a few days. Unfortunately, Tara once again had to stay on board due to quarantine regulations, though still got lots of exercise as I would take her swimming in the dinghy close by *Deusa*.

"Hey, Tara, how about a swim?" I'd ask as we stood on the deck in the hot sunshine. "You haven't been off the boat for ages, so boring for you, little girl." Bright-eyed with enthusiasm, she'd hop up and down, running to the stern ladder and back to me as if to say, 'come on, what are you waiting for?'

I had a stick that I threw for her, and she would leap from the dinghy into the water, swim like crazy, seize the stick and bring it back to me. I would haul the dripping dog and stick into the dinghy, and the routine would start again. Tara swallowed a lot of sea water playing this game, which made her very thirsty. Not only would she pee a lot more as a result, but it also gave her diarrhoea. The survival journals do not recommend drinking sea water, and say it's better to drink your own urine - as long as it lasts!

Friend Paddy and I enjoyed visiting the village, chatting with the children as they walked home after school. The women and young girls made a living by weaving fine mats and baskets. Two of the schoolgirls befriended us, and asked if they could visit our boats one day, so we told them we would pick them up on the shore. The islanders loved to come on board the visiting yachts, fascinated by all the electronic equipment, the gimballed stove, and the bathroom ('head' in nautical terms) with toilet and shower. Most of them didn't have luxuries like this.

Paddy spent the morning baking two fine cakes, and Ken went to pick up the girls, but only one of them - Moli - arrived, explaining that her friend was sick. She climbed on board *Imago*, refused a cup of tea, wouldn't eat the cake, didn't want to look around, but said she wanted to come over to *Deusa*, then go home.

Most strange. I went across to *Imago* to pick her up in the dinghy.

As we headed back to our boat Moli began to speak. "I've got a present for you," she whispered, shyly (I could barely hear her above the chugging motor).

TARA

"Oh, how nice, Moli, what is it?" I asked as we arrived at the stern of *Deusa*, whereupon any hope of further conversation was dispelled by Tara's barking.

"Hello, hello!" I shouted above the dog-din, "I've got a visitor. Please grab Tara."

Once poor Tara had been reluctantly hauled away, Moli and I sat down in the cockpit to resume our conversation.

"So, you said you have a present for me, Moli, how very nice of you."

Moli fished in the plastic bag she was carrying, and drew out three little place mats.

"I made these at school, and I brought them for you." Moli said, handing over the mats, and I saw the price tag of US$3.00 dangling from one of them. I went to get her the money but she waved it away.

"I don't want the money," she said, "I want to trade these mats for your camera."

My camera! I was quite shocked. How could she think that my precious camera was worth only three small mats? I realised she was speaking to me in all seriousness, however, and, in her mind, this was a fair trade.

So I went to get one of my diaries that I kept on our travels and showed it to her.

"Moli, I would love to give you my camera but it's the only one I've got. I take pictures for my diary, so I must keep it."

I gave her the money and some small gifts that we kept for visitors – a tea towel and pot holder for her mother; a bright orange-and-gold bead clasp for her.

Once she realised that she wouldn't get my camera Moli said she wanted to go home. However, a large cargo boat had pulled up to the jetty, and she was too shy to go back to the dock and have everyone stare at her. Finally, she had me drop her on the nearby shore, and waded through the ankle-deep water to the beach and wandered home. I felt a bit hollow after her visit. To Moli, the mats had just as much value as my camera; after all, she had made them by hand, whereas I'd simply bought the camera.

⁎‘⁑

It was with relief that we finally dropped anchor in Suva harbour after a four-day, long and hard sail to Fiji. Sea state was rough, and the wind was a continuous 25 to 30 knots. Robert had not been feeling well for several days, and I got seasick: Tara took it all in her stride. There was a cyclone warning, too, but it was still some distance from us, and nothing to worry about. However, as I like to worry, I worried about that!

It was here that Robert stayed on board with Tara while I flew to England for a family wedding. This was the first time the two of them had been alone together since Robert got Tara in Miami, and gave them the opportunity to once again share quality time, and Tara didn't have to challenge me for her favourite place on the settee.

Robert took on the amazing task of getting the whole of *Deusa's* interior re-varnished. It must have been very difficult, living on board and keeping out of the way of the two Indian varnishers, never mind persuading Tara not to knock over the varnish pot. Besides all the dust from sanding down the old varnish, Robert also had to clean up after the varnishers at the end of each day, and sweep Tara's dusty pawprints from the settee and bedcover in the aft cabin. This also meant cleaning the toilet – not his favourite task, especially when it's been used by others apart from yourself! This was the longest time he had spent on *Deusa* on his own with no help at all, and he soon realised what a lot of work it takes to keep a boat clean, particularly with workers on board making dust storms of old varnish.

Besides being boat cleaner, bottle washer and dog-minder, Robert also ran the SSB radio net, which was usually my job. We had built up quite a following, and spoke every morning around 9am, giving a brief weather forecast for the next couple of days, and local information pertinent to arriving sailors. One morning, Robert was out early on shore when he suddenly remembered the net, so leapt into the dinghy, hurried back to *Deusa* and scrambled up the stern ladder, where he nearly fell over Tara as she greeted him with great enthusiasm, leaping around his legs. Hurrying below he turned on the radio to catch the first yacht calling "*Deusa, Deusa.*"

Hearing Tara barking on deck, he asked the caller to stand by a moment and poked his head out of the companionway to see who was coming. No-one was arriving, but the dinghy was departing, on its own: in his haste he had forgotten to tie it onto the stern rail when climbing on board, and now it was drifting away.

"Oh, bloody hell," Robert swore to himself, making a general announcement to the radio listeners that he would call back in half-an-hour. Fishing his flippers out of the dive bag he jumped into the water in his shirt and shorts, and struck out for the runaway dinghy as fast as he could. A splash behind him let him know that Tara had joined him in this great game of catch the little boat. Tara could swim just as fast as Robert, and it was an even bet as to who would get there first. Luckily, there was no wind in the harbour that day, and it hadn't drifted too far. Hauling himself and Tara into the dinghy, Robert started the motor and returned to *Deusa*, this time tying the dinghy to the aft railing so that it couldn't go walkabout again.

∞CЗ

I arrived back from England after a month away to a sparkling new boat – and an exhausted Tara and Robert. He had even laid new carpets as the old ones had got so dusty. It was great to get back to my home and the routine of living on board: back with beloved Robert and beloved Tara, my close family. I gave them both lots of hugs and kisses, and told them how much I had missed them. Travelling and seeing friends and relatives was wonderful and a good break from sailing, but I was very happy to be home, and to continue our adventure through the Pacific islands.

Whilst we were in Fiji, Robert – who needed to have a cataract removed from his left eye – heard that there was a very good eye surgeon nearby. Friends and family were rather doubtful about the wisdom of this: how could there be a good ophthalmologist on a far-away island like Fiji; surely it was a risk to one's sight to have an operation there? However, the more we heard about Guy Hawley, the more we were convinced it was a good idea. Every year, Guy used to sail to the Marianna Islands and carry out free cataract operations for the islanders, so had vast experience.

Robert bit the bullet and had the operation, and from when he went into the surgery until he was back on *Deusa*, promising not to go sailing for the next two weeks, took just two hours.

"Now, be careful," Dr Hawley advised him. "You're a big, strong man, and there must be lots of jobs to do around the boat while you wait. Leave them alone; be patient, otherwise you can dislodge the new lens, and that's very serious. Avoid picking up heavy weights, and don't bump your head. You've got a good, strong wife: let her do some of the things you normally do!"

Tara was most surprised to see her beloved master with a patch over his eye, and insisted on climbing into his lap when he sat down, licking his face as if to say, 'I can make it better!'

The next day we went back to Dr Hawley's surgery, and joined a queue of Fijians who had had their cataracts removed the same day as Robert. Judging by the crowd who filled the waiting room it was obvious that he was a good surgeon.

"You're fine," said the doctor, as he took off Robert's eye cover and looked at his handiwork, "you'll be able to see all those marker buoys guiding you into harbour – you won't need your binoculars any more. Good sailing and fair winds." He patted Robert on the shoulder and called in his next patient.

We weren't planning on leaving too soon so Robert's eye healed very well, and there was no bruising. Some years previously he had had the right eye done in England, which entailed staying overnight in hospital. He had the most dreadful bruising, as if he'd been in a bar fight. For all the fancy letters after his name, the English surgeon was not half as good as Dr Hawley.

‎✣‎

Once Robert was ready to travel again we said goodbye to Fiji and sailed on for Vanuatu, arriving three days later at Port Vila, the major town of Efate Island, where we had to check in.

The fishing was good; so good, in fact, that Robert had to put away the rod as we had too much fish in the fridge. We caught a 48lb yellow-finned tuna and a nice wahoo of about 20lb, so that filled our fish quota. Wahoo is a delicious fish to eat, with white, flaky meat, and is also known as dolphinfish and dorado because of its spectacular green-and-gold colouring when it first comes out of the sea. Robert was really disappointed as he loves to fish - as did Tara.

When Tara was very young she ate puppy biscuits, but as she grew older we moved her onto rice and fish with, when we had them, some cooked vegetables chopped into her dish. At first, we thought this might be too much protein for her, but she thrived on this diet. For snacks she loved avocado pear, apple, bean sprouts, and coconut. Coconut was her favourite and, if she found a broken one on the ground, she would roll in it for perfume, rather like other dogs would with much more disgusting smells, such as dead frog and human excrement.

The people of Vanuatu were very friendly, but shyer than the bold Fijians. Very dark-skinned with fuzzy hair, and not as tall and solid in build as the Fijians, they were much more Melanesian than the Fijians, who had mixed with Polynesian explorers of long ago. Fortunately, we could take Tara ashore here, which was a great relief to her: she so missed her walks, and the possibility of chasing chickens!

Port Villa had an extensive fruit and vegetable market under a large open shed, and we learned about a local delicacy called lap-lap, made from bananas and yams. Grated and mashed into a paste with coconut cream and herbs, it is sometimes mixed with seafood or pork, wrapped in banana leaves, and cooked in an earth oven or umu. Later, we tried some and it was delicious.

While exploring the market we got caught up in the 50-year jubilee celebration of the Presbyterian church as the participants paraded through the main street pulling a large outrigger canoe on a trailer. The missionaries, when they arrived in the islands to spread the Lord's word, were horrified at the sight of the bare-breasted, golden-brown girls, and quickly invented a cover-up type of smock for them to wear so that they would no longer offend the Church. The ladies paraded past us in their sunshine-yellow missionary dresses, followed by little girls with flowers and bows in their short, frizzy hair. Everyone was singing and dancing, and it was such a happy sight.

Sitting on deck one evening enjoying the sunset, someone motored up and tapped on our hull. Tara leapt from her perch on the life raft with a loud bark, hurrying to her place at the stern to ward off marauders. The visitor was our neighbour from the nearby catamaran, who we hadn't yet met.

"Hi, folks" said a solidly-built man with tousled hair and a lazy Australian drawl, "does your dog bite?"

"No, no," we hurriedly assured him, "she's very noisy, but not dangerous." We called Tara back to the cockpit.

"I'm Grant, mate" said our surprise visitor, "I was expecting guests this evening but they haven't turned up. Now I've got all this good wine and snacks going to waste. Come and help me enjoy them."

The offer of a free cocktail and nibbles was most attractive, so, leaving Tara on guard, we jumped into the dinghy and went across to the very luxurious catamaran anchored nearby. On board, we met a tall and glamorous lady in jangling bangles and a flowing sarong that barely covered her sapphire-blue bikini. Grant was an ex-pilot for Qantas, and Stephanie was his girlfriend.

Over the next few days we saw quite a lot of Grant and Stephanie. They had drinks with us; we had tea with them. One makes friends quickly in the sailing world as we all lead such itinerant lives, and enjoy each other's company while we can.

One day we stopped by the catamaran on the way back to *Deusa* with some shopping, and imagine our surprise when Stephanie greeted us in floods of tears. "I'm going back to Oz – Grant's wife is arriving tomorrow."

They had been living together for five years, and had been planning to set off on a three-year cruise. In Australia, the two of them had built a house together on Stephanie's property, and her daughter from a previous marriage was looking after all their financial affairs whilst they were away.

"Grant's still got a wife in Sydney; they never got divorced," she sobbed, leaning over the lifelines as we hung on to the side of the boat. "She's found out where we are and is going to make trouble for Grant because he took the boat out of Australia. It's in her name, and she's arriving tomorrow in Port Vila with a warrant for his arrest. She's told him I've got to get off the boat."

Stephanie was clearly in a state of shock, and quite dazed. Poor woman: she had left her job, rented out her house, and prepared herself to sail the oceans for three years. But what was she thinking of, running away with a guy on his wife's boat?

"You know," she continued, getting more and more angry, "he's not tidied up his life and now his wife is coming to take him back. He's telling me not to worry, just go and stay in the hotel for a couple of days and he'll send Mavis back to Australia. They've been married for 25 years and have three kids. She's not going to let go, I'm sure of it." She sat down in despair with her head in her hands.

Later, Grant came across to see us, obviously to fill in his side of the story. Robert and I decided that, as a pilot of Qantas, he had been playing these two ladies along very skilfully, saying he was off flying, when really he was off visiting one or the other. Nice game as long as it didn't catch up with you. Now that he had retired it obviously had!

"I love them both," sighed Grant as he stared into the glass of neat whisky Robert had poured him. "They're both fine people, I can't choose one over the other. I just don't know what to do."

The next day I went to see Stephanie in the hotel that she had moved to, as I really felt sorry for her.

"Mavis arrived yesterday," she fumed, "and he's gone and put her up in this hotel, just down the corridor from me. How can he, what the hell is he playing at? Do you know what he said? 'Don't worry, everything will be fine. Leave the door open a crack and I'll come and visit you.'"

Later, Stephanie and I sat on a bench in the park and watched Grant move Mavis out of the hotel and onto the boat. Mavis didn't know Stephanie, and thought she'd gone back to Australia. As Mavis stood on the jetty while Grant ferried her bags to the boat, Stephanie walked right past her to check her out. Stephanie was younger and much more attractive, and knew it, but this was the wife and she had first claim. Interesting point, here: both women owned sewing machines. Stephanie had taken hers off the boat and Mavis had moved hers on board! It was almost as if the sewing machine symbolised possession of territory!

I told Stephanie I would take her to the airport if Grant was otherwise occupied; they both came over later for her to say goodbye. Whilst Grant sat in the cockpit with Robert, Stephanie came down below.

"I made the bastard take me over to the catamaran to meet Mavis," she said with a fierce glow in her eyes. "You should have seen Mavis' face. She hid behind Grant, screaming at him to get me off the boat. Then she rushed, crying, into the cabin and slammed the door. I followed her, and told her I wanted to see the woman who had lived with such a spineless, gutless worm all those years!"

Whilst Stephanie was talking to me in the back cabin, Grant was telling Robert that he still loved them both. His wife had an arrest warrant to have him hauled away in handcuffs, but the police were reluctant to do this, not wanting to get involved in tourist tiffs.

Whilst all this had been going on, Grant had found a totem pole floating in the bay, and handed it to the authorities. It was very old and precious; probably stolen from a sacred site. The first officials who came to collect it off the catamaran turned grey under their dark skins and wouldn't touch it, saying they would have to call a holy man to remove it. It was a mystery why it was floating in the bay: maybe a yacht had bought it cheap from the thief, and then thrown it into the sea for fear of reprisal. Maybe the thief himself had got cold feet at the thought of all the ancestors who might haunt him. Vanuatu is full of spirits, magic and animistic rituals, which may be why the authorities didn't want to arrest Grant, as he had done the right thing with the totem pole.

We never saw Grant and Mavis again. Did they stay together, did she go sailing with him, or did she return to Australia? There are a lot of unfinished stories amongst sailing friends.

છ∞જી

On the nearby island of Tanna was an active volcano that I really wanted to see, but we had to check in first at Port Vila to be legal. This was the official port of entry to Vanuatu, and the authorities could get very upset if yachts ignored their rules, so we didn't stop there on the way. Now was a good time to go, however, so, one afternoon, we set out. As it was quite rough I took a seasick pill, and Tara lay on the settee below looking miserable. Robert doesn't suffer seasickness like Tara and I do, and she always recovers much sooner than I. It's not recommended to give dogs pills that humans can take, and we didn't know of any canine medication for this problem.

We were ploughing into rough seas beating on the bow, and I wondered if I really wanted to do this. Robert didn't care whether or not he saw a volcano, but he would definitely put up with rough seas and high winds if I did. We turned back and, as we did, I slipped against the cockpit table with a crash, feeling a sharp pain in my side.

"Oh, bugger," I said, "I think I've cracked a rib."

I felt very depressed at being such a wimp and not getting to Tanna. I'm a fair-weather sailor and don't like the rough, pounding seas and rocking boat that make me feel so sick. I also get very frightened when the waves are building and crashing onto the deck. My imagination kicks in and I think awful thoughts, such as what if Robert is washed overboard? At least we can put Tara down below, but Robert is on the helm steering *Deusa*, particularly in rough seas when the autopilot can't cope. We always wear safety harnesses that attach by wire cables to padeyes (solid U-shaped bolts at strategic places) in the cockpit, in case of just such an eventuality.

Now, we had to check back in at Port Vila, having left just the evening before. Rowing the dinghy ashore with Robert was very painful, and I was even more convinced I had cracked something. There was really nothing to do but wait for it to heal, though, and not cough or laugh too much, and certainly not pick up anything heavy: not so easy on a yacht. My injury pained me for at least two or three weeks, and then began to ease up, though I still had to be careful not to overdo it, and find myself full of aches and pains the next day.

₴℡

We stopped at several islands on our journey through Vanuatu, and at Ngouna Island, one Sunday, we were invited to a church service by a smiling, round, brown lady called Betty. The church was rustic and simple, with leaf walls and roof, wooden benches, and a sand floor. We soon realised we had sat on the wrong side of the church, however, when all the men arrived and sat on the same side, with the ladies the other side of the aisle.

Down by my feet I found a nest full of speckled eggs, and all through the service a black hen tried to come into the church to lay another egg. First, she tried to gain access via the open window, flying up with a cackle only to be shooed away with an open bible. Then she tried the door, sneaking surreptitiously around the corner with a beady eye on the congregation. A child spotted her, and once again she was chased out with a flap and a flurry. We could hear her cackling indignantly outside in the hot sun, waiting for the prayers to end! Thank goodness Tara wasn't with us: she would have soon chased away the intruder.

Most of the people were Presbyterian, and the church service was held in Bislama, the local dialect, with the women the main participants, leading the prayers and singing, reading from the bible, and giving the sermon. The church played a very strong role in their lives, though there were some 'custom villages' who still maintained their traditions, rejecting all western ways, clothes and teaching. The men wore penis wrappers made out of plaited leaves that tucked into a bark belt; the women wore grass skirts. The children didn't go to school but learnt the ways of their elders.

As we walked into the bright sunshine after the service the resident pastor, Willie, approached us.

"Please come and join us for a meal: it's been cooking while we were at church. You'll be able to see how we celebrate our Sundays together."

We received another lesson in how to make lap-lap, grating yams, manioc, bananas and any other starchy substance, and kneading it into a paste. Rather like a pizza, it was then spread in a large circle an inch thick on banana leaves. Some tasty herbs from the jungle were sprinkled over it, and chunks of fish, octopus, chicken, pig, or even beef, was decoratively arranged on the circle. More banana leaves were laid on top of the great, round, doughy dish, and it was laid in the umu, a traditional oven dug in the ground, sandwiched between hot stones, and left to cook slowly.

Burning logs were used to heat the stones in the umu, and these retained their heat long enough to cook all the food that had been prepared for the feast. It was a great way to cook for a large crowd.

The result was quite delicious: well, I certainly thought so, though Robert had his doubts! Several ladies spread large, woven mats under a big, shady mango tree, and more ladies brought the steaming bundles of food in their banana leaf wrappers, carefully laying them in two long lines. The banana leaves were peeled back, revealing a multitude of colours. The banana was yellow, the pumpkin orange, the yam was almost purple, and the manioc grey. An old lady cut the lap-lap into wedges with a sharp shell, and our plates were heaped with hot, fragrant food. Those who didn't have plates just took a handful and began munching. We all ate with our fingers, which was quite easy to do as the dough base made a good platform for the toppings.

Of course, the delicious smell of lap-lap lying in the cool shade drew the dogs, chickens and pigs, who were chased away with a large stick. Some persistent chickens were even so bold as to fly in over the feast with a cackle and a flutter. It wasn't the most hygienic of circumstances, but, presuming one has to eat two bushels of dirt in one's lifetime, this was a good moment to catch up.

Willie came over to talk with us.

"How are you enjoying our Sunday feast?" he asked with a twinkle in his eye. He could see we weren't used to sitting on mats, eating lap-lap with one hand, and chasing away chickens and dogs with the other.

"Thank you so much, Pastor Willie, it's a great privilege to join your group." Robert replied. "Please tell us how you manage to have all this lovely food and there are no shops anywhere near your village."

"We grow it all, and what we don't have we trade with the nearby village. For instance, we have a good yam crop this year so we traded for some manioc. A lot of us fish, and we only take what we can use on the day as we have no refrigeration. See that washing line over there? It's made from a jungle vine. And the clothes pegs – look closely, they're split bamboo. Our plates are banana leaves, our ovens are wood-fired, and we use stones to preserve the heat."

Looking around we could see that what he said was true. These island people seemed to be very environmentally-friendly, and we could learn a lesson from them. They didn't take more than they could use or trade with the next village. It all came from the jungle around them, their vegetable patches, or the sea. We couldn't see any rubbish or plastic lying around because everything was biodegradable.

TARA

Moving on to Epi Island in Vanuatu, we stopped at the small village of Leman. Some yachting friends told us to look for Mackin, a school teacher who had a problem with her computer. Robert was just the right person to ask as he was considered the local computer expert amongst the sailing community.

Off we went to look for Mackin at the little two-roomed school sheltering under a large tree.

"Are you Mackin?" Robert asked a pretty girl of about 24 who answered our knock on the schoolhouse door.

"Yes, I am, how can I help you?" she replied, surprised to see these two sunburnt foreigners standing in her yard.

"Well, maybe I can help you," said Robert, "someone said you have a computer problem and I know something about them, particularly if it's software."

Mackin's face lit up. "Oh, yes please, you can't imagine how difficult it is for me to run a computer. We have no electricity on the island, but I have a small generator behind my house. Sometimes I don't have enough money to buy fuel until my next pay cheque arrives. Please come in and have a look at the computer. There's enough fuel at the moment, and maybe you can help me sort out a few things."

She led us around to her house at the back of the school and invited us in. It was a typical Melanesian home where everyone sits on the floor on palm leaf mats, but Mackin had a small table and chair in one corner where she did her computer work.

"You'll have to excuse my lack of knowledge," Mackin smiled shyly, "I'm totally self-taught so I have lots of questions for you."

Robert is very good at helping people, not only with computer problems, but also anything else that he could fix with the tools and materials on *Deusa*, whether it be soldering a loose wire on a radio, or using epoxy putty to mend a hole in a canoe. He is a very capable person, whose lateral thinking means that nothing is impossible in his eyes!

While Robert talked with Mackin, I went back to *Deusa* to fetch a couple of litres of petrol for her generator, and Robert asked me to pick up a book on Windows he wanted to give her. By now, my cracked ribs had completely mended, so I didn't have to watch what I carried.

"Guess what, Tara?" I said as I climbed the stern ladder and she gave me a big, wet kiss on the cheek, "you and I have at least twenty minutes to go to the beach and have a swim. Robert's going to be quite a while helping the schoolteacher."

Tara leapt with joy and ran around in circles as I fetched her collar and lead. 'Swim' was one of her best words, and she could hardly wait for me to pull in the dinghy before she jumped into the little boat, yipping with excitement. Dogs are such fun and good companions to have on board: it's almost like having a third person to do fun things with, talk to, or complain to in difficult and trying times.

We stayed in Leman for a couple of days and Robert was able to help Mackin a lot, though there was so much still for her to learn that we could have spent a couple of months there.

ഇഇരു

Washing clothes is always a challenge on board, and even though we had a water-maker, I would always go ashore with the laundry whenever I could, taking Tara with me.

We were anchored off the village of Ranon on Ambryn Island, where I met a very kind lady called Eslin. She invited me ashore to use the village tap, lending me her large, aluminium bowl. I never realised, though, that I was to be the entertainment for the day as she, her family, and friends all sat around in a circle to watch me do my washing.

As the water went into the bowl I added a generous handful of soap powder, which bubbled and foamed to the brim. There was a gasp of amazement from the audience, who couldn't believe anyone would use so much soap at one time. The children were delighted with the bubbles, and tried to catch them as they blew away in the light breeze. But that was not the only shock the villagers were in for. The amount of clothes to be washed was a goodly heap of towels, sheets, pillowcases, and many, many T-shirts and shorts, as well as underwear.

This was my first opportunity to do laundry in a couple of weeks so everything was brought ashore. However, this pile of clothes represented the entire wardrobe of several families. They had very little, and would even share a shirt or dress for special occasions. It was a mistake to wash so much stuff in front of them, I later realised.

I felt very awkward sitting there with an ever-increasing audience, muttering and pointing, watching my every move, so I tried to speed up the operation, washing everything faster and faster, and doing a thoroughly bad job of it. The ladies must have noticed this and thought that not only did I use too much powder, but I didn't even scrub the clothes clean!

It was with relief that I finished the job and hauled it all back to the dinghy. The rest of the soap powder I donated to Eslin and the other women of the household, who seized it with delight. I knew it was going to last them a lot longer than it would have lasted me. Once I arrived back at *Deusa's* stern, Robert and Tara were there to help me get the dripping wet laundry onto the deck and hung up. We tied washing line all around the rigging in a spider's web of patterns, and pegged the wet clothes to these, where they dried very quickly in the sunshine and breeze. However, if there was a howling gale, we would thread the line through parts of the clothes, such as a shirt sleeve, a shorts leg, underpants waist, bra strap to keep them from blowing away. Sheets were very tricky, though, and I frequently lost a pillowcase or towel overboard. Sometimes I could see them lying on the sandy bottom, and Robert would dive for them, but at other times the wind and the current whisked them away to King Neptune's palace.

We had an amusing stop in the anchorage of Asanvari in Pentecost Island. The villagers had built a rustic little yacht club where they put on a show for the yachties, charging about US$8 a head for custom dancing, a string band, kava, and dinner. Ten adults and four children came to the party, which was excellent.

TARA

The headman's son, Jacob, ushered us to our seats on concrete blocks left over from building the school. The rest of the village was bamboo and palm fronds!

"Welcome to Asanvari," Jacob said, "we are very proud of our culture and traditions, and tonight we will do some songs and dances for your entertainment. Before each dance we will tell you what it means. Afterwards, we shall treat you to a kava drink, and I shall explain that later."

The men who would be entertaining us were standing around, short grass mats around their waists, white-painted stripes and spots on their bare torsos and faces, a headdress of leaves and feathers, rattling seedpods around their ankles and wooden spears in their hands. At the clap of Jacob's hands they melted into the surrounding trees.

Suddenly, with a great shout and a chant the men rushed at their unsuspecting audience from around the corner of a house, and we all nearly fell off our seats, much to their delight. For the next twenty minutes we were treated to a foot-stomping, spear-shaking song-and-dance cabaret, some of which was very funny, like the song about the rooster chasing the hen.

After the dancing we were offered a kava drink, much stronger than the Fijian brew. Once again, Jacob was there to explain how it was made.

"Do you see this bundle of stems and roots I'm holding? This is our sacred drink 'kava.' We grind these green roots and stems with a stone, strain the juice into a coconut shell, and drink it down in one go, saying the word 'malo.' Okay, who's going to be the first to try it?"

I'd already tried it in Fiji where they used the dry roots, and, as I quite liked the taste of it, I put up my hand.

"I'll go first," I said, terribly pleased with my boldness as I took the coconut shell, said 'malo' loudly and gulped it down. To my surprise it was not nice; in fact, quite nasty. Rather like drinking a thick milkshake tasting of bitter green jungle with a peppery aftertaste. The effect was almost immediate: a slight numbing of the tongue, my leg muscles went weak, and I felt a heightened sense of awareness. Some people went back for a second coconut shell but I decided that one was enough. A very garrulous lady was sitting next to me, gabbling on and on, and I wished she'd shut up. All I wanted to do was be quiet and observe everything going on around me. All she wanted to do was talk and talk. We were all affected in different ways. One yachtie from another group a week before had had three cups, and fell down flat in the sand with his eyes wide open, unable to move or speak. He could hear everything but was unable to respond. It took him a long time to get the sand out from under his eyelids.

In Luganville Harbour, Espiritu Santo, the northern and largest island in Vanuatu, we heard a strange story. A lady on a sailboat had lost her thumb in a freak accident, and was now in the Northern District hospital. Apparently, the lady, Heather, and her husband, Brian, had already left Luganville on their way to Malekula when they hooked a big fish, and brought it on board. It was flipping and flopping around in the cockpit, splashing blood everywhere, so Brian asked his wife to shut

continued page 89

Tara broke her right hind leg and was most unhappy in her plaster cast.

It was the greatest fun to haul the freshly-washed, wet laundry out of the tub!

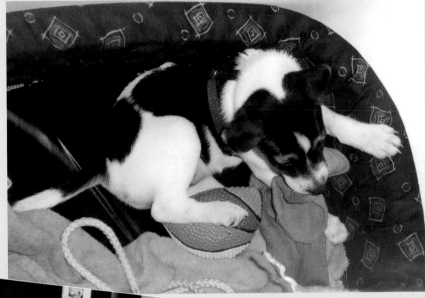

An old sock was a good way to relieve the discomfort of growing teeth.

There were so many strange and interesting things to learn about in Tara's young life.

Deusa and Inl were rafted together to transit the Panama Canal.

When we didn't want Tara to get wet we would carry her ashore.

On deck Tara loved to make herself comfortable in the cockpit, gazing out to sea.

There were many places on board where a little dog could catch a quick nap while sailing on a passage.

The dinghy was Tara's transport to the beach, where she would spend hours playing in the shallows, chasing after little fish.

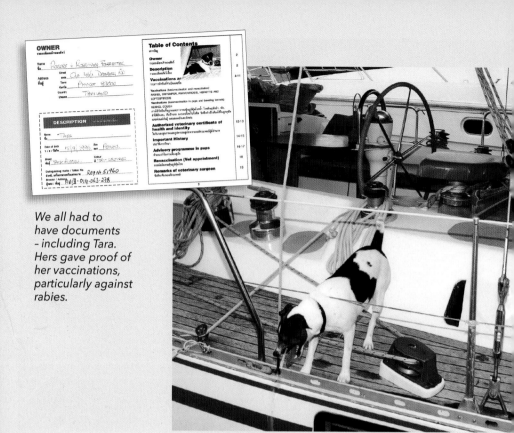

We all had to have documents – including Tara. Hers gave proof of her vaccinations, particularly against rabies.

Tara always considered it worthwhile to gaze into the water in case something swam past.

One of Tara's favourite vantage points was looking out of the stern portholes.

A cool spot for Tara to hang out when we were at anchor, was on the cabin roof in the shade of the awning.

Even though she could jump down Tara always asked permission to come below.

Tara and Robert really enjoyed each other's company.

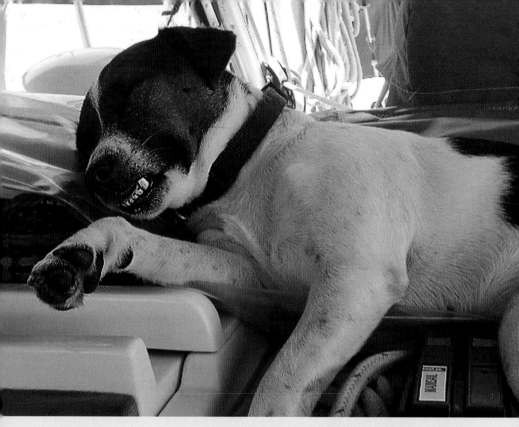

Dogs also get seasick and Tara was no exception, collapsing in her bed in disgust when she was stricken.

The ocean had a great fascination for Tara and she was always on the lookout for dolphins.

After a rousing game of chase the ball, Tara and Robert would sit in the saloon and catch their breath.

A sail bag was a secure and comfy spot to have a sleep after a busy day on the beach.

Wading in the shallows, Tara would pounce on little fish brushing past her toes.

When we were at anchor Tara would sit on the cabin roof, watching intently for anything interesting to happen.

Big trees in the coastal forests provided cool shade on lovely walks.

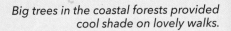

These handsome Thai fishing boats used to come very close to us, driving Tara into a barking frenzy.

the door into the saloon. Their boat had a large, heavy door instead of a companionway with weather boards, and, as Heather went inside and slammed the door, she noticed something flying past her and falling to the floor. Looking at her right hand, she saw she was minus the thumb: it had been neatly chopped off just below the first joint. With amazing control and presence of mind, Heather picked up her thumb, called her husband, and together they tried to secure it back on, packing it all around with ice.

The nearest hospital was Luganville, so they turned around and motored back into wind for four hours. With only the two of them on board, Brian decided to drop Heather on the public dock, where she caught a taxi to the hospital, whilst he anchored the boat and joined her later.

Luckily, the one thing the doctors were good at in Vanuatu were accidents where bush knives had chopped off toes and fingers. They immediately took an x-ray of her hand, saw that the bone was very mutilated, and told her that they could not save her thumb but would clean up and stitch the stump. Poor woman, what a terrible shock. The hospital was very dilapidated, built at the beginning of the century by French nuns, and abandoned after independence.

I went to visit Heather, walking from the dock up to the hospital on the hill.

"Hello, Heather," I said, "we're in the anchorage with Brian and heard all about your accident. What a terrible thing to happen. Are you okay – can I bring you anything, food, magazines, books? By the way, my name is Rosemary."

"Thanks very much," Heather replied, "but Brian comes to see me every day and brings me what I need. When I first got here there were no sheets or pillowcases on the bed, just a bare and dirty mattress, so I got Brian to bring my pillows and a couple of sheets. As long as I have this drip in my arm I'm going to have to stay right here."

Heather was in a white-walled room with a couple of other iron bedsteads containing stained mattresses, but she was all alone. A door led out onto a grassy patch full of weeds, with dismal, custard-coloured buildings forming a quadrangle.

"You know, we haven't been sailing for very long," she continued, "and I dread the passage back to New Zealand with my injured hand. I hope Brian will find crew to help us."

I could imagine just what she felt like. I'm not, as I've said before, a very brave sailor, and I would have hated to have to cope with a crippled hand. I visited Heather several times while she was in the hospital, and she told me an extraordinary story.

"Can you imagine," she said, "I was fast asleep one night when I felt someone kissing me on my cheek. I woke up with a helluva fright, and there was a man bending over my bed. I couldn't move as I had this drip in my arm tied up to a stand, and my other arm bandaged because of the thumb. So I screamed and screamed and shouted for the night nurse. Of course, the man ran away because of all the noise, and they couldn't find him.

TARA

"The next day they told me that he was an escapee from the psychiatric ward across the courtyard, and meant no harm. What the hell was he doing in my room, in any case? The door should have been locked. I'm going to ask Brian to sleep here at night: it's not safe."

A scary encounter: fortunately, they let her go back to her boat the next day.

৪৩৫৩

As we moved around to Palikula Bay on Espiritu Santo, the engine developed a strange noise. Robert discovered that a bearing had gone in the fresh water pump. This was quite disastrous as we carried no spare, having been told in Cartagena that fresh water pumps never go wrong!

Robert took the pump to pieces to find that the bearing was totally shredded. He got a lift into Luganville and searched everywhere for a bearing to fit the pump, without success. That meant ordering one from Australia, which would take two weeks to arrive. Being unable to run our motor and charge the batteries, we had to be very careful with using our power, relying on our wind generator to trickle energy into the bank of batteries. However, we couldn't have been in a nicer anchorage, with a white sand beach for Tara to run on and clean sea water for swimming.

Now and then small boats used to go past *Deusa*, and the ever-alert Tara would rush up forward, challenging them loudly to come any nearer. As they ignored her and drove on, she would become very frustrated, and tear into the nearest object with her very sharp teeth ... and that happened to be our jib sail, carefully tidied away on its roller furling mechanism, right up at the bow. We eventually had to sew a sacrificial patch of suede to the foot of the sail, so that when it was put away, all Tara could bite was this patch. Once she had shredded it into tatters we would renew it with spare pieces, kept for just that reason. Tara and I would sit on the foredeck in the sunshine, the sail dropped at our feet, replacing the patch with a strong needle, twine and leather sewing palm. We never cured her of this habit and, short of smearing mustard all over the lower part of the sail, we didn't know the answer!

While in Western Samoa – and later in Fiji – we had come across a rare delicacy – Palolo worms. These worms bury their heads in the hard substrate of the coral reef, and spawn in a reproductive frenzy of eggs and sperm on two successive full moons in October and November. For a long time, scientists were mystified by the headless worms writhing on the ocean surface, until they discovered that the heads remained buried in the coral, and the worms released their bodies to float to the surface, growing a new body for the next year.

The islanders made a big celebration of the Palolo worm rising, dressing up for the occasion, and almost turning it into a carnival atmosphere. In Vanuatu they lit fires on rafts and floated them on the sea, attracting the worms to the light to be scooped up by the bucketful. When we returned to *Deusa* one evening we looked for the worms around the boat. There they were, hundreds of them, like thin strips of shiny paper, wriggling in patterns of scrawled writing, moving very fast with a jerky motion, some of them very long ribbons shining in our torchlight.

"Quickly," said Robert, "get a bucket, there's dinner all around the boat."

I clambered up on deck to get a couple of containers, a sieve and another torch for the worm-fishing session, forgetting to secure Tara. Next minute, she had jumped into the dinghy with us, straining over the side of the pontoons to see what we were catching. With us all dabbling and scrabbling in the water, it became quite chaotic and we never caught a thing.

However, Robert found a lady in the market next day, selling worms she had caught the night before. Being less squeamish than I, he bought a scoop of worms and we carried them back to the boat. Unfortunately, our wonderful cookbook, *The Joy of Cooking*, that tells us how to skin a porcupine and roast a grizzly bear, does not cover Palolo worms! In the absence of a menu, I sautéd them lightly in butter, garlic, and finely-chopped onions. Shredding some lettuce leaves on each plate, I delicately arranged the tangled mass of worms as best I could, enhancing them with a slice of lemon. You guessed it – they were disgusting: never again!

ten

Solomon Islands

Saying goodbye to Espiritu Santo Island, we headed for the Solomon Islands, passing through the Banks and Torres that form part of Northern Vanuatu, en route. This small island archipelago was named after a Portuguese explorer of the 16th century, Luis Vaz de Torres, and Sr Joseph Banks, the botanist and naturalist.

As we arrived in Gaua Island a canoe paddled out to greet us.

"Hello, I'm George, welcome to my bay," said a cheerful, brown-skinned man wearing a colourful, knitted beret, trying to speak above Tara's loud barks. "Come ashore once you've dropped the anchor. I'm a sculptor, and I'd love to show you my work."

"Can we bring our noisy dog, George?" I asked, "She's been on the boat for several days and would love to run on the beach. We'll keep her on a lead in case you've got any chickens."

"No problem," called George as he paddled away, "I'll see you later."

You might wonder if we ever bought chickens from local people when we felt like a change of fish diet. However, the scrawny things that Tara liked to chase would not make a delicious meal, even if stewed for hours. Plus, there was the nasty thought of having to pluck it, even if someone else killed it. If we wanted chicken, it was frozen chicken from the rare supermarket we came across or no chicken at all. I would de-scale and clean a fish any day – but not a chicken!

ಬಂದ

The next morning Tara, Robert and I climbed up to George's house on the bluff overlooking the bay. It was a really attractive setting with a traditional custom house, shady trees, and lots of people. He showed us his paintings on tree fern plaques, carved sticks and wooden spoons, then took us into the jungle to see the big carvings.

"I'm going to ask one of my sons to lead the way, I can't quite remember my secret path." said George, who was definitely a showman. "I'll send him ahead to hack away the undergrowth."

"Oh, yeah," we thought, "he thinks we're a couple of inexperienced tourists, instead of the world travellers we like to see ourselves as." After several minutes of wild swipes at inoffensive bushes with a long-bladed bush knife, we suddenly found ourselves in a little clearing in which stood several tree fern statues with great, bulging eyes and extended stomachs. It was a really spooky and dramatic setting for their alien and otherworldly appearance.

George pretended he was very pleased his son had successfully guided us to his forest art gallery. "I've an American who just loves my work and buys all he can," he told us with pride.

"The yachting folk can't be too much help to you, George," remarked Robert, pointing to the huge statues, "we couldn't fit even one piece onto our boat."

"You're right," said George, "but I've got some much smaller stuff you might like to look at."

Back at George's house I gave Tara a drink of water from the bottle I was carrying in my backpack. Robert bought a carved 'nalo' stick as a memento of our visit, and we thanked George for his hospitality.

"Wait," said George, "before you go, I've got a surprise for you. Have you ever heard of water music?"

Looking at each other we shook our heads. Maybe in the distant past at school musical appreciation we had heard Handel's Water Music, but surely we wouldn't be listening to a full-scale orchestra under the coconut palms?

Leaving George's house on the hill, we all walked down to the beach, where George waved a skinny brown arm. Out from the trees came twelve young girls, giggling and pushing each other forward, crowns of bougainvillea woven into their curly black hair. Dressed in shirts and shorts, the girls waded waist-deep into the calm sea, looking more like a wet T-shirt contest than a musical group. Somehow, they scooped air into the water with a cupped hand, producing a booming sound; then the same hand lifted the water into the air and the hands were clapped together through the spray, giving a high-pitched note. Done with rhythm and co-ordination it was very good, but they couldn't keep it up for long, falling into the water in a heap of laughter and exhaustion.

Tara rushed to join them, excited by all the hilarity, but I stopped her, sure that the girls didn't want an over-enthusiastic Jack Russell swimming round them, trying to herd them ashore.

We loved the show and gave all the girls new T-shirts from our collection on board. We also traded more shirts for vegetables and bananas. A friend of George's, Richard, invited Robert to look for lobster in the bay, and they were most successful. Richard gave Robert his radio to fix, which was quite a challenge, but Robert found that a wire had come loose, and was able to solder it back on.

Later, Richard paddled by the boat to pick up the radio, and had a question for Robert. "Do you have any sucurros?"

"Sucurros?" asked Robert, most puzzled, wondering what a 'sucurro' might be.

"Yes, I need sucurros and all mine are finished – surely you have some on your boat?"

"Well, yes, maybe I have, but I'm not quite sure what they look like. Can you point one out to me?"

TARA

With a look of total exasperation, Richard stood up in his wooden canoe and pointed to *Deusa's* toe-rail, where screws attached the lifeline stanchions.

"Oh, screws!" said Robert with a big smile as it dawned on him what 'sucurros' were. "Yes, I have all sizes – what would you like?"

Richard was so pleased at finding a supply of 'sucurros' that he brought his one-eyed friend, Mac, for a visit in the afternoon. Mac needed glue for the pastor's canoe. This was a bit more complicated because the two-part epoxy we used for our own repairs wouldn't work too well on a wooden canoe.

Our boats were a treasure trove for the islanders, who had so little, and it was always worth their while to come and ask, though this time we couldn't help.

ঙ০জ

Waterfall Bay on Vanua Lava Island, just a short sail away, was not half as friendly as Gaua. As we arrived, we were besieged by three canoes.

"I'm Jimmy Edwards," said a short stout man in the first canoe, "I'm the port captain around here, and if you want to see the waterfall you can't come ashore until you give me a T shirt."

We were most surprised at this brusque greeting – the islanders were normally such gentle, polite folk – that we decided to stay on board. Later, another canoe paddled out from the beach.

"I'm Patrick, don't listen to that man, Jimmy Edwards, I take care of the waterfall; he's got no right to demand things from you."

There was obviously quite a dispute over waterfall rights, and we didn't want to land up in the middle of a feud. However, the next day, Jimmy Edwards went off to a wedding so Patrick invited us ashore to look at the waterfall, do some washing of clothes, and entertain Tara. There was always washing to be done, and I would seize any opportunity to use fresh running water available on land, as opposed to using *Deusa's* precious purified water-maker water.

Patrick wanted to build bungalows for tourists on his piece of land, and asked us to write him a letter saying what a good idea this would be. With several letters like this he hoped to get a grant from the Ministry of Tourism, but we never learned whether he achieved his dream. It looked like there was too much fighting over land rights for any development to go ahead.

ঙ০জ

The check-in point of the Solomon Islands was Nendi. Our good friend Scott of *Ini* was there to greet us, and show us where the immigration office lay hidden amongst the trees.

What a miserable island Nendi was: full of malaria and a kind of typhus called Santa Cruz fever. The Spanish explorer Mendana tried to set up camp here in 1595, but his men mutinied and he executed the camp commander. Forty-seven of them died of malaria in the first month.

They called it "a corner of hell in the claws of the devil." As you can imagine, the camp was abandoned.

Malaria was a big problem in this part of the world, and there were two theories about how to handle it. One was to take the anti-malaria pills that tourists are often recommended to take on short trips into malaria-infected areas, or not take anything at all and wait to get malaria, then take the cure. We spoke to several doctors about this, and the general recommendation was not to take anything as we were travelling in malaria areas for such a long time, and the anti-malaria pills can be damaging to the liver and eyesight. The danger of taking prophylactics are that they can cover signs of malaria, if you are unfortunate enough to get it. A bad cold and sore throat *could* be malaria, and, by the time you are feeling really rotten, it could be too late ...

So we took nothing and carried malaria remedy with us. I caught malaria in Honduras and self-medicated, and we both got dengue fever in Fiji, but there is no remedy for that: just rest and no aspirin, only paracetamol for the headaches and aching joints. (Aspirin thins the blood and can cause internal bleeding with dengue.)

We had yellow fever and tetanus shots, and Tara had a regular jab each year for rabies.

We tracked down Willie the immigration man and took him back to *Deusa*. He was most friendly and polite, which always gives a good impression of a country. This was the first time that an official had actually asked to look inside our drinks cabinet at the half-full – or empty – bottles, but didn't ask for one!

Whilst travelling through the islands we heard of a yachtie being eaten by a crocodile in this part of the world, and asked Willie about it.

"Oh yes," said he, with a broad grin, "the crocodile was working for immigration because that yacht should never have stopped where it did without first checking in here at Nendi."

"That's a very sick joke," Robert said, frowning at him, "what really happened?"

"It was a Swiss boat," Willie explained, "and like you yacht folks often do, he dived in to check that the anchor had set properly. The water around these islands is quite murky, and he didn't know about the sea crocodiles – the Australians call them salties."

"His wife was sitting on deck smoking a cigarette when she suddenly saw him surface, frantically waving to her and calling for help. Then he disappeared. The villagers found the body a couple of days later, and laid it on a slab where they normally cut up fish. They insisted she took photos of her dead husband for identification, as they didn't want to be blamed for manslaughter."

We shuddered to think of the trauma this poor woman must have gone through, a very long way from home, all alone on the boat, with her man killed by a crocodile. Thereafter, whenever we went swimming or took Tara out along the beach, we asked local people if these fearsome reptiles were in the area.

TARA

We didn't stay longer at Nendi than was necessary, and moved on to Pigeon Island, in the tiny group of sixteen islands named Reef Islands. Imagine our surprise when we saw a white man rowing out to greet us. A white man? We hadn't seen any white folk in ages, except for fellow yachties.

David came on board. We handed him a cold beer and listened to his story.

"My wife and I are out from Scotland to teach the grandchildren of Diana Hepworth who owns Pigeon Island. She's been here for more than forty years. Tom and Diana originally sailed here from England in their 70-foot ketch, with thirty British pounds in their pockets, and a sense of adventure."

"You'd certainly need a sense of adventure with only thirty pounds to your name" said Robert, getting up to fetch David another beer from the fridge.

"Well, this couple realised there was trade to be done amongst the islands, so they bought copra and sold dry goods and tinned food. Rather like a floating store. The folk of the Reef Islands were so pleased that a trading ship came by now and then, that they asked them to stay, and they did. They got a long lease on Pigeon Island for something like two pounds a year, and had a girl and twin boys."

"My goodness," I said, "what do you guys do for communications: what if someone gets ill?"

"Right now the nearest phone is thirty miles away by canoe in Nendi, where you've just come from. There's no airstrip on any of these Reef Islands, and our only communication is via VHF radio. There are no roads on the islands. If any of us get sick, and the local clinic can't handle it, then we have to go by motorized canoe to Nendi, and from there by air to Honiara, the capital."

It must have been quite an adventure for David and his wife to leave the comfort and convenience of Scotland to land up in a place as remote as this. Of course, the situation was the same for us living on yachts. Any emergency for us meant sailing to the nearest harbour and hospital, wherever that might be

David took a long pull at his beer and continued talking.

"Diana's twin boys are about forty now, and still live on the island. Ross has married a local girl, and it's their three children I'm teaching. Diana was so cross that he married a Melanesian girl she didn't speak to him anymore, and threw him off the island, so he went to live with his in-laws."

Robert looked thoughtful. "What do you expect if you bring your kids up on an island: who else is there for them to meet and marry?"

"He soon moved back again," said David, "mother holds the purse strings! You'll see his house when you go ashore."

The next person to visit us by canoe was Ross, who asked us to come and meet his family and join in the school fête festivities the next day. We asked if we could bring Tara, but he shook his head and said there were a lot of cur dogs around, so it wouldn't be a good idea.

"By the way," he said, "there's someone here writing Mum and Dad's biography, so you might bump into her. She's Lucy Irvine, and has written a book called *Castaway* about when she and her boyfriend stayed a year on a little island north of Thursday Island in Australia. Mum thought she would be a good person to write about their lives on Pigeon Island."

Ross' house was a sprawling bungalow filled with people lounging on the sofa, armchairs, on the floor, spilling out onto the verandah, dozing, sleeping, just waking up. What a lot of bodies! As Ross explained, they were his extended Melanesian family taking it easy in the heat of the day.

Diana, a slim, sunburnt lady of at least seventy-six, was busy painting a drawer for a cupboard when we arrived for coffee. We asked if she had made the drawer.

"Oh, yes" she said, putting away her paintbrush, "I do all my own carpentry work and maintenance. Before we have coffee, come and see my husband's grave, it's in the garden. He died four years ago and it's so nice to have him right here where I can chat to him."

We found that a lot of people in the South Pacific islands buried their dead close to home, and it was a nice custom. Easy to tend the grave and have casual chats with a loved one.

Over coffee Diana told us a fascinating tale about a previous teacher who had come to educate the grandchildren.

"The silly girl, she wanted to study the stars," said Diana as she handed round some homemade biscuits, "so off she went one evening in a small canoe with her star book. Lying back with the book in one hand and a torch in the other to read the pages, she gazed into the glittering night sky. Of course, with the canoe rocking in the gentle swell, she fell asleep."

"Oh my goodness," I looked at Diana in horror, "what on earth happened to her?"

"Well, we realised she was missing when she didn't turn up for school next day, so we checked the beach, saw a canoe was missing, and started a search party. We even got a spotter plane to help us but found nothing."

"After three days we had to phone her parents in New Zealand and tell them the dreadful news that their daughter had gone missing from the island, presumed dead. Meanwhile, she had drifted 70 miles in her little canoe to the island of Utupua, where she staggered ashore and collapsed in a heap. Some villagers found her and took her to the main town, where she stayed for three weeks before a freight boat called in and found her there."

Diana poured us another cup of tea, then went on with her amazing story.

"Later, she told us what happened. Waking up at sunrise, she realised she had fallen asleep and drifted out with the current. The island was only a distant blur on the horizon. In a state of shock she had grabbed the paddle, to try and head back, but it was a futile effort. Realising she would get fried by the hot tropical sun, she lay under the length of cloth she had used as a wrap-around against the cool night air, and tried to paddle after dark.

"The freight boat picked her up, and finally delivered her back to our shores en route to another island. She was lucky to be alive. We phoned her parents, who insisted she come home immediately: they couldn't bear for her to be so far away now that she had come back to life again!"

છબ્છ

We had to be very careful when walking Tara on beaches in the Solomon Islands due to custom and tradition, so we always asked the village chief or elder for permission. On one particular island we stopped at, we asked a friendly guy called Justin about walking Tara. He drew us a map in the sand to show where she was allowed to go, and off we set with our eager canine.

The first stop was just a sand spit where she could run and run, racing after hermit crabs as they scuttled away in their borrowed shells, and then we moved on to a nearby island that was still small enough to let her go again.

Next morning I met Justin on the beach.

"Oh, you're in big trouble," he said, "you went to the wrong island and the chief who owns it wants compensation."

"What do you mean?" I asked him. "I went exactly by the map you drew in the sand."

"No, you didn't. I said only go to the sand spit. The chief gets paid US$10 for every tourist who visits the island you were on, and he wants his money." Justin looked very stern, as if I'd committed a criminal offence.

I went and fetched US$10 for him but made a mental note to double-check next time I took Tara out.

On our way to Honiara, the capital of the Solomon Islands, we thought that two small islands en route looked interesting for a visit. Our friend on *Inl* was sailing with us, and we decided to look for an anchorage to spend the night, but as we got closer, all we could see were steep reefs and very deep water. We motor-sailed into the bay, and were met by a sailing canoe filled with men.

"Stop your engine" demanded a large man in a ragged shirt, "we're coming on board."

Tara immediately challenged the men as they came close, and wouldn't let them put their hands on our toe-rail, showing her teeth and snarling.

"Tie up your dog," shouted another man over the racket, "we want to come on board."

"I don't think it's a good idea," said Robert sternly, "and we are certainly not going to turn off our engine!"

"Where you come from; where you check in?" said a third man, missing several front teeth. "We want to go to Santa Cruz, we need gasoline, give us gasoline." He waved a 20-litre fuel jug at us as we continued motoring forward, and they hurried to keep up with us.

An old man huddled in a grubby coat in the middle of the canoe kept muttering about dollars, 'give us dollars.'

There were too many of them, too few of us, and we didn't like the feel of it at all. Thank goodness they were frightened of Tara, and she kept them at bay. Calling *In* on the VHF radio we told Scott not to come into the bay, as it was highly unsuitable, and aggressive men in a canoe were trying to board *Deusa*. They soon gave up pursuing us, thankfully, as they were wasting what precious fuel they had, and we weren't going to stop, obviously – and Tara would bite them if they laid a finger on the boat.

We had very few incidents like this, fortunately; never saw a weapon or knife, and most of the time it was fishermen, begging for cigarettes or water. Tara acted as a very good deterrent, and the fishing boats would only come close enough to shout across the water to us, so we would throw them a couple of plastic bottles of water, which we kept for just this sort of occasion.

So, giving Tara a hug and a cuddle, and thanking her for her good guard duties, we continued on our journey to Honiara in Guadalcanal Island, arriving there late in the day and finding a spot to anchor off the town.

ଞଔଓ

Robert had been bothered by a sore tooth for some time, and dabbing it with Tea Tree oil, bathing it in hot salt water, and dousing it in TCP™ hadn't really helped. In the end he knew he wasn't winning and the tooth should come out, so when we arrived in Honiara he looked for a dentist.

We soon discovered that any self-respecting expat flies to Australia for their medical and dental needs. However, Robert took his courage in both hands and went to the hospital in Honiara, where he found a local dentist with a rickety chair and a pair of pliers. The dentist pulled out the tooth, pushed a plug of cotton wool in the hole, handed Robert a slice of gauze, and told him to mop the blood dribbling out of his mouth. He then pushed him out of the chair and shouted "Next, please" as some unfortunate Solomon Islander shuffled in, clutching his swollen jaw.

Poor Robert had to take a bone-shaking bus trip back to the yacht club where *Deusa* was tied up to a very dubious-looking stone jetty. Tara and I welcomed him back on board, and she sat on his lap giving him dog kisses to make him better, while I poured him a stiff whisky. Robert was in good health, so the gum didn't take long to heal, and I dosed him with the supply of antibiotics we always carried on board. In fact, if you had looked in our medical supply drawer you would have thought we were a floating pharmacy.

A few days after Robert had visited the dentist, we heard some interesting stories about life in the Solomon Islands from a Frenchman who had a dive centre where we filled our air tanks.

As Jean-Pierre checked our tanks before filling them, he chatted to us.

"You just won't believe this, but it tells you how crazy these islanders are. The local telephone company – Telekom – wanted to put up a repeater station on the corner of a villager's land. They offered the landowner about US$5000 as compensation, telling him that he would hardly notice the small building on the edge of his vegetable patch. The

99

fellow said no thanks, he wasn't interested. He wanted US$100,000 or nothing at all."

Jean Pierre stopped to speak to some tourists about scuba diving, then continued his story.

"Telekom told him there was no way they would pay that much money. They would go and put the building in a swamp nearby which would cost them more money to construct – but nothing like the US$100.000.00 the villager wanted. So they tried to convince the guy that it was a good deal for him, that he would be US$5000 richer (and that's a lot of money in the islands), but no, he wouldn't budge. It was all or nothing – so he got nothing!"

When the tanks were filled, we invited Jean Pierre to join us for a beer at a nearby bar.

"Listen to this one," said Jean Pierre, as he took a gulp of the ice cold amber liquid, "some earth-moving equipment was going to be used for making a road to a mining project. The best way to get the equipment to the site was to unload it onto a nearby beach, and drive it two hundred metres onto a track that would take it to the destination. The alternative was to cut a track from Honiara, which would be a horrendous job."

The bar was filling up, and getting quite noisy. The sun was setting and we needed to get back to Tara and *Deusa*.

Jean Pierre saw us looking at our watches, and hurried through the rest of his story.

"The beach belonged to a nearby village, so they were offered about US$2000 for the use of it for a couple of hours, whilst the vehicles were landed and driven up to the track. The villagers wouldn't hear of it, though: they wanted 25% of the value of each vehicle for the right to cross the beach. So, once again, it was all or nothing. And once again they got nothing. And what's interesting is that they don't care. They don't seem to have a commercial or capitalistic attitude towards things!"

Downing the last drops of our beer we hurried back to *Deusa*, apologising to Tara for being late as we climbed aboard.

"Have you been a good girl, Tara?" Robert asked as he cast an eye around the deck, but she very rarely ever chewed on anything except the jib, and her basket when she was a young thing. Now she had more important things to do, like guard the ship and chase off marauders.

She looked up at him with shining eyes as if to say, Me? Of course I've been good; aren't I always good?

There seemed to be a lot of complications with land ownership in the Solomon Islands. We met the owners of a lodge at Tavenipupu Island, who told us a complicated story on this subject. Denis and Keith had come to an agreement, signed a document with the previous landowner, and built their beautifully-designed, five-star resort. A couple of years later, the landowner's son paddled up in his canoe and demanded an astronomical sum from them for occupying his land.

"What do you mean?," said Denis, quite surprised, "we signed an agreement with your father, and paid him handsomely."

"Ah," said the canoeist, "that agreement was with my father, and he has now died, so the agreement is null and void!"

"Well," replied Denis, "in that case, the house that your father built for you kids in the village no longer belongs to you. Your father has died, and therefore it is no longer your property."

The local fellow thought about this for a while, scratched his head, and then paddled away, never to be seen again.

Here's another nice story. A couple on a yacht anchored outside the Honiara yacht basin had caught a lift into town with another yachtie, leaving their dinghy tied to their boat. They imagined it would be easy to get a lift back when they returned with their shopping. But it wasn't.

A local lad approached them. "I can swim out to your boat, untie the dinghy, and row it back to you here on the jetty."

"Good man!" they exclaimed. "We'll give you something for your troubles when you come back with our dinghy."

They watched him swim off to their boat, clamber up the stern ladder and go down below, disregarding their shouts and arm-waving. Finally, a fellow cruiser turned up and gave them a lift out to their boat, where they discovered that the lad had locked himself down below and refused to open the hatch.

They had to break in, and found total chaos. The rascal had helped himself to all the alcohol he could find, dressed up in the wife's clothes, and thrown flour, oil and coffee grounds all over the furnishings. That was the last time those two took a lift from anyone else!

೮೦೦ವ

Whilst in the Solomon Islands we were cruising in the company of our friends on *Inl*, an American boat, and *Dokusan*, a Japanese boat. On Thanksgiving Day I decided to invite them both to dinner. I found a tin of turkey breast in the local supermarket, and bought a pumpkin for pumpkin pie. We thought it most humorous to have our American and Japanese friends sitting down to dinner on an English boat in the Solomon Islands, where Japan and America had such terrific battles during the Second World War. I'm glad to say they found it amusing, too!

Robert decided to treat me to dinner one night in a nearby resort as it was very hot cooking on board, with tropical temperatures of around 32 degrees Celsius.

When our meal arrived, Robert found that the potatoes and vegetables were stone-cold, so he walked back to the kitchen with his plate to ask someone to heat them up. The head cook, in his tall, white hat, came out and looked at Robert's plate, grabbed a handful of the potatoes and vegetables and took a bite out of them!

"Yes," he agreed, "they are cold, aren't they?"

Throwing the remaining vegetables in his hand back onto the plate, he carried it away.

"I'm not touching that food again," grimaced Robert in horror, as he walked back to our table. Of course, he didn't eat his meal when it eventually reappeared from the kitchen, and instead made himself a snack when we got back to *Deusa*. In this context, it's important to bear in mind that, traditionally, Solomon Islanders eat with their fingers ...

TARA

Some fascinating rituals were still performed here, such as shark-calling on the island of Laulasi in the Malaita Province, whose people believe that the souls of ancestors inhabit the sharks, so feed them pieces of cooked pig in an amazing ceremony.

A young boy, painted with white stripes, stands on a submerged rock in about a foot of water, holding a basketful of pork, while the villagers beat together stones under the water to call the sharks. The high priest calls to the sharks by name, one by one, to swim past the boy, who feeds them a chunk of meat. The smallest sharks are fed first, and, should one try and jump the queue, it is called by name and told to wait. The oldest and largest shark is given the biggest piece of pork in honour of the ancestor's spirit, and the priest tells the shark to wait alongside the rock so that the boy can climb onto its back.

The shark then swims once around the lagoon, bringing the boy safely back to his rock. This is an extremely serious ceremony, and the dances are performed to perfection. The people believe that, should they make an error, it might anger the ancestors, and a rogue shark might take them during the ceremony or whilst out fishing.

Interestingly enough, the reason why the sharks don't attack is because of the white stripes painted on the boy, which resemble those of the banded sea snake that the sharks avoid. In olden days, human sacrifice would have been what was offered to the sharks, rather than pig. Red and black are taboo colours on the island as black is the colour of the local pigs and red is the colour of blood – both of which stir up sharks!

We gave up wearing our fancy red and black swimwear. We told Tara she should take off her black and white jacket when swimming, but she said it was too difficult.

Tara had ripped her security net to pieces during the course of our travels. We had originally bought some black netting and string in Panama, and tied the netting onto our toe-rail and the lower of the two lifelines, making a barrier of about 15 inches (37 centimetres) so she couldn't accidentally slip overboard.

Every time curious children rowed up to watch the little dog bark and bite the netting, the holes got bigger and bigger, until Tara could have very easily fallen through in her excitement. We visited a fisherman's house and bought a whole length of coarse black net that he was no longer using. First, we laid out the net on deck, and carefully measured the width we needed, then cut it with strong scissors. The final part was to loop it onto the lifelines and the toe-rail with strong, black string. The operation took a couple of days, but we weren't in a hurry to go anywhere, and we certainly didn't want Tara falling overboard!

Sailing across to Marovo Lagoon we caught the most enormous sailfish – about two metres long and extremely heavy. So heavy, in fact, that I had to lasso its tail while Robert gaffed the head, with Tara barking encouragement behind us, tied up in the cockpit. Poor fish, it was so big we couldn't eat it all, so we took a slice from the lower back and decided to give it to the first canoe arriving at *Deusa*.

Whenever we anchored near villages, swarms of canoes filled with villagers would paddle out to sell their carvings, baskets and bowls. Tara was always a good deterrent for people leaping on board without invitation, as happened a short while previously when the aggressive men in a canoe approached us on our way to Honiara. The villagers were desperate to make a sale, and would often clamber, uninvited, onto visiting yachts, which many people found most irritating.

Even though Tara was just a little person, she had huge presence, and, what with her noisy bark and sharp teeth, no-one was prepared to confront her. You'd never think that a Jack Russell terrier would frighten off all-comers. She was probably taller than the average Jack Russell, to be fair, with her long, white, stockinged legs: more the height of a Fox Terrier.

The first canoe to arrive contained one-armed-Willie: small and wizened, burnt to a crisp by the hot sun. We tied up our noisy dog in the cockpit and invited Willie onto the back deck as he was on his own, and, with one arm, was no match for strong Robert.

"My name is Rosemary," I said to Willie as I took his basket and helped him on board, "and that is Captain Robert over there with our dog, Tara."

"Hello, Willie," said Robert, extending his hand in welcome. "Would you like a fish: it's far too big for us, and maybe it would be useful to the village."

Willie's eyes lit up. "Oh, yes, very good, very good fish. We make big party in village tonight. You come along?"

Robert shook his head "Thank you, but we are tired from sailing, so we'll stay on board. But what happened to your arm, Willie? It must be very difficult to fish or carve wood."

"You know Malaita Island?" he asked. We nodded. "Malaita islanders, him folk very bad people, like to fight too much. Cut off my arm, me nearly die."

We had heard this before. Malaitan islanders were known to be the most aggressive folk in the whole island chain, and, whenever there was a fight or someone got beaten up, there was invariably a Malaitan somewhere in the brawl.

Willie had some very attractive coconut wood salad bowls, and we bought one from him as a memento of our visit to Marovo lagoon.

ဒပ္ပေဒ

The Solomon Islands had some great dive sites, with spectacular coral reefs and vertical drop-offs plunging into deep blue infinity. The coral would be about two or three metres below the surface (six to nine feet), full of corridors and nooks and crannies for fish to hide amongst the bright and varied corals. We would be swimming along, admiring the magnificent scenery below us, when suddenly it would drop away into a deep blue void. It was quite tummy-turning and scary, wondering what might be looking up at us out of that cobalt darkness.

The corals along the walls were quite magnificent, and some of them looked like a child had been painting with wonderful shades of purple, pink, peach, lime green, and deep red; splashing the rich colours at random onto the dark rock.

There was great happiness to be found doing this, as both us and Scott on *Inl* were scuba divers. It's usual, when diving, to have a dive buddy, and go out in pairs as a safety precaution, but as there were only three of us this became more of a challenge. Scott and Robert were independent-minded captains of their own yachts, who, as soon as they were in the water, would set off in different directions, to leave me swimming in agitated circles between them, rather like a sheepdog who has lost control of the flock, and is nipping madly at their heels, trying to bring them back together again.

There's no talking underwater, unless one has some very fancy equipment, so all signals were made by hand or rapping on the air cylinder with a dive knife to attract the attention of fellow divers. If I got close enough to my errant companions, a smart tap on the shoulder or a quick pull at a finned foot got their attention.

On one dive, waterfalls of gleaming fish poured over the underwater cliffs playing follow-my-leader in flowing bands of colour, admired not only by us but by three grey whaler sharks. The sharks thought we were pretty interesting, too, as people didn't often dive in this remote area. I kept on frantically pointing them out to Robert and Scott, who merely shrugged in a macho way and continued to explore the reef. They weren't very big sharks – maybe a metre and a half – but they certainly bothered me, so I kept very close to the wall, and Robert. After all, no self-respecting fish is going to take a bite out of something as large as him, and I felt safe hiding behind him, even though I still carried my short, sharp, shark-stabbing spear for protection.

We often sailed in the company of *Inl* and, one afternoon in a quiet anchorage off a palm-fringed beach, we noticed a lot of squid around our boats enjoying the shade. Robert had a special lure and managed to catch several squid off the side of *Deusa*, flipping them on board and into a bucket of water before they could squirt us with ink. After a while, the others vanished in a puff of black dye, not to return.

"Hey, Scott," Robert called over to our friend, "can I come and catch some squid off your boat: ours have all swum away?"

"Yeah, sure," drawled Scott in his lazy American accent, "Invite me to dinner and you can catch all you want."

Robert rowed over to *Inl* armed with a bucket and the lure. Tara glared at him through the deck netting, willing him to take her along.

"No, Tara, you and fishing don't go together. You watch from where you are. Be a good little girl; I'll be back shortly."

Tara gave a huff of disgust and came to sit beside me in the cockpit.

Robert soon hooked a big one and swung it over to Scott to untangle and drop in the bucket of water. The squid was full of ink and just needed to draw water to arm itself for an ink attack. Scott peered into the bucket to admire the catch of the day, and got a shot of jet black ink right in the face. Furious, he grabbed the squid to stop it slurping up more water. All he achieved was a fire hose effect as the squid spurted ink all over the dodger, cockpit cushions, lee cloths, and even down the companionway into the saloon. Scott had recently beautified his boat, re-covering the cushions, making new lee cloths, and new dodger, all in a deep maroon colour. The black ink did nothing to enhance the effect.

Robert bellowed with laughter, "Oh, my goodness, just look at you, Scott, what a mess, you look like one of Al Jolson's black minstrels!" He could hardly hold his fishing rod he was laughing so much.

Scott wasn't amused. "It's not bloody funny, you stupid bugger, look what you've done to my boat."

The more Scott yelled and screamed, the more Robert fell about laughing. The more Scott waved the squid around the more the ink sprayed everywhere.

I wondered what on earth had happened to cause such a commotion, and only learnt when Robert later returned, the proud possessor of a squid dinner which we all enjoyed; Tara, too. He helped Scott clean up the mess but squid ink sticks like crazy and is almost indelible, as we could see from Scott's face when he came over later. *Inl* then became known as Inky!

&OG

Our fridge had been giving us lots of problems, and we discovered that we could get it checked out and re-gassed at the Japanese Solomon Island Taiyo factory in Noro. The tuna fishing boat fleet was repaired there, and they allowed us to tie up on their dock. Frozen fish were being unloaded from the boats, which Tara and I watched with interest from *Deusa's* deck, while Robert went to look for the fridge man. Instructions were being shouted in Japanese, and great, slippery netfuls of shining tuna were hauled out of the boat holds and dumped into waiting containers. Many fish cascaded onto the dirty, slimy dock, where they were casually scooped up by a local worker and thrown back into the container. Hopefully, they were washed before being processed into bright little tins of 'fresh from the sea tuna.'

It was a tough, rough bunch of men who worked the boats and the dock. When things slowed a bit, a lot of them came to stare in ragged rows at our boat, and the frantically-barking little dog. It was the same old questions – Where you from? What's your name? But the answers didn't really mean much to them, outside the boundaries of the Solomon Islands.

Finally, Robert returned with Marcos, a small, wizened gnome of a man with a cheerful grin, dressed in blue overalls, who would – we hoped – be able to fix the fridge. They both disappeared down below to look for the problem.

A little while later Robert popped his head up through the companionway.

"Marcos has found a hole, it's in the line by the cylinder; no wonder all the fridge gas was leaking out. We would never have found it. He's going to take out the line and cylinder and mend it in his workshop."

Marcos came trudging back along the dock some time later without his cheerful smile.

"Mr Robert" he said rather seriously, "we mended the line but the fellow doing the welding, him bugger up, he's made a big hole in your cylinder. It's now 4.30 and we are knocking off. You'll have to come back tomorrow."

"Oh, damn!" both Robert and I said together. It was horrid being tied up to the dock all day, not only because it was so hot but also because of the staring curious crowds and constantly-barking Tara.

One moment when Robert had gone into the workshop with the repair man, a few of the lads jumped on board, and started messing around at the bow, showing off.

"Hey, you guys, get off the boat right now!" I was furious and, as I shouted, Tara made a rush up the deck. I certainly didn't want Tara biting them as that would have caused huge trouble, but, between shouting at them to get off the boat and shouting at Tara to come back to me, I was not winning. The kids tried to out-stare Tara and me for a while, because if they got off the boat on the orders of a mere woman, they were going to lose face in front of their buddies on shore. With all the racket Tara was making, a more official-looking older person appeared on the dockside, so the young men reluctantly strolled off in a nonchalant fashion. My heart was pounding, and I felt seriously outnumbered. Until the older man appeared there had been no one around to give me moral support except for the loyal little Tara.

After all the work on the fridge, we discovered that it *still* had a leak, so had to return to the Noro dock for further repair. Once again, the fridge man worked all day on *Deusa*, bringing with him a big, heavy compressor to vacuum the system of all air bubbles. At least this forced stop gave us a chance to buy a couple of cases of Taiyo tuna, some of it called Solomon Blue, and excellent for Tara's dinners, and some other very hot stuff with a red pepper in the middle. We had to rinse it several times before we could eat it, but it was excellent trade material for the islanders, who liked their food spicy.

By the end of the day it was time to return the compressor to the factory. Strong Robert managed to haul it up on deck, tied several ropes around it, and called to some men standing around on the dock.

"Please help me take this compressor off my boat," he asked politely. "I'm going to pass you these ropes and you hold on tight while I guide it from our deck to the dock."

Willing hands stretched out to grasp the ropes, but one eager fellow put his hands on the hot metal exhaust of the compressor.

"Aaaahhh," he yelped in pain, "too hot, too much!" and, with that, let go of his side of the compressor.

Feeling the dragging weight of the machine, and seeing their companion leaping around in agony, all of the others let go, too! Robert tried desperately to hold on to his end, balancing precariously on the edge of *Deusa's* deck, but it was impossible, and, with a loud splash and a hiss, the compressor hit the water and disappeared under *Deusa's* belly, leaving a trail of silver bubbles as it sank to the sandy bottom below the dock.

A group of stunned faces peered over the edge. Robert asked if the factory had a diver. They all shook their heads. No diver.

"Well, it looks like I'll have to dive for it," he said, going to look for the wander-lead that attaches to an air tank, and allows him to dive to at least 10 metres (30 feet).

He took a long rope down with him, first handing one end to the men still standing around looking rather shocked. He told them that when he gave a sharp tug, they should start hauling on the rope. This time, everyone held on tight, and the compressor was soon on dry land again, dripping seawater everywhere. Tara gave everyone encouragement with a paroxysm of barking, and Robert went to speak to the manager to tell him about the disaster.

"I am so sorry; your compressor dropped off my boat into the water. You'll have to strip the motor, wash it well, and saturate it in oil, and then, hopefully, no damage will have been done. The sooner you can do this, the better."

The manager looked none too happy as it was their only large compressor for vacuuming the big fishing boat refrigeration systems. Robert promised he would come back in a couple of weeks to see if it was working all right. If not he would pay to have it fixed. Luckily, it did work again because of the quick action of washing out the seawater.

The Japanese bosses of Taiyo lived in a separate compound to the Solomon Islanders, and had imported Japanese cooks to look after their meals. The Japanese captains of the boats had only Japanese crew, and rumour had it that they got paid higher salaries. There were Solomon Islander captains and crews, but they got paid less. The bonuses were the same, but somehow the Japanese always caught more fish.

The local folk spoke well of the company because it gave incentives and loans for the islanders to buy their own boats and outboard motors to transport workers to the factory. They were paid for this service, so could pay back the loans and finally own the boats. The factory also trained the locals to become mechanics, welders, electricians and boat captains, and so were seen to be helping the island communities.

❧❦

While in the Solomon Islands we heard of an agricultural school at Vanga Point on Kolumbangara Island, run by the Catholic Marist brothers. A yacht called *EOS* was in the anchorage, and the owners, Harry and Susan, had been working with the brothers for the past six months, planning an integrated farming scheme, together with ecotourism. Harry worked on the project and Susan helped in the kitchen, and gave the boys a cookery class each Wednesday.

"Why don't you join me at the cooking classes?" suggested Susan, a pretty and cheerful Australian, "It's such fun, and I'm sure you've got some good ideas you can share with the lads."

TARA

She brushed her curly blond hair out of her eyes. "Think of things that grow around the villages, so they will be able to make the recipe."

"I'll look through my notebook and see what I've got. Is there a lesson this Wednesday? Why don't you and Harry come over for a drink this evening and we can talk more about it?" I replied.

On Wednesday I met Susan at the classroom, and was ready to give the students a pawpaw and ginger jam recipe. Every garden has pawpaws, and ginger grows wild. The only trouble was I had to try and explain the recipe in pidgin English.

"You takem this goodfellah pawpaw, take out little blackfellah seeds, takem off skin, choppem small small."

I struggled on through the recipe until it came to crushing the ginger.

"You takem ginger root and killem good. Don't killem dead, just killem good!"

The kids thought I was the funniest thing they had heard in years, their white teeth flashing with merriment in their brown faces. It was great fun, and I passed around some pawpaw jam I had made on *Deusa*, which they all thought was quite delicious.

Tall, slim Harry, with his Scottish accent and dry sense of humour, had worked as a town planner and landscaper in Australia. He helped the Vanga farm by writing up its projects and drawing a large-scale map of the area, designating the production on each section, and even planning ecological walks for future tourists. Harry described the farm to us. "They've got two-year courses for young guys who've left school. They can become mechanics, electricians, carpenters, and market gardeners. They can study pig- and cattle-rearing, chickens, and bee-keeping."

We peered over Harry's shoulder as he pointed to his colourful map, on which he had marked off all the different sections.

"The headman of the village chooses who will study at Vanga. Very often they are lads who can't afford to go on to further schooling, or they haven't done very well at school. What's great about Vanga is that the training is so good that anyone coming here is guaranteed a job when they leave. There's a long waiting list to come here, and I reckon it's one of the most successful ventures of its kind in the Solomon Islands.

"The Marist brothers hope that these kids will go back to their villages and pass on their new farming skills to their people. However, the chiefs and elders don't think the young folk have the right to tell them what to do with their newfangled ideas. What was good enough for their grandfathers is good enough for them."

Harry sighed and tossed his cap on the table. "The students get very depressed when they discover that they can't put their hard-won learning to good effect, and must look for work far from home. Some of them have even returned here to become teachers."

৪০৫৪

The farm ferry travelled once a week between Vanga and Gizo, the main town, and we could sometimes catch a ride on it to get essential provisions like coffee, tea, sugar and flour.

One day when we were in Gizo the lights went out, and we soon learnt why.

The local bulldozer had been put to work tidying up the decaying road system, and it was scraping away with its heavy metal blade when the driver's eye was caught by the sight of two local lovelies strolling by. Gazing at them in rapture, rather than looking where he was going, he slammed the bulldozer into an electric light pole, wrapping it around his blade like a toothpick. Luckily for him, this tripped out the generator station, and everything in the town stopped dead. Thank goodness there were no live wires lying around.

Now came the next problem. The felled pole was located halfway through the small town so everyone below it had no power, including the government offices, the police station, Solomon Airlines, and a small company selling frozen meat. A new pole had to be ordered from the capital, Honiara. A general shudder ran through the town at the thought of this, as everyone knew how long that would take.

But wait, an alternative solution appeared possible! The driver who mowed down the pole was hired as a regional driver, and knew where there was a spare pole lying around waiting to be used; available right there in town!

Meanwhile, some enthusiastic soul had decided that, with the electricity off, now was an ideal time to trim some large trees drooping over the power lines, completely unaware that the electricity board had tidied up the mess, installed a new pole, and switched on the generator again. In his enthusiasm for trimming, the individual concerned miscalculated, and lopped off a huge branch, that promptly crashed down onto another electricity pole, throwing it to the ground in a heap of twisted cables. We weren't around to hear who said what and to who, but we understand it wasn't very pleasant.

৪১০৪

Thank goodness we bought a huge mosquito net in Gizo before we went to Vanga, as we had been told that the flies there were fearsome. Flies in the daytime and mosquitoes at night. In order to cover the entire cockpit and the open saloon windows, we cut the net and wrapped it around the mast, bringing it right back over the boom and as far as the mizzen mast, creating a large and spacious, pest-free living area. Tara didn't see it this way, unfortunately, and insisted in wriggling out from under the net to rush up to the bow, barking at passing dinghies as they motored between the many yachts in the bay.

As soon as she stopped moving the flies settled all over her, drinking at her eyes, and crawling into her ears and mouth. She couldn't work out how to get back under the net as it covered the deck, so, scratching frantically, and snapping at flies, she would look at us imploringly, as if to say "For God's sake, hurry up, let me in, the flies are driving me crazy!" But no sooner had we brushed the flies from her, dragged her under the net and told her not to go out again, she was off, barking at someone else. The only solution was to take her for a good, long walk and a swim out on the reef, rinse her off in fresh water, dry her, and bundle her down below.

ಬಿಂದ

The nearby island of Simbo was home to Megapode birds, which I had always wanted to see. They are unique in the bird world in that they gather great mounds of leaves into a pile, like a compost heap, in which they lay their eggs. The heat of the rotting leaves incubates the eggs, and the male bird takes care of the mound, moving leaves this way and that to control the temperature. The chicks hatch out fully-feathered and able to fend for themselves immediately. They don't even have a hook on their beak to break out of the egg, but use their strong toes to crush the shell, lying on their backs and digging upwards, scratching away the cover with their powerful legs and feet. In fact, their name, Megapode, means 'big feet' in Latin.

Lenore, a happy, red-headed Irish girl who worked as a lawyer with the VSO (Voluntary Services Overseas), invited us to lunch to meet a couple of her friends, Ross and Jackie, who had just stepped off the Simbo ferry. Ross was a Megapode research man, who looked like he had been in the bush for months, stalking birds through dense scrub. With his straggly beard, hair a matted tangle, clothes all ripped and barefooted, Ross was the epitome of a determined ornithologist, unused to civilization.

His girlfriend, Jackie, looked much more presentable in clean clothes, hair neatly brushed, and pretty sandals on her feet.

"I've been living in Simbo village," she explained, "working with the local ladies to revive their ancient craft of weaving. I've even got the shops in Gizo to sell what they produce, so I'm very pleased with the success I've had. It gives the ladies pride in their culture and traditions, as well as some pocket money at the end of the day."

Jackie unrolled a bundle she was carrying. "Have a look at this. I even learnt how to do their complicated reverse-style weaving, and I made this mat for my sister."

The mat was beautiful: so intricate and well finished. I'd have been so proud of that mat if I had made it, I wouldn't have given it to anyone, but kept it for myself to show all my friends!

Ross sat silently through most of the meal, eating ravenously as if it was the first square meal he had seen in weeks. I eventually asked him about his work.

"I've been living with the Simbo people for some time," he said between mouthfuls. "There's an understanding between man and bird. They farm them like chickens, gathering the newly-laid eggs for consumption, and also to sell at local markets. Egg-gathering is strictly controlled by the chief on a sustainable basis so that enough chicks hatch each year to maintain the species. The birds are wild. They visit their great nesting mounds to lay and then fly away to feed in the forest. The trouble is that, lately, greedy village chiefs are exploiting the egg trade for their own pockets."

"Do you think we could go there for a visit?" asked Robert leaning back in his chair with a glass of wine in one hand.

"Don't expect to be welcomed," said Ross, "they don't like visitors, and will charge you a lot of money."

We decided against that plan ...

eleven

Papua New Guinea and Australia

We wanted to visit Australia, so, before we left Fiji, we found out what sort of documents and injections Tara would need in order to be allowed into that country. The rules and regulations for rabies were very strict, and a dog had to be out of rabies-infected areas for more than six months prior to a visit, as well as have all the valid vaccination certificates, and a microchip.

"We'll need to run several blood tests," said Vanessa, the friendly vet, sweeping her long, blond hair back off her shoulders. "They're very strict down under, and you'll have a lot of forms to fill in. For starters, she's going to need a bar code chip for identification."

"Oh, that's interesting," said Robert, holding Tara under one arm, as we chatted to the vet. "What size is a chip?" He was obviously imagining something the size of a postage stamp that one would use in a computer or digital camera.

"It's tiny," replied Vanessa, smiling at Robert, "I know what you're thinking, but it's only the size of a rice grain. I'll place it in her shoulder under the skin, then give you a strip of paper with the bar code on it, as well as a vet's certificate. For goodness sake, don't lose it – put it in your diary – it's just like the bar codes you see in supermarkets. You can even take Tara to the checkout counter and run her under the bar code reader."

"Ha, ha," laughed Robert, "I can't see a supermarket allowing a dog on the counter for a read-out."

"I'll come over to your boat tomorrow afternoon around 3pm, and place the chip in Tara," said Vanessa, "but you are going to have to give her this Valium pill, as it's quite a big needle I use to inject the bar code. Give her the pill at about 2pm so that she's nice and sedated by the time I arrive."

"Right you are." Robert pocketed the pill and we headed back to *Deusa*.

∞◌∞

The next day we gave Tara a morsel of chicken with the pill cunningly wrapped inside. An hour later Vanessa knocked on the hull to come aboard, and there was Tara leaping around barking; not sedated at all.

"Oh, my gosh, look at your dog," gasped Vanessa, "that pill should have knocked her out. Here, you're going to have to give her another one: tough little dog, this!"

She fished in her medical bag and brought out another Valium. We found a bit more chicken and Tara swallowed it with pleasure. Robert, Vanessa and I then sat down to wait, had a cup of coffee, chatted about life in Fiji, life on a yacht, life with a dog. We waited for Tara to grow sleepy. She didn't. At 4pm Vanessa looked at her watch.

"I can't believe it! Two pills can knock out a Great Dane: what's with this little terrier?"

Robert and I looked at each other and smiled. We knew 'what was with' this little terrier. She never gave up, never gave in: a tenacity of spirit that would later save her life.

Meanwhile, we drank more coffee, and chatted on and on, until, finally, Tara's eyelids started to droop and her back legs wobbled.

"This is it," said Vanessa, getting out her large syringe, armed with the chip. "You hold her firmly, Robert, and this won't take a moment."

I wondered if Tara would wriggle and Robert get the chip in his arm. Well, at least we would be able to take him into Australia!

It all went well, however, and now Tara was chip code AVID801480638278.

8003

As soon as we set sail from the Solomon Islands out went the fishing lines and we hooked a large one, the reel screaming and the rod bending with the weight. Tara was tied up, complaining bitterly that she only wanted to help, as we brought the big fish on board.

"Oh, no, not a barracuda, couldn't the sea have given us something else?"

I glanced at Robert as he struggled with the pliers trying to get the barbs out of the barracuda's mouth. Whenever we could, we would return unwanted fish to the sea but this one was so badly hooked we couldn't save it.

"We'll find a local fisherman and give it to him," he said scanning the horizon.

Unbelievably, for once, there was no one around, There was always *someone* out and about, fishing or offering vegetables and fruit to the yachting community. Finally, we caught sight of a lone paddler and hailed him over, sending Tara down below into the saloon so she wouldn't be a nuisance.

"We've caught a big fish and it's too much for us: would you like it?"

The ragged fellow in his torn shirt clung to the side of the boat and looked suspiciously at us. Who in their right mind would be giving away a fish?

"How much money you want?" he asked, his face breaking into a broad grin as we told him 'no money,' and flopped the fish into his canoe. "May God bless you, this will feed my family for many days."

Sailing on into the night, we finally caught up with Scott on *Inl* who had left a couple of days earlier and had been quite a long way ahead of us. It was a calm night and he had hove to, dropping his sails so he could snatch a little sleep. The most remarkable co-incidence was that we were exactly on his track. In the great, wide ocean, to see another yacht, even on the horizon, produced great excitement, so to come across *Inl*, right on our GPS course, was extraordinary in the extreme. We had not planned to meet up with Scott, we did not have his GPS position, and he was two days ahead of us. But *Deusa* was the faster boat, and, as a single-hander, Scott would stop and catch up on much-needed sleep now and then.

It was my watch, well after midnight, and I could see a faint light twinkling on the sea. Drawing closer, I took over from the autopilot, and hand-steered around *Inl* as she lay in the moonlight, gently rocking to the rhythm of the deep, quiet ocean.

Tara was sitting beside me in the cockpit, sharing the lonely night hours.

"Look, little girl, it's our friend, Scott, fast asleep. I bet he's curled up with his cat."

Tara stared at me. She knew the word 'cat' and pricked up her ears, looking around in surprise. "There's no cat here, you daft thing." She seemed to say, but then caught sight of *Inl's* mast light.

"Don't say a word, Tara, let them sleep: it's a tough life, being a sailor on your own. Just keep your bark to yourself as we sneak past."

Easier said than done, and she let out a few muffled squeaks as I wrapped her in my warm jacket to prevent her seeing the boat so near to us.

Poor Tara: she had been very bored these last few weeks, hardly getting off the boat except to accompany me to do laundry in streams by the anchorages. She always had to stay on the lead because of chickens, dogs, goats, and other domestic animals. But at least on a passage she had our company all the time, and wasn't left alone when we had to go to town or do the shopping.

After several days of calm sailing, we arrived in a peaceful anchorage in the Louisiades with no people, no villages, and no chickens! Tara could run free to her heart's content. She was so pleased to leap into the sea, swim to the beach, and scramble across the rocky shoreline, without a long lead to restrain her. Her agility was amazing and, like a mountain goat, she leapt from rock to rock, climbing ever-higher. Our one concern was that she would tumble down into a cave and be unable to get out. Of course, clambering on the rocks filed down her nails very well. Living on the boat meant she got very long nails if she wasn't able to run on sand and rocks from time to time. Cutting them was a major operation, involving a muzzle and a lot of calming words. Once we nicked the quick by mistake and she objected strongly to pedicures after that.

⋈

Whenever we arrived in a new country the first thing we had to do was check in with our passports, boat documents, crew list, and any other papers that might be required. In Papua New Guinea the nearest port was the small and squalid harbour of Missima, with its broken-down docks on the edge of a muddy lagoon, dotted with small fishing boats, canoes, and one lone tug boat.

The customs, immigration and quarantine officials came down to the dock and waved frantically to us, so we picked them up in our dinghy and ferried them out to *Deusa*.

"We don't want to sit in the cockpit," said the plump, sweaty Customs man, his shirt straining across his belly, a Customs badge lopsidedly pinned on his chest, "we want to go down into your saloon, its cooler." He sniffed loudly, and blew his nose into a rumpled handkerchief. All three had streaming colds: Robert and I glanced at each other.

"That's not a good idea," replied Robert, "we have a dog down there and she can be quite a nuisance. You'll be fine up here under the awning; look, there's a breeze coming from the shore."

However, the quarantine man was very determined, and once we had shown them all our documents, he insisted on looking around, taking off his shoes to clamber down the companionway, accompanied by us. Tara let him know that he was trespassing on her patch by baring her teeth and flattening her ears, but Robert laid a calming hand on her head, whilst the official ignored her totally.

He opened all of our lockers, peered into the storage facilities under the saloon seats, checked the plastic containers of flour and sugar, counted the bottles in the drinks locker, and picked up the binoculars to look through them. Some officials would ask for things like whisky, money, or clothes, but not him. Opening one cupboard, he saw a tin of mushrooms, and wanted to take it back to his family ... Mushrooms must have been quite a rare luxury in this Papua New Guinea outpost.

Once all the formalities were completed and they were ready to leave, I asked where we should dispose of our rubbish.

"Oh, chuck it in the sea," they replied with a dismissive wave of a hand!

⁝⁞

It was here, at a nearby island, that we discovered a beche-de-mer industry. The owner, Peter, showed us how they processed the sea slugs harvested from the ocean floor. (This is the same animal we met earlier in our travels, which was called a sea cucumber on that island.) Slow and defenceless, the creatures were harvested in great number from the sea bed.

"We take the slug in the left hand like this," Peter said, picking up a large, black specimen, "then slit open its belly with a sharp knife and pull out all the guts."

"Do you want to try?" He offered Robert a fat slug. I had backed off to a safe distance so I didn't have to become involved in this revolting process.

"Now, we drop the slugs in this half 45 gallon drum full of boiling water, and cook them for a while."

From where I stood I could see a coconut husk fire blazing under the barrel which bubbled like a witch's cauldron, full of slimy, shrivelled bodies.

"Finally," said Peter, "we spread them out on these palm fronds to dry in the sun, then ship them to China and Japan. There are all sorts of varieties, and each has its market price."

It was obviously a good business as the family owned a couple of small boats for harvesting the sea slugs, as well as a transport boat to run the dried slugs to Port Moresby.

ಖುಡ

Australia was now only three days away. The weather along the Queensland coast can be quite rough, influenced by the high pressure zones that move along the bottom of the continent, and we had to wait for a break in the highs to make a run for it. But, however carefully we had watched the weather, we miscalculated; we were impatient to leave the Louisiades and continue our travels. The first day was motor sailing but then the wind filled in and got stronger and stronger and stronger, with an average of 30 knots, gusting to 45 knots. The south-west swell rose higher and higher to about 10 metres, with breaking cross waves on the crest.

"Oh, dear, I don't like the feel of this at all, little girl," I told Tara, holding on tightly to her sitting on my lap down below on the settee. We gazed up through the companionway at Robert, dressed in his heavy, red, waterproof jacket, standing at the wheel, guiding *Deusa* through the rough swell.

"Do you think it's going to calm down at all?" I shouted up to him.

"I can't hear a thing," he called back, "I know you're asking me something, but there's far too much noise up here. Put on a jacket and come and help me reef the mainsail: the wind's getting stronger and we've got too much sail up."

That was just what I *didn't* want to hear, and my tummy turned over. I wasn't seasick, yet, but fear can bring on that queasy, dizzy feeling very fast.

"I'll be there right now." Apologising to Tara for moving, I struggled into my foul weather jacket, lying beside me. "You're the lucky one, dear dog, you only have to go out to pee. I have to go out to help Robert!"

Leaving the warm comfort of the saloon, I stood by the roller furling winch, waiting for Robert to release the mainsail so I could roll it in a little, and shorten the amount of sail.

"Okay, here we go" signalled Robert, freeing the big sail enough for me to begin winding it in.

The sail flapped wildly above my head as I frantically wound in the line around the winch, while Robert steadied *Deusa* against the strong wind and breaking waves that were starting to spill over the deck.

"That's enough. We'll give it a try and see how that feels."

"No, no, let's take in more," I called in panic, "we can always let it out again, if you think we're slowing down too much."

Robert knew *Deusa* was a good, strong ship that could handle heavy weather; it was his crew who was faint-hearted, and would prefer to sail with a pocket-handkerchief fluttering on the mast.

But Robert also had his anxious moments, though he never let me know at the time. He was always a rock of dependability to off-set my nervous disposition, telling me it was my imagination running away with me; that he didn't have any concerns.

But this was not true, because, in the calmness of a tranquil harbour, sipping a whisky or having a glass of wine, he would comment, "Well, that was a rough passage, wasn't it?" Too bloody right it was!

The wind grew stronger, the sea piled into breaking waves on top of the swell, and I became more and more miserable. We took two-hour watches, because our auto pilot could not always handle some of the rogue waves that knocked us sideways. It became tiring, constantly helming the boat. The daytime watches I could handle – I could see and knew what sort of wave was about to crash into us. It was the night-time that boggled my mind and created images of half-sunken containers about to rip a hole in our hull; enormous seas stalking us in the dark; Robert being injured or washed overboard, even though we wore harnesses at all times. Would I be able to pull him back on board as he dangled helplessly in the turbulent water?

Sleeping was very difficult, and in the aft cabin nigh-on impossible. We had a wind generator mounted on a pole by the dinghy davits on the aft deck. It helped supply energy to the batteries, which, in turn, ran all the electronics in *Deusa* – such as the GPS, radar, SSB radio, and auto-pilot when we switched it on to take in a quick coffee break or meal. The wind generator blades whirred around in light winds and rose to a shrill shriek in stronger winds. The aft cabin, being directly below the deck, resounded like the inside of a guitar, so the shriek became intolerable to my ears, increasing panic level to maximum.

Looking for other places to sleep, I tried lying in the corridor by the Pullman berths, but this gave me the weirdest feeling as *Deusa* heaved and sank with the waves, making me feel quite sick. Tara joined me for a while, but soon hurried back to the settee to wedge herself into a corner. She was lucky: she didn't get thrown around as much.

Robert was able to grab some much-needed rest on the settee; he also avoided the aft cabin because of the noise factor. The alternative was to switch off the wind generator, but then we would have to run the engine to keep the batteries topped up.

On one particularly rough night, Robert came up to relieve me from my two-hour watch, showing me a bump on his head, oozing blood.

"Look at this," he said, pointing to his forehead, "I went to have a pee in the forward head, and *Deusa* bucked like a mad horse, throwing me against the mirror. I've cracked the mirror, and it looks like I've cracked my head as well. This really is a bloody awful passage, I'll be relieved when it's over. By my reckoning, and if all goes well, it's only another 36 hours until we get to Arlington Reef, off Cairns."

I took a close look at Robert's head, wearing a worried frown, and staggered below to get some antiseptic to clean it with. Luckily, it was only a surface wound, and would soon heal.

TARA

"Dearly beloved Robert, are you okay to go on helming with your sore head?"

"No problem," he replied with a wry smile, "it will be better before I'm twice married!"

When I went back down below to return the antiseptic to the medical aid drawer, the bookcase in the aft cabin tore away, and the books scattered all over our bed; the door of the toilet slammed open, giving me a terrific fright, and came off its hinges.

"Oh, shit!"I shouted in anger and despair, "I can't stand this bloody sailing life," then burst into tears of misery and wretchedness. By now I was feeling thoroughly ill, and swallowing seasickness pills with gay abandon.

Water was coming in everywhere: the saloon windows, the forward hatch and corridor hatches, soaking everything. The saloon settee and cushions were sopping wet, and the mattresses of the forward and corridor berths were drenched ... but at least our bed remained dry. The awful mess and the effort of cleaning it up was horrific. The bilge pump kept on blocking, and it was a dreadful job to lean down to unblock it, adding to the seasickness and general misery.

Now and then, when Robert was on watch, I would bring him a mug of steaming coffee and stay to chat with him. Wedging myself under the dodger in the cockpit, I made sure I didn't block the instrument panel, though, when I accidentally did, I realised that Robert was not as calm as he appeared to be.

At last we made it to Arlington Reef, a big horseshoe of coral about 18 miles from Cairns in Australia. Exhausted, we dropped anchor, and fell into bed for some much-needed sleep.

But it was not to be. Even behind the reef we were getting 30 knots of wind, and metre-high waves, which snapped three anchor rodes (a short piece of rope attached to the anchor chain to act as a spring) one after another. *Deusa* bounced up and down, like a restless horse champing at the bit.

"This is just too much," groaned Robert, rolling out of bed, as he heard the anchor chain rumble, a warning that something was wrong, yet again. "I'm not going to replace the rode; this time I'll just wrap the anchor chain around a cleat (a solid, T-shaped fastening securely bolted through the deck). "Sorry, Rosemary, I know you're exhausted, and so am I, but we'll have to do an anchor watch through the night: this anchorage is just too dangerous in case we drag the anchor. There are reefs all around us. It would be a pity to crunch *Deusa* on coral, when we have come so far."

Tara was looking quite miserable, too, and, like us, hadn't eaten much on this journey, preferring to lie huddled up with one of us, when we were below taking a quick, off-duty, nap.

As soon as we could see the surrounding reefs the next morning we picked our way out into the ocean again and headed for Cairns. It took us 8 hours to do 18 miles against wind and current. What a journey from hell. Our friend, Scott, on *Inl* had left at the same time as us, and such was the force of the wind and waves on his smaller boat that he had to veer off, and ended far up the Australian coast. It took him nearly a month of waiting to get back to Cairns to join us.

ଽଠଔ

Customs, Immigration and Quarantine came on board as soon as we had found a good place to anchor, and asked us to fill out form after form.

Tara was shut in the forepeak, and when the bustling little quarantine officer asked to see her to check she was healthy, we told him to brace himself, and let her out. With typical Jack Russell enthusiasm she leapt all over him, smothering him in dog kisses and slurps, until he called for help and proclaimed her 'very healthy!'

The paperwork we did in Fiji should have been correct for the Australian authorities, but when we showed them our file, bulging with documents, we got quite a shock.

"Canberra doesn't tell us what to do here in Cairns," said the officious little man, scratching his sparse and bristly moustache with the end of his pen. "This document might authorize temporary importation of your animal, but that is in Canberra. You are in Cairns, and your dog will be quarantined on board." He tapped his clipboard importantly and cleared his throat. "What is more, you will not bring your yacht alongside any dock to take on fuel or water; nor may you take your yacht into a marina. You will stay at anchor. When you leave the boat, your dog must be shut down below so that she can't jump off the yacht and follow you."

"We will come by your yacht once a week to make sure your dog is still on board, and you will pay a fee for this service. If you want to quarantine the dog on shore, you will have to pay for a special kennel and handlers to fly her to Canberra where she will stay, at your cost, for the next six months."

Well, what could we say? We tried reasoning with him, furious that we hadn't been told about these restrictions beforehand. Having finally made it to Australia, it was hardly likely we were going to turn around and retrace our steps. All our plans of buying an old car and exploring the country drifted out of the saloon windows, together with some choice swearwords.

As we stood there, glumly looking at Tara panting happily on the sofa, the quarantine officer suddenly spotted our pot plant. This plant had travelled several thousand miles, and it gave us much pleasure to see its green and glossy leaves as it dangled from a special hook in the saloon.

"You can't have that coming into Australia," said the nasty little man, waving his clipboard at the plant, which visibly shrunk as if from attack, "it will be carrying all sorts of awful diseases. I'll have to take it away and destroy it."

We were horrified, and Robert loudly protested the proclamation. "If you're going to inspect the dog each week, you can easily inspect the plant as well: I doubt it's going to jump overboard."

With a lot of grumbling and mumbling, the jobsworth got out his Polaroid Instamatic camera and took a picture of dog and plant. But when the time came to reveal the photos, there was no film in the camera. We smiled and suggested he come back another day; better prepared.

After a good night's rest in a quiet anchorage, we went ashore to gaze at the city sights ... and what a lot of sights there were to see after two years of wandering amongst Pacific islands. The last big city we'd been in was Panama.

We had to be very careful about crossing the street, looking left and right like country bumpkins, holding hands and crying 'now!' as we raced across the busy roads. Then there were the throngs of people; such a lot of very pale people. We hadn't seen so many white faces in years, and it was quite strange. Where were all the graceful Polynesians, the burly Melanesians, the dainty Micronesians? All we saw were fat, white tourists with sunburnt faces, short shorts, and wobbling backsides – not a pretty sight!

The big adventure was the supermarket – a supermarket such as we had not seen in years. Enough to bring a lump to the throat and tears to the eyes. Shining fruits laid out in gleaming rows, crisp green vegetables, lettuce, potatoes, English potatoes, garlic, and *real* onions.

Saying a little prayer for self-control we proceeded along aisles groaning with good things to buy, and helped ourselves to just a little cheese, some bread, a box of wine. The BIG shop would come later.

The very varied conditions we had lived through made us appreciate calm anchorages, good supermarkets, sunshiny days, and enough water to do the washing. And there was an awful lot of washing to be done after our soaking sail to Australia: a week later we were still trying to dry out *Deusa*.

For the next month or so we sat at anchor in Cairns harbour. Friends came to visit. We visited friends, but always came back to *Deusa* before dark to let Tara out of her prison. She didn't get much exercise at this time, but was happy to run up and down the deck, barking at all the passing boats.

We couldn't help asking ourselves 'what was the point of getting Tara vaccinated and chipped, if she wasn't allowed off the boat?' It really didn't make sense having different rules in different parts of Australia. What made the situation worse was that every time we got ready to go onshore, she looked so excited, wagging her tail in anticipation, only to be disappointed every time. It was heartbreaking to see.

We bought a couple of bicycles, which made getting around so much easier. Lots of small things needed repairing on the boat, and we were able to go shopping and find what we needed without having to catch buses or taxis. Dentist appointments were easy, even if they were 5 kilometres away. A bad shock was that the dental bill cost more than my bicycle!

One day I was cycling right behind Robert when he stopped suddenly at a traffic light. I wasn't looking where I was going, and crashed into him, knocking us both to the ground in a tangle of legs and spilled groceries. The passing traffic looked at us in amazement as we sat there laughing and laughing. They thought we were strangers who had bumped into each other.

After a lot of time spent doing repairs and maintenance, we moved on up the coast along the Great Barrier Reef to the northern most point of Australia, Cape York. There was a short cut on the inside of York Island, between the Cape and the island: a narrow channel that would reduce the distance to our destination, Thursday Island.

Robert carefully studied the popular *Cruising Guide to Australia* as well as a chart of the area, and noted a sandbank that changed the course of the channel to port halfway through. It would make much more sense to take this route rather than go all the way around York Island.

"Go and stand at the bow, Rosemary. I want to make sure there's nothing dangerous lurking in the water. I know there's a sandbank we have to avoid, but just to make sure, I'd feel happier with you keeping a lookout."

"I can't see a thing," I shouted back to him, once I was in position, "the water's really murky."

The jib and the main sails were poled out wing on wing, each side of *Deusa*, and we were moving fast with the current – at least 6 knots over the ground. Lots of tourists clambered around on the rocky shoreline, and I waved to them like I was royalty. All of a sudden there was a terrific bang and I was thrown into the air, coming down with a thud on the deck, the wind knocked out of me.

Deusa came to a sudden stop, the round TV aerial on top of the mizzen mast spinning off like a flying saucer. Robert lurched into the wheel and bruised his ribs. We had hit an uncharted pile of rocks, and were now pinned hard against them, slowly turning sideways, a terrible grinding sound coming from the keel and hull.

Robert leapt down below and started our very powerful diesel Volvo motor, shouting to me as he disappeared. "Quickly, get Tara off the deck."

She had been sitting next to Robert by the helm, and had been hurled to the cockpit floor. I scrambled to my feet, ignoring the pain in my back, and staggered along the deck. Tara was beginning to bark at the sails as they flapped wildly out of control.

"Come, Tara," I said as calmly as I could, "you jump down below, where you'll be safe. We've got to get ourselves out of this terrible situation."

Robert was back on deck in a flash.

"Let's get these sails away. This is really serious. We might lose the boat!"

Together, we worked frantically to wind in the wild sails, and then, with black smoke pouring from the exhaust, Robert tried to reverse. But *Deusa* didn't move. She was held in a vice-like grip. It was impossible to know what sort of demon had us in its teeth, as we could see nothing in the dark water, but we *had* to get out of its deadly grip.

"We're going to have to pull out the jib sail again and heel her over, it might release the keel, the motor's not moving us an inch." Robert hauled on the jib sheet and the big sail billowed out, filling with wind blowing down the channel. *Deusa* began to heel ever so slightly, and the motor strained to move the 14-ton boat off the rocks. Inch by painful inch we started to creep backwards, accompanied by terrible grinding and grating noises. The keel was very solidly fibre-glassed into the hull of the boat and we hoped that wouldn't come apart – what worried us was a possible rock gnawing a hole in the hull.

It must have taken us half-an-hour to break free, when we were able to put away the sail and cautiously motor out of the channel to a safe, shallow anchorage. The current slowed and we could inspect our wounds once we had dropped anchor. We were both very shaken and shocked.

Our friend, Scott, on *Inl* had been following some distance behind, but when he saw what had happened, he took the long way round York Island, and met us a couple of hours later where we had anchored. That 'short cut' nearly cost us our boat ... and took twice as long!

The first thing I wanted to look at was the bruise on my backside. I had fallen very hard, though – thank goodness! – had not broken anything, but I had a huge purple and red patch coming up in great blotches. What if I had been tossed overboard in that fast-flowing, crocodile-infested water? What if Tara had fallen overboard when we hit the rocks?

Robert lifted the boards covering the bilges.

"Oh, my God, look at this, there's water leaking in."

In dismay we watched the bilges slowly fill with water. The automatic bilge pump came on, sucking out the steady flow. Lying on our tummies, we felt around where the water was coming in, and could see where the fibreglass had lifted up. There was no chance of diving overboard to look for the damage because of the saltwater crocodiles – large and dangerous animals in Australian waters.

In our ship's supplies we had underwater putty, and our only hope was to mix up a batch of this and push it into the crack where the sea was bubbling in. First, Robert ripped up rags and stuffed them down the tear in the fibreglass, then packed in the putty, the whole time pumping out the water with the bilge pump and our high-capacity hand pump. Initially, the pumps couldn't keep up so Robert also bailed out the water with a bucket. It was completely exhausting work, and I gave him a break now and then, but I didn't have the strength to go for long, and soon collapsed in a helpless heap. Eventually, we got control of the inflow so that the automatic bilge pump came on only every ten minutes or so.

It was essential to haul *Deusa* from the water as soon as possible to see what had happened below the water line. We could imagine all sorts of dreadful scenarios: our keel dangling half off, or a great gash in the side of the hull. After a sleepless night at anchor, we cautiously set off for Thursday Island, where we hoped to find some sort of haul-out facility, listening the whole time for suspicious sounds of our keel ripping away from the hull. If it did fall off, it would be catastrophic: without a keel *Deusa* could flip right over, due to the weight of her masts – a sailor's worst nightmare. It was a horrid and nerve-wracking, six-hour journey. Even Tara sensed it was time to keep quiet, and out of the way.

৪০০৪

"Yeah, mate, we can haul your boat," said Marvin, a solid, down-to-earth fisherman who ran a boat yard for the fisher-folk of Thursday Island. "We've never hauled a yacht before, but there's always a first time. You bring her in first thing tomorrow and she'll be fine as the tide will be two hours into rising." He ran his hand through his short, curly, grey hair. "We'll have to reinforce the cradle, mind you. Our boats don't have keels."

Robert and I looked at each other nervously. We didn't know what kind of damage had been done to *Deusa,* and the cradle looked far too small for our boat.

Next morning, the current was running strongly past the yard, with a fierce wind of 25 knots. It was a huge challenge for us trying to get our big boat onto a very flimsy-looking wooden contraption. Yard workmen gesticulated excitedly, steadying the cradle in the water, shouting to us to bring the boat in. Down below, Tara could hear all this commotion, and added her voice to the general cacophony.

As we approached the slipway Robert had to point the yacht into the current, at the last minute swinging the bow onto the cradle with a burst of power from the motor. On the first attempt we could hear the keel grinding on the concrete ramp as the winch pulled us out. There weren't enough planks fixed onto the frame of the cradle for the keel to rest on. Back into the water we slid as the yard folk readjusted various lengths of wood, hammering them home with long nails. We could hear the automatic bilge pump working continuously, so knew that all this shuddering and grinding up the slipway had unseated our temporary filling of the hole in the hull.

Once again we attempted this horrifying haul-out. There was no other option as the next boat yard was in Darwin, hundreds of nautical miles away. This time, we attached heavy lines to the bow and stern of *Deusa,* then threw them to the waiting men on shore. They could now help guide us in against the ever-faster flowing current battering us sideways off the cradle.

The Australians running the setup were a cool bunch, and finally had us high and dry on the concrete apron. *Deusa* shuddered in the wind as they securely tied us down with lengths of rope. These guys weren't nearly as anxious as we were, laughing and joking as they went about their business. All we could think of was our precious home toppling off the homemade cradle, lying forlornly on her side in a fishing boat yard.

"What about Tara?" I asked Robert, really worried now. "We're not allowed into marinas or docks, and here we are on dry land. They'll take her away, they'll lock her up, we'll never see her again!" I was feeling a little hysterical after all the drama, and could feel tears welling.

Robert, ever the optimist, soothed my anxiety.

"It shouldn't be a problem: we have an emergency and this is an island. I'll speak to the yard manager."

"Don't worry about a thing," said Marvin when Robert asked him, "Conrad's a mate of mine, he handles quarantine around here, I'll talk to him."

Conrad was most understanding, and even said Tara could come down off the boat and walk in the yard if we kept her on a lead.

The first thing we had to do was inspect the damage. Luckily, we had hit the rock at the top of the keel where it joined the hull. A foot higher and it would have gone right through the hull and sunk the boat within an hour. The bottom of the keel was also quite badly damaged by many chips and gouges. The fibreglass on the main hit was pulverised and squashy where the sea water had filtered through into the bilges, but our makeshift repair job had prevented a lot of water from getting in.

Old Bill, in stained and torn overalls, a floppy hat shading his wrinkled face, was the fibreglass expert at the yard, and knew exactly what to do.

"Pull out all that muck you shoved in the hole, and then we'll dry everything. You're bloody lucky you didn't sink; this is one tough, strong boat you've got here."

He patted *Deusa* on her bow admiringly. "It's your good fortune to find me here; my work is a dying profession. Tried to teach my two sons; they're just not interested. Don't want to stay on Thursday Island: they want the bright lights of the mainland cities."

The wind blew and blew, and *Deusa* shook and shook on her cradle. We spent restless nights fearing the worst. Bill struggled with the fibreglassing in gusts of up to 40mph. Our good friend, Scott, of *Inl* lent a hand, helping to paint on antifouling and providing moral support. After four days, Bill's patch on the hull and keel had dried, and *Deusa* was ready to go back in the water. The only person who wasn't concerned with wind and wobble was Tara, so pleased was she to walk in the yard and smell all the exciting Australian smells. It was her only chance of semi-freedom since we had arrived.

Looking back on the accident I realised how very lucky I was not to have been flicked into the water like the TV aerial, and washed away in the current, battling crocodiles and swimming for my life. And Tara was lucky, too, as she only fell to the cockpit floor. Robert and I suffered a lot of bruising. I had a purple, blue and yellow backside for several weeks, and heavy work caused Robert's ribs to hurt.

Bill recommended we have his repair job checked out in Singapore to make sure there was no moisture caught in the hull. How lucky we were to come across Bill – there aren't many like him around anymore ...

ঙ০ও

Continuing on our journey west we headed for Darwin, stopping at Gove en route, where we saw many sad and ragged Aborigines hanging around in the streets. An NGO had set up an arts and crafts centre where one could buy some of the beautifully-woven baskets and intricate dot paintings created by the Aborigines.

In Darwin we re-provisioned for our passage to Indonesia, and looked up some cousins who lived in a town with the wonderful name of Humpty Doo. They owned a banana plantation, and told us the reason why Australian authorities were so strict about animals, plants and foodstuffs coming into the country: they bring diseases that could wipe out his banana crop.

As it was, boats staying in the marina in Darwin had to be checked for bearded mussels coming in on the hulls.

A good stopping-off place on the way to the Indonesian island of Roti was Ashmore Reef, belonging to the Australians. It was full of refugee Indonesian fishing boats that had been impounded by the Parks Board which patrolled the area. The people on the fishing boats were sent back to Indonesia, and the boats were towed out into the deep ocean and sunk. What a shame. Some of them were beautiful wooden boats, with high, sweeping bows, but Australia didn't want them in its territorial waters. The only problem with sinking these vessels was the large amount of diesel stored on board, which had to be taken off and stored somewhere. The best place to store it was in the tanks of the visiting yachts, who were delighted to jerry-jug hundreds of litres of free fuel to their boats.

All of us at the anchorage pooled our resources, dinghies and fuel cans, jerry-jugging fuel to each yacht in turn. As we didn't know the condition of the diesel we filtered it very carefully before putting it into our tanks, but fortunately, didn't suffer any problems later in our journeys.

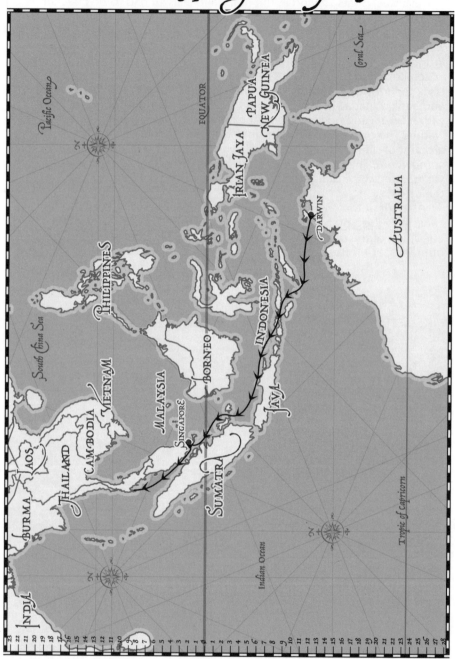

twelve

Indonesia, Singapore, Thailand and Malaysia

The islands of Indonesia are great for cruising and exploring, each different to its neighbour, with its own culture and customs, and even though the religion is Islam they are still strongly animistic. The Muslims have strict laws concerning dogs which, like so many religious rules and regulations, are to do with health. The Muslim faith considers that dogs are unclean, and if a Muslim should touch a dog, he or she must wash their hands seven times in holy clay before they can pray in the mosque. Dog saliva was a big problem, and, of course, dogs carry rabies, as well as many parasites.

We had to be very careful where we took Tara for walks, and not let her come into contact with any of the inhabitants of the islands. One thing we noticed was the absence of the mangy and abandoned dogs that we saw in so many other countries and islands.

One day we were sitting at anchor off a small island when a skiff approached us, wanting to sell bracelets and shells. We said no thanks, but the fellow was very persistent, tying his boat to the stern of our dinghy, and starting to climb into it. Tara spotted him from her lair up in the cockpit, and shot onto the back deck, barking furiously. The invader got the fright of his life, leaping back towards his boat, now some distance behind our dinghy. He nearly didn't make it, hitting his shin quite painfully against the anchor on the bow of his boat.

With a howl of pain he shouted back at us, "Your dog threw its bite at me. Give me money, I'm hurt." Robert looked at him in astonishment, "You're crazy, the dog is here with me, she was nowhere near you."

The man glared and shook his fist at us, muttering under his breath as he untied his boat and drifted away with the current. Later, we asked some Indonesians what he was talking about. They explained that it was a form of magic: dogs could 'throw' their bite at people they didn't like. We congratulated Tara on her new-found abilities to drive away unwanted visitors and persistent salesmen, even from a distance ....

Malaysia is also Muslim and, on occasions when we stopped in marinas, I had trouble with the local attitude towards dogs. If the marina was clean enough, I would let Tara swim around the pontoons where *Deusa* was tied: she loved to hunt the little fish as they nibbled on the barnacles and seaweed growing on the pylons. As soon as she caught one she would ask to be hauled out onto the pontoon to give the captured fish a quick death shake – just like killing a rat – and then jump back in the water. Afterwards, I'd rinse her off in fresh water as we didn't want a salty dog down below.

One day I was doing just that, washing Tara with our hosepipe, when one of the staff on a nearby power boat summoned me over.

"Wash that water off the dock right now, your dog has polluted it. If the owner of this boat comes past, he won't even walk where your dog has been. The whole dock has been fouled."

I looked at him in amazement, but there was no point arguing with people like that, so I dropped Tara back on board and hosed down the offending spot.

Another time I was chased out of a park close by the Sheraton Hotel because the irate guard told me that a Muslim owned the land, and dogs were forbidden to walk on it. As we had previously obtained permission from the Sheraton manager to walk our dog there, this was worth a fight. So, 'Big Robert' took Tara for her walk the next time, hoping to confront the guards, but, coming across them, they took absolutely no notice of him and his little dog. Robert is a large presence, and these people were cowards, preferring to intimidate women.

Robert found an interesting article in a newspaper which I cut out, as it helped us better understand the Muslim attitude towards dogs –

'Muslims can keep dogs to protect their home or farm, but not as pets. This is because any contact with the dog or its saliva or droppings is taboo, because the saliva or droppings are considered najis (faeces).

'In order for Muslims to perform prayers, they must be free from najis. Otherwise, their prayer is useless and will not be accepted by the Almighty.

'There are three types of najis, one of which is najis mughallazah, from pigs or dogs. We can touch dogs or pigs with our bare hands or with any part of our body but all surfaces – man and creature's – must be dry. When one or both are wet, then it is considered najis.

'A Muslim may not know whether a place has been frequented by a dog before, and if you don't know, it is not a sin.

'But if it is publicised that dogs have been to a particular place, Muslims would avoid going there – unless the Muslim is certain that the dogs did not leave anything behind or lick anything that he/she may be in contact with.'

There is a health reason behind these rules. A dog's saliva is to do with rabies, and dog droppings can contain worms. Also, a lot of street dogs have mange, which is a good reason for not touching them.

ЮĆ3

Marinas had other challenges, too. We'd tie up our boat with the bow facing towards the dock and walkway, as we liked to gaze out of our stern portholes at a nice view when lying in bed, and not have passers-by staring into our aft cabin. But sharp-eyed Tara liked to frighten people, rushing to the bow suddenly and barking loudly so that they nearly fell into the water, or dropped the parcels they were carrying. She was very naughty and loved the drama she caused. Fortunately, we didn't often stop in marinas ...

∞∞

In Singapore we had the boat hauled out to check the repair job done on Thursday Island in Australia. Bill had done a brilliant job; the yard manager said he couldn't have done it better himself.

While waiting for a vacant space on the hard, we anchored by the boat yard in Changi. One day, coming back from shopping at the local grocery store, we were met by a very worried Tara, who kept running back and forth towards the bow. Normally, she would prance all over us on the back deck while we tried to get our parcels out of the dinghy, but this time she was acting very strangely.

"Okay, Tara, what is it you're trying to tell us?" I asked as we climbed past our parcels and followed our excited dog.

"This way, this way, come quickly!" She seemed to say, glancing over her shoulder as she ran to the front of *Deusa*.

Arriving at the bow she scratched and whined at the anchor locker cover. As we lifted it up she plunged amongst the chain, and came up with a great black rat in her jaws. A quick shake of the head and the rat was no more, its sharp yellow teeth protruding in a death snarl. I stepped back, horrified. The rat had swum out to *Deusa*, climbed up the anchor chain and into the locker. Needless to say, Tara got an extra big dinner that evening, and Robert sat her on his knee, petting her, saying "What a clever little girl you are, you don't know what trouble you've saved us by that rat not getting into the boat."

Rats are a menace on board and a boat-owner's nightmare. They nibble at electrical cables, and can start fires; hide in the bilges; creep around at night, spoiling stowed fruit and veg, and pee and poop everywhere. So a cat or a dog is a very useful companion on board.

∞∞

We still had a house on an island in Brazil, and it was time to return there to check everything was all right, particularly as there had been some bad storms, and rainwater had washed away a supporting wall. It was no problem to leave *Deusa* in a marina for a couple of months, but what about Tara? She certainly couldn't come with us, as we would fly via England to Brazil, visiting family on the way.

We had sailed to Phuket in Thailand, and were talking with a friend one day, telling him about the problem with our dog, and did he have any suggestions? We couldn't have asked a better person. Phil said he would consider looking after her, but he needed to meet her first. What an offer!

We hurried back to the boat to have a serious conversation with Tara about good behaviour.

TARA

"Come here, Tara. Come and sit between us in the cockpit; we want to have a chat with you," said Robert, patting the wooden seat invitingly.

Our little black-and-white dog, ever-ready to join in whatever was going on, obligingly hopped onto the bench with us.

"We're going away for a bit and you can't come, too. We've found a really nice man to look after you and, for the first time in your life, you're going to stay in a house, with a garden."

She cocked her head quizzically at us – she didn't know the word 'house' or 'garden.'

"You're going to have to be a good dog."

She knew *that* word, however, and wagged her stubby tail. She loved Robert dearly and hung on his every word.

"No barking at strangers, no chasing neighbourhood cats, no trying to escape through the fence to visit strange dogs in the street. Uncle Phil is going to come and visit you to see if he likes you. Please be on your best behaviour."

Phil came over the next day for a cup of tea, and Tara couldn't have been more charming, sitting quietly on her bed in the cockpit, paying attention to Phil's every word, ignoring passing people. Phil was enchanted, and said he would be happy to look after her while we were away. What a relief, it had been such a worry: Tara had been with us day and night now for four years, and we'd never been parted. We weren't sure how *we* were going to cope with a separation, never mind Tara.

While we returned to Brazil, Tara learnt to speak Thai with Phil's lady friend, learnt to enjoy spicy Thai food, and live in a house. Now *that* was a new experience for her. She had always lived on a boat and her toilet was on the foredeck. What would she do in Phil's house? Amazingly, she always went outside for her toilet needs, and never had an accident indoors. The one thing she found very tempting was Phil's fish pond, full of pretty Oriental fish, flashing in and out amongst the lily pads. This was just too much for Tara, and the day we took her to Phil's home, she dived in headfirst, snapping frantically at the darting fish.

"Bad dog, Tara," I scolded, "no fishing in Phil's house."

"What? " she seemed to say, "we always go fishing together. I kill fish and you congratulate me."

ଝଉଏ

On our return from Brazil four months later, we found a very fat and happy Tara. She was so excited to see Robert she peed all over his shoes, and when she caught sight of me, she couldn't stop jumping up and running round and round until I picked her up and gave her the biggest hug ever. In return she licked my face all over until Robert had to rescue me. Phil and his girlfriend were sad to see Tara leave, but we reassured them that all three of us would see them often, as we would be land-based for a while.

Now that we had made it safely back to Thailand, we needed to do some extensive work on *Deusa*, rent a house to live in, and invest in a car to get from the house to the boat yard and back. The contractors estimated that it would take four or five months to do all the work of a new teak deck, changing the colour of the hull from blue to white; replacing the old davits with a new pair, and the necessary carpentry work on the nav station below. It sounded like a long time, but we realised we would just have to be patient; major work like this had not been done on *Deusa* since we bought her in 1987, and it was now 2000.

The house was a simple, two-bedroom place down a side road, amongst other houses owned by Thai families. Luckily, it was furnished with a sofa and chairs in the living room, a dining table with four chairs, a double bed and chest of drawers in one room, and a single bed with cupboard in the other. The kitchen had a single burner stove with no oven, and was quite a challenge to cook on, but all was solved with a wok, cooking Thai-style.

Living in a house meant we could get a lot of laundry done as we got very dirty working on the boat all day. I had just done a large wash of clothes, sheets and towels one day, and hung them out on a makeshift washing line behind the house, when it started to rain ... and then rained solidly for four days. It was monsoon time. No gentle showers, these, but great, roaring downpours with high wind and tossing trees (luckily, there were no tall trees around the little house we rented). The ditches and gutters filled and overflowed, the frogs croaked in delight, and the birds fled for cover. The laundry was rinsed, and rinsed, and rinsed again, until I had to bring it into the house, dripping wet, and hang it in the bathroom in soggy bundles.

And what about the work on *Deusa*, now hauled out in the yard, wrapped up under plastic covers to try and keep out the rain? The contractors now estimated it would take six or seven months to do all the work we had requested. The old teak decks had been removed, the topsides sanded, both masts pulled out, and all hardware taken off the deck. A terrifying sight: we hoped the Thai notations carefully inscribed on every piece meant that each would be returned to its correct place with the right bolts in the right holes. The mind boggled at the possibilities of what could go wrong in this foreign land with a strange tongue. Many small and slim, golden-coloured people swarmed over our boat, as busy as ants, with screwdrivers and spanners, ratchets and hammers. Easy to pull apart – how about putting it all together again?

ഌരു

Robert bought us a white, four-door Toyota truck registered in 2563! This puzzled us no end until it was explained that the date was from the Thai Buddhist calendar, and not our Western one. It had a Buddhist blessing smudged in ashes on the inside roof over the rear-view mirror so we felt well-protected. As it was a second-hand vehicle we took it to a local mechanic to check the oil, which was so black and sludgy it would hardly run out of the drain hole. The mechanic kept muttering in Thai, and held his head in his oily hands. He didn't know how much he could roll his eyes at Robert because he wasn't sure how long we'd owned it, and we couldn't tell him we'd just bought it.

TARA

As Thailand is a Buddhist country we found a number of vets with small animal clinics. We'd known we would have to spay Tara sooner or later, and now was the time, while we had a house and a vehicle, with the boat in a yard. She was nearly five years old, and the chance that she would get pregnant while we were 'grounded' was just too big a risk to take. Much as we would have loved a bunch of mini-Taras running around, it just wasn't practical.

When we went to collect Tara after the operation, the vet met us at the door to his surgery.

"Your dog, she very tough, she no go to sleep quickly. I give three injections. Normally, one injection okay."

We looked at each other in horror. My God, what had they done to her? There was Tara lying on her side in a wire cage, looking very groggy, just managing to wag her tail.

"We'll take her now: how much do we owe you?" Robert asked as he walked towards the cage.

"No, no, cannot take now, dog must stay seven days. Make sure everything all right."

"There's no way she's staying here," Robert replied, "we can look after her perfectly well." It was awful that we had to put our beloved animal in the hands of strangers. The wire cages had no blankets, just chicken mesh on the floor ,and several pathetic-looking dogs in cages gazed at us longingly, asking us to liberate them.

Now the vet said something very strange.

"Dog too fat. I no take out ovaries. Too dangerous, might damage kidneys. I tie tubes, no more puppies."

Which meant that Tara would still come on heat, would still attract male dogs if she was on the beach, but wouldn't present us with a litter of puppies. It was possible that Tara being too fat was an excuse, and that the Buddhist vet did not take out her ovaries because of his belief that all life should be protected.

We were furious. Tara's operation was a botched job. It was a nasty experience for all concerned, and she took a long time to come back to her senses, staggering around the house with a glazed look in her eyes, and partially deaf. I thought she might have been permanently damaged, and sat on the floor holding her and talking to her with tears running down my cheeks.

"I'm so sorry Tara, so sorry. Can you hear me, can you see me? What have we done to you, dear dog?"

It took two long days and nights for Tara to return to the world from the strange place the anaesthetic had sent her, and we felt as though we had been through hell together.

ဆဂ္ဃ

Because it was so difficult to communicate, I decided to take Thai lessons so that at least we could say a few words of greeting and shop in the market. It was lots of fun, but not easy, as there are at least five different ways to pronounce the same word as it is a tonal language. There is a neutral tone, low tone, high tone, question tone, and descending tone. Can you imagine trying to get it right, let alone hearing it when spoken?

For instance, the word for 'far' is 'glai,' said in a neutral tone. And the word for 'near' is also 'glai,' said in a descending tone. So there we were in the hot midday sun in the middle of Thailand, asking how far it was to the next town. Was it "glai" or was it "glai"?

How about the word for horse? This is 'mah,' said in a high tone. And for a dog? Well, that's 'mah,' too, spoken in a questioning tone. I think we may have told the Thais that we had a small horse, who we carried around in the truck with us; who liked swimming in the sea and trying to catch fish. And she was a very good watch-horse, who doesn't allow anyone on board.

Here's another: 'suay,' meaning both 'beautiful' and 'very bad luck.' Someone came to visit us with their small child, and I carefully pronounced that their daughter was very bad luck. Oh, dear, what a way to win friends and influence people!

And what about 'suea,' which can mean a tiger, a mat or clothes? I put on some new mats, and shake out the tiger lying on the front doorstep. As you can imagine, it was a long time before I dared open my mouth. But I loved copying out the wonderfully curved and decorative Sanskrit writing that looked so exotic to my Western eyes.

୫୦୦୫

We were out most of the day working on the boat, so never really got to know our neighbours. However, one evening, we were invited to a child's birthday party by the people in the house next door: a Thai girl who was married to a Swiss guy. A wonderful meal had been prepared of satay chicken, a soup, noodles with seafood, a sour mango and cabbage salad, lots of white rice noodles, and many hot, fiery sauces.

We learned a great way to eat cockles and mussels. Take a lettuce leaf and lay it on your plate. Now take a generous pinch of rice noodles in your fingers and lay these on the leaf. Next, stretch across the table to the bowl of mussels and pick one, prising open the shell, pulling out the mussel, and laying it on the noodles. Finally, choose a spoonful of sauce from one of the many side dishes, and pour this over the whole leaf. Parcel it up and pop it in your mouth – delicious!

One wizened old lady, the grandmother of the birthday girl, was a betel nut chewer, and when she began preparing her betel nut she asked if anyone would like to give it a try. I had wanted to try betel nut ever since the Solomon Islands, but never had the right ingredients of nut, lime and a leaf, so here was an opportunity not to be missed. I volunteered.

"Chew on this," she said in Thai, handing me several withered brown pieces of nut, and demonstrating that I should pop them all into my mouth. It was absolutely horrible: bitter and disgusting, and dried my mouth like a crab apple. I pulled a terrible face, and she told me to keep chewing. She then got out a leaf and gave it a generous dab of lime paste, rolled it up, and signalled for me to add it to the very nasty mixture that was churning around in my mouth. She showed me how to spit the saliva into a can lined with a plastic bag (I remembered that this shouldn't be swallowed, otherwise it will make you feel quite ill), and wedge the gooey mixture against the inside of my lower lip.

It tasted sooo bad, but I had to go on chewing while the Thais rolled around with laughter, thinking it the funniest thing they had seen in a long time. Robert said I was very brave, watching with interest to see what would happen next. To add to this awful mixture the little Thai granny offered me a twist of tobacco, showing what to do by vigorously rubbing some across her betel nut-stained teeth and tucking it into her cheek. I baulked at this latest delicacy. The end result of all my chewing was that I felt quite giddy and my legs felt hollow. The effects did wear off, leaving a mellow peacefulness, almost as if I had swallowed a tranquillizer. Despite this, I decided not to repeat the experience.

∞∞

Our lives now took on a different routine. We woke early, had breakfast, and piled into the truck, Tara sitting between us on the front seat, for a twenty minute drive in the mad Phuket traffic, with scooters weaving in and out around us, to reach the Ratanachai yard, where we parked the truck in the shade if possible. We would then pick our way amongst the railway lines, fishing boats and yachts, to where *Deusa* sat on her cradle.

Tara was tied up on a long lead, and we clambered aboard to see what had to be done that day. At 10.00am everyone - yachties and yard workers - had a coffee break, and the choice was sweet, milky coffee, black tea or Milo (chocolate and malt powder mixed with hot or cold water or milk), plus a 'sticky bun,' which could be a boiled rice dumpling stuffed with minced figs, rice flour and sweetcorn cooked in a banana leaf, or a shivering jelly of many colours that tasted slightly salty! In order to get one of these goodies we had to rush to the table before all the Thai workers scoffed the lot. It wasn't that there was not enough to go round - there was ample sufficiency for all of us - but the workers would wrap up extra goodies to take home at the end of the day.

After our break it was back to the boat, and while Robert kept an eye on the carpenter as he made a new set of shelves for the navigation table, Tara and I sat below with a great big basin of soapy water, scrubbing all those lines and ropes that had gone green from mould in the many months we hadn't been on board. Every now and then, Tara would sound off with mad barking as the cleaning ladies walked past.

The cleaning ladies were like army ants - anything in their path disappeared - so we had to hide anything we wanted to keep. Small things like scrubbing brushes, soap, sponges, bits of cloth, were swept up never to be seen again. One time they gathered up a bottle of Listerine from another yacht and came and asked me what it was for, as they couldn't read our Roman letters any more than we could read their Thai squiggles. I gave them a very good mime of gargling, rinsing and spitting it out, and they were delighted.

We couldn't really communicate with each other except for me to say "My name is Rosemary – what is your name?" and then there were lots of giggles when I didn't understand the answer! Later in the day they drifted back with their brooms and black plastic bags, and one of them tried the only English she had learnt. "I love you!" she pronounced carefully, but I decided to ignore her and went on scrubbing. This was obviously a good phrase for picking up single sailors.

There was another break for lunch. A Thai lady ran a rustic restaurant with three tables on the verandah about a hundred metres up the road, cooking everything in a wok in front of her clients. Essentially, it was rice or noodles with something scattered over them: squid, prawns, chicken, beef. We learnt to say 'cow pat' for rice and seafood, and 'gwa tiao pat' for the noodles and seafood. Now and then we would head into town when her menu became too monotonous.

Tara always came with us for lunch, and we'd ask if we could take her into the restaurant. The Thais like dogs and were kind to Tara. One particular restaurant had an outside patio where we were going to sit, and, as I walked towards our table, something suddenly streaked across the floor and launched itself at our unsuspecting dog. Next minute, I was in the middle of a dog and wild animal scuffle, trying to extricate myself and Tara, who was barking shrilly and trying to bite. Well, the attacker turned out to be a territorial lady cat with a bell around her neck, and a no-nonsense attitude towards dogs! I got bitten and scratched on the leg, but the two animals didn't hurt each other, thank goodness!

⋙⋘

Deusa had been in Thai waters for six months now, and the permit was about to run out. Thais are very strict about foreign boats and impose huge fines if either the visa is not extended or the boat in question does not leave the country. As work was being done on our boat, the yard had to write a formal letter to Customs, requesting an extension on the time limit. Normally, Customs would grant a month, but we were warned that they were becoming more and more difficult about this.

Armed with our letter we went to Customs, and presented our application. We were told to bring photos of the boat so they could see why we were requesting an extension. This we did, dropping them around at Customs the following day. As Robert was driving he stayed in the truck and parked in the street, while I delivered the photos. Two fat officials, bulging out of their brown uniforms, were sitting outside the door on the veranda, enjoying the cool of the morning. Of course, they stopped me and asked where I was going and what I wanted. I explained that we had already submitted our documents and were merely bringing in back-up photos to accompany the request. The larger fellow took the photos and said it would be very difficult to get permission. However, if I gave him 4000 baht (US$100) he would see what he could do.

"I'm not carrying that sort of money on me," I said, looking him in the eye.

"Well, what are you prepared to pay?" the official asked in heavily-accented English.

TARA

This was getting complicated, so I said I would have to speak with my husband and beat a hasty retreat.

By midday the men were down at the yard, demanding to speak with Robert, hot on the scent of a bribe. This could be a big problem because if they insisted we leave in ten days, we would not be able to get *Deusa* back in the water in that time. Fat men in military uniforms with little minds and huge power always gave us the shivers.

This fellow sat down next to Robert, patting him warmly on the leg.

"How much you pay me?" the same question he'd asked me earlier.

Robert thought quickly, he was obviously going to have to pay something so he may as well ask for as much time as possible. We had originally asked for two months; Robert upped the stakes.

"I will pay you something if you give me a four month extension."

The roly-poly man nearly fell off the concrete bench where he was perched.

"That's impossible – too much time – you cannot stay so long!"

The two of them haggled back and forth for a while, and we finally got two months for US$25, a much better deal than the original request for US$100. This would give us time to finish repairs on *Deusa,* and leave Thailand for Malaysia.

ഇൻഡ

The managers of the yard, a young Thai couple, decided to give their employees a dinner to thank them for all their hard work. They had recently finished a large, wooden tourist boat, and been paid good money for it, so, whilst it was still hot in their pockets, they gave their staff a treat. They very generously invited the yacht owners whose boats were in the yard as well. There were three couples in all, and we went along to a nice restaurant on the edge of the bay.

A long table had been set up for about thirty people, and we all sat down to enjoy a spectacular meal! In true Thai style, the dishes were brought in, one by one, and as each course was finished, old dishes were removed and new ones appeared. The meal started with batter-fried prawns and grilled prawns, with various little dishes of hot sauces to dip them in. Then chicken in cashew nuts, chicken with Chinese mushrooms, fried chicken, boiled chicken, chicken soup, and chicken in a basket made of noodles. And just when we thought we had eaten enough, the fish started to arrive: fish in ginger, fish in garlic, whole fried fish, little fish rissoles, big fish rissoles, and great urns of steaming jasmine rice.

The Thais drank Thai whisky and got merrier and merrier. The yachties drank beer and also got very merry. Robert and I couldn't do full justice to the dinner because some of it was hotter than hell because of tiny red peppers known as 'rat shit peppers.' I had been eating a wonderful cold salad with lettuce and radish, bean sprouts and other delicacies, when, all of a sudden, it felt as if my mouth was on fire. Trying to ram slices of cucumber into my flaming mouth, I could hardly breathe. The Thais found this hilarious, and fed other unwary visitors with little bites of fiery food, sitting back to watch the inevitable reaction.

thirteen

Life in Phuket

Every year the Vegetarian Festival was held in Phuket. This began in 1825, when a travelling Chinese opera company visited Phuket to entertain the local Hokkien Chinese working in the tin mines. It was a very swampy island, and there were lots of fevers, malaria and other unidentified ills around. Many miners died as a result, and when the entire opera company became sick, everyone was very dismayed. The Chinese visitors kept to a strict vegetarian diet to honour two of the emperor gods, Kiew Ong Tai The and Yok Ong Song The, and when the sickness afflicting them disappeared, the local people were astonished, and asked how could this be? It was explained that ritual vegetarianism, with its attendant ceremonies, had cured them. Consequently, the miners of Phuket were sufficiently convinced to adopt the faith.

Every day there were street processions during the morning, and events at the various Chinese Buddhist temples in the evening. Our route from the house to the yard took us straight past a Chinese temple, and we invariably landed up in an enormous traffic jam, at which point we would jump out of the truck with Tara on her lead, and walk up ahead to video what was going on.

One particular procession contained trucks full of flowers, small altars with golden Buddha images, and people in trances shaking their heads and staring with vacant eyes at the respectful crowd lining the street, all dressed in white. Other mediums were walking, quivering and shaking, distributing amulets and flowers to outstretched hands, being guided by carers who made sure they didn't stumble and fall. Some of the mediums must have been well known holy men as people in the crowd bowed to them with the formal Thai gesture of respect, their hands held in a prayer position to the forehead, then reached out to touch their garments. Some trucks had small boys sitting in the back clashing cymbals and banging drums, in a rhythm unfamiliar to our western ears.

In amongst this jumble of humanity were Thais in trances who had stuck skewers, swords, TV aerials, half-inch stainless steel piping, etc, through their cheeks, ears, the side of the neck, the tongue: a very gruesome sight. There was no blood, and they appeared to be striding along quite normally, though with a glazed look in their eyes. Some of the pipes were up to two metres long, and stuck out each side of their face, with pineapples threaded on the ends to add weight, or a sack of oranges, or even a child's tricycle! Helpers walked on each side of them to prevent the crowd knocking into the rods.

The little pamphlet we picked up described these mediums –

"Ma Song, or entranced horses, are devotees whom the gods enter during the festival. They manifest supernatural powers and perform self-tortures in order to shift evil from individuals onto themselves, and to bring the community good luck."

The most bizarre thing we saw was a great stalk of bananas, the stem of which had been sharpened and pushed through the cheeks of one individual, from one side to the other, and at least three inches of the stem was sticking out the other side. It made our tummies turn over. The medium was supporting the bananas with both hands, and the procession must have gone on for at least an hour. Robert and I can hardly manage to carry a stalk of bananas between us from the market to the dinghy!

One man must have tried to pierce his cheeks and failed, as blood was frothing from his mouth and splattering his T shirt. He was in a trance, shaking and nodding his head, and behind him walked an assistant carrying a large skewer. The crowd was extremely reverent to this man; bowing and touching the cloth wound around his waist.

This part of the procession was quiet and dignified, but another part of it was totally wild and raucous, and we could hear it coming before we even caught sight of the white-clad figures rushing down the street, carrying a litter on which bounced and swayed a fearsome-looking god with snarling face and great, bushy, black hair. Firecrackers were going off everywhere, creating dense clouds of acrid, choking smoke with deafening explosions. The litter bearers had wrapped white scarves around their faces, giving the impression, as they came racing through the smoke curtain, of a street riot in a war zone. More and more strange gods and effigies appeared borne high on litters, leaping and swaying, rushing forward; stopping suddenly. Very dramatic, very scary – and this was the purpose of it all. The firecrackers – the louder the better – were to chase away evil spirits.

Tara was with us throughout this extraordinary commotion, and wasn't scared at all, just barking, barking, fit to burst. Nothing frightened this little dog: she didn't know what fear was and had enormous courage against all adversity, prepared to take on all devils coming her way!

One evening we went back into town without Tara, to watch bladed ladder-climbing at a temple. There were 36 steps up and 36 steps down, mounted on a very strong, wooden structure in the middle of the temple grounds. In place of each rung was a long knife blade: the mediums were going to climb up one side and down the other, barefoot. A lot of incense was lit, and many people were praying in the various rooms in the temple where the gods we had seen earlier in the street were positioned above the altars, glaring down at the crowd. These temples were wonderfully ornate, painted in red and gold, full of carved dragons and mystical symbols.

We saw many people with wounds in their cheeks and necks from the morning procession. Some of them looked very clean and not at all swollen; others were puffy and sore. We knew that the implements were pulled out once the procession had ended, but did they go back in again the next day, we wondered (the processions went on for at least five days)? Apparently, the wounds healed with barely a scar, though one medium died of blood poisoning the previous year.

Many mediums were ready to climb the ladder, and almost as many TV cameramen crowded around to get good shots, so it was difficult to see what was happening. However, once they had ascended several rungs we could see that they were, indeed, climbing barefoot on the knives, their hands gripping the blades above them as they clambered skyward. The previous year a tourist had decided that this was all a hoax, and gave it a go. He was rushed to hospital with badly lacerated feet, even though he had been wearing strong shoes ...

ഇ൪ങ

We were driving into town one day when Robert took a corner a bit sharply and hit the curb, which punctured the tubeless front tyre. We stopped abruptly in the middle of the road, Tara landing on my lap with a thud, catapulted from the back seat.

Robert eased the truck to the side of the road, jacked it up and took off the tyre. Rather than try and get the spare from under the back bumper where it was stored, he looked for a taxi to run him to the nearest garage. Phuket had a lot of motorbike taxis, and one soon stopped, beckoning for Robert and his tyre to leap on the back.

"You can't take a ride on that," I called to Robert from the curb where Tara and I were sitting. "It's a tiny bike and you'll never fit - you'll fall off and then we'll have to repair the tyre *and* you."

Robert laughed at my concern. "Look, the garage is just around the corner. I'll be back in no time, and of course I can fit - the driver seems to think so!"

The spindly little Thai driver was interested in getting the fare, so he balanced the tyre behind him, and then Robert on the last ten centimetres of the pillion seat. There was nowhere for Robert to put his feet, so he stuck them out on each side of the driver, and off they went, weaving and wobbling their way around a corner and out of sight. I don't know how the motorbike didn't rear up on its back wheel like a nervous horse. Needless to say, Robert came back in a car, as the motorbike ride was quite enough ethnic adventure for one day! Tara and I were very pleased to see him: we were growing bored of sitting in the sunshine, surrounded by petrol fumes and noise.

ഇ൪ങ

Our extended boat permit allowed *Deusa* to stay for an extra two months, but that didn't include us, so we had to drive to the Myanmar border, get stamped in, and out and return to Phuket.

TARA

It was a very pretty 300km (185 mile) drive through lush, green countryside, rice paddies, coastal resorts, and forest-clad mountains. As we hadn't done this drive before, we decided to stop the night at a National Park called Cow Sok. Stone cottages had been built right on the edge of a gurgling river that rushed past the veranda under tall, shady trees, and a small restaurant prepared delicious Thai food. Tara was with us, and we took her for a walk along one of the many jungle trails in the park. When we got back I wandered over to the restaurant for a couple of beers. One of the Thai tour guides looked at my foot and pointed out a leech. A LEECH! I had never seen a leech before, let alone one attached to my foot. There it was, bloated with blood, nestled on my foot with its mouth buried into the soft skin between my toes, drinking its fill.

"What shall I do? What shall I do?" I squawked, wildly looking around at the surprised Thai faces. "Shall I burn it off by fire, or douse it with alcohol?"

"Oh, just pull it off," said the guide, very nonchalantly, turning back to his companions at the bar.

Bracing myself, I grabbed the leech between finger and thumb and wrenched it off. It wriggled and squirmed in my fingers, trying to bite me again. Oh, horrors! It was the shape of a banana and a brown, slimy colour. I couldn't tell which end was which as I hurled it into the garden.

"Aaaggghh" cried the guide, "you can't do that, it will have hundreds of babies and invade the place."

Well, there was no way I was going to hunt for a leech in the dense undergrowth, even if it meant, that, in a couple of weeks the restaurant would be invaded by an army of slithery leeches, hungry for tourist blood! But I learnt a thing or two about leeches, that day: they don't like tobacco, so rub yourself liberally with a nice twist of Silk Cut; don't wear longs (long trousers) and tuck them into your socks because they will burrow through the socks and travel up under the longs, and then you will have leeches where you really don't want them! I never felt the leech bite me, so they must use a kind of anaesthetic, and also an anti-coagulant. My toe bled profusely for a good four hours afterwards: no wonder they used them for blood-letting in the old days! We checked Tara over to see if she had any leeches lodged between her toes or on her soft underbelly, but she was leech-free, thankfully.

The next day the three of us drove up to the Thai/Myanmar border and checked out with Immigration in the town of Ranong, Tara riding happily in the back, barking at stray dogs and errant chickens. She very seldom ever growled; barking was much more her favourite form of expression. At the dock we hired a water taxi to take us across to an island in the middle of a large bay, where the Myanmar Immigration post balanced on a rock.

"You take little dog with you?" asked the nervous young Thai as we stepped aboard his wobbly wooden boat. "She not bite me?"

"Oh, no, she doesn't bite," we said crossing our fingers behind our backs. "She's very friendly and loves boat rides. Just makes a lot of noise."

Off we set across the bay, the sun sparkling on the sea, the short, sharp waves splashing over the bow. Tara raced around the boat, snapping at the spray, barking at the water traffic, happy as only a dog can be.

The Myanmar Immigration office had to win the prize for the strangest immigration post we had ever visited in our travels around the world. A tiny tin shed perched on the edge of a minute rocky island; the only landing spot a couple of slippery, sea-washed steps. These led into a hut of four square metres, crammed full of uniformed and gold-braided men, eight of them sitting at a table, eating; the other four waiting to be fed.

Was this an Immigration convention or a shift change, and why did they need so many officers to man this postage stamp island? We never found out, but they were extremely friendly and chatty and spoke excellent English, because when Myanmar was known as Burma, it was a British colony. The officers dutifully stamped us in and out of their country in all of five minutes, admired our dog waiting impatiently in the boat, and wished us a safe ride back to Thailand.

෫෮෬

Working on *Deusa* in the yard was a great challenge. Not only did we have the topsides and cabin roof sanded, faired, filled and painted shining white, we also had the woodwork of the navigation station remodelled, the aft head floor repaired, the workshop table and floor repaired, and new stainless steel davits made. To complicate the workload we also thought it would be fun to varnish the entire interior.

We must have been out of our minds. At what point of lunacy would one presume to do varnishing in a yard full of sandblasting, grinding of the antifouling paint from the hull, spray-painting, dust storms, rain storms, and a nearby fish sauce factory belching black, stinky smoke? *Deusa* was filled with cutting machines, sawing machines, polishing machines, stapling machines, and air guns. One could hardly walk amongst the spaghetti tangle of cords and plugs. As the varnishing went from bad to worse, with stains and dribbles, mottles and gaps, we cancelled that project, which did not endear us to the contractors. They had probably quoted too little for all the work, in any case, so tried to cut corners to economize. Talking with other boats, it seems we were certainly given good prices on the painting and teak work. Funnily enough, the actual haul-out and hardstand costs varied from boat-to-boat, and wasn't based on length but on how adept one was at persuading the yard manager to give a discount.

One of the items that was economized on was Sikaflex, a horrid, sticky, black putty used for re-sealing the deck hardware (when it rained, the deck leaked like a sieve, so we had to re-bed a lot of the fittings). Whilst doing this job, somehow, the workers got Sikaflex all over their clothes, which then spread to the cushions of the V berth as they wriggled and squirmed to tighten the bolts below deck. Not content with this, they also dropped a generous blob of black goo on the saloon sofa. To add a little texture to the black smears, the guy varnishing the newly-made navigation station must have tripped over the tangle of electrical wires, hurling his pot of shiny varnish across the seat opposite him. I was furious and shouted and screamed at Robert, Tara, the workers, and anyone else within hearing range. Our home was a disaster, and I wept out of sheer frustration at the awful mess.

And to this chaos add a rat. No, add two rats. We spotted the first whilst *Deusa* was still on the hard. It had made itself quite comfortable in a nest of ropes and dock lines under a seat in the saloon. Goodness knows how long it had been on board, but the boat was there a total of four months, so it might have taken out a long lease. Luckily, we were lent some traps and soon caught it before we moved back on board with Tara the ratter.

ॐ⃝ℬ

Once *Deusa* was back in the water looking all new and shiny – a sparkling white boat with a golden stripe through her portholes along her topsides, instead of the midnight blue she used to have – we gave up our rented house on land. One evening, a couple of days later, I heard a strange, nibbling noise that certainly wasn't fish or crabs, exploring along the waterline, moving around under the floorboards. It was another rat which, because of all the small holes through the bulkheads carrying wires, pipes and cables, was free to roam where it would. Each night we could hear it grating its long yellow teeth on something ... but what? The wires of the GPS, the radar, perhaps, or maybe a vital link on the autopilot? We kept our food in buckets and stored them on deck at night, hoping to starve out the rat so it would take the bait in the traps. Tara could smell the creature, and it drove her frantic, but she had no chance of catching it as *Deusa* had so many hidden nooks and crannies.

During this rat-catching drama we had to make a passage to Malaysia as we had run out of time with our visas in Thailand. Setting off in bad weather, it was an uncomfortable journey, with a swell coming in from a cyclone that had passed through the Bay of Bengal. The voyage took us three days, because we went slowly in order to rediscover our sea legs, put *Deusa* back together – and catch the rat!

The first night we baited three traps with cheese, checking hopefully next morning for a victim. Nothing. So the following night we tried bacon. Nothing. Then sausage. Nothing. We felt total despair as each night we could hear it gnawing away. What was it eating, for goodness sake? Tara felt despair, too: she was as eager to catch it as we were.

New evidence was found as tooth marks in the soap in the forward head. We never knew rats ate soap, though now we do! Two kinds of rat liked to climb on board boats in South East Asia: the black Norwegian rat that travelled the world in sailing ships and is found in every port, and the brown, fruit-eating Thai rat.

The final insult was when the rat managed to crawl into the fruit hammock, and ate a large slice of pawpaw. That was the clue. It had to be a fruit-eating Thai; not a black Norwegian.

So, on the eighth night, the traps were baited with pawpaw. The next morning the trap had been sprung in the forward head, and there was a small pool of blood on the floor, but no rat. Tara, the rat tracker, was called in, and she insisted that it had gone up into the forepeak, so we hoisted her onto the bunk. In a flash she flushed out the rat from behind some books, and, as it leapt from the bookcase, seized it in mid-air and killed it with a quick shake of her head. What swift ratters these Jack Russells are! We had one very pleased dog bustling about feeling most important afterwards.

We were so relieved to see the end of the rat that had had us fooled for nine days. It was a different colour from the black rat we had caught earlier on, with a brown back and biscuit-coloured tummy. We checked carefully to make sure it was not a nursing mother with swollen titties. Rats have to survive, and generally I wish them no ill, but it is very dangerous to have one gnawing through unknown wires and cables, especially at sea!

ഇഐരു

To add to the general woes of learning to sail again after so many months as landlubbers, someone – who shall remain nameless – forgot how to store eggs! The eggs were left on a counter top, and on one particularly large ocean roll, inevitably fell to the floor, shattering and oozing all over the cabin sole, and down into the bilges. Regrettably, it wasn't only the eggs that self-destructed, either, as a fair quantity of bright red anti-fouling paint, left over from painting the hull, was balancing precariously in the basin of the forward head. This also had suicidal tendencies, it seems, as it, too, cast itself to the floor with a great crash and a splat, painting half the floor scarlet and adding a touch of interesting speckles up the door. The smell and the colour were overpowering, so we shut the door and hoped it would go away, which some of it did, into the bilges, to join the eggs. Eggs Benedict or Eggs Anti-foul. Yuk!

We were very glad to get to the marina and clean up *Deusa*, putting Tara down below in the saloon as she always barked a lot on arrival anywhere. She even carried on yapping out of sight in the saloon, and Robert would shout at her to be quiet. Any onlooker seeing me standing at the bow with a dock line in hand, must have been most surprised as Robert bellowed "Shut up!" and "if you don't keep quiet right now, I'm going to muzzle you!" It got even worse when Tara gave Robert a wet and slobbery kiss on the lips as we were quietly having a cup of tea in the cockpit. All the neighbours could hear was "Aaaghh – not on the lips! I hate being kissed on the lips by you!" People thought we had a very strange relationship.

The marina organized a Christmas Day potluck lunch for those yachts that didn't have any celebration arranged, and this entailed taking enough food for the captain and crew of one's own boat, and sharing it with others who were doing the same thing.

After the meal the tables were cleared and people began dancing. The Thai restaurant staff were also joining in by this time, and one gay waiter was bold enough to haul Robert off his chair and onto the floor. Now, Robert was a rock-and-roll star in his youth, and the crowd couldn't believe their eyes when this large man who had been sitting quietly in the background, took off like a rocket. The timid Thai waiter was amazed at what he had fished from the sea of foreigners, and fled back to the kitchen. Robert was given a warm round of applause for his exhibition, and had to be cooled down with a large glass of cold beer.

Some Japanese tourists, to their shock and horror, became swept up in the line of cavorting, laughing, snorting Westerners leaping around like mad things. They must have thought it was a very ethnic and tribal experience and joined in cautiously, rather like we would at a Fijian or Samoan get- together.

Phuket had a large sailing community that ran weekend races and several regattas during the year. Our friend Phil (Tara's uncle, who looked after her when we travelled) suggested we joined the Phang Na regatta, which continued over several days, and was lots of fun.

Thirty-eight yachts signed up, with around 260 participants, including organizers, captains, and crew. Having never joined a race or a regatta before, this was all very new and exciting for us. The skippers' meeting was especially interesting, and we had to pay attention to all sorts of information, such as ten-minute warning signals, categories of yachts, flags of different colours, committee boats, marker buoys, and gates to go through. We were handed a printout of the courses to be raced over the next three days, together with mud charts of the islands.

Robert and I were not racing sailors, with no experience of tacking back and forth behind a start line, keeping out of the way of the multi-hulls and racing-class yachts. All quite traumatic for us beginners, but thank goodness the speedy racers and multi-hulls went first, and the cruisers – being slower boats – were last in the line up. There was very little wind and, fortunately for us, it was a calm start.

The participants in these regattas were extremely enthusiastic and competitive people. They removed all excess weight from their boats – anchors, dinghies, fuel, water, bed linen, crockery, pots and pans, etc – so, really, they shouldn't have been classified as cruisers. We had three anchors, carried the dinghy on davits, were full of diesel and water, and weighed down with many tins of 'make your own beer' from Australia, so consequently staggered through the start line amongst the tail-enders. There was only about 5 to 7 knots of wind, which did not move our fat lady weighing 18 tons very fast.

The first leg was to windward, and we weren't doing too badly, making about 4 knots just keeping up with the pack, with a few stragglers behind us. Then came the great challenge as we cleared the first buoy and bore off downwind. The spinnaker. Dear Lord, we prayed, let's hope we get this right. We hadn't used the big sail for more than a year, so, holding our collective breath, we hauled it up in its sock behind the jib, attaching the sheets to the clew and the tack of the large sail.

Robert rolled up the jib, I hauled on the sock and up it shot, releasing the spinnaker. How pretty, how dazzling in stripes of blue and white – but how strange, it does not want to fly, and flops around like a wounded butterfly as everyone pulls ahead of us in their rainbow sails of bright colours.

Something was very wrong, so we hauled down on the sock, changed the tack for the clew, and the clew for the tack and started again. Basically, we had it back to front! This time it worked and, miracle of miracles, we caught everyone up as they had sailed into a wind shadow and were lying this way and that, their spinnakers like popped balloons at the end of a children's party. We were still coasting along on a tiny puff of breeze, and landed right amongst the yachts, which was a grave tactical error. On this mammoth learning curve that we had unwittingly subjected ourselves to, we discovered that it is not clever to put yourself in the middle of a pack of drifting boats that are looking for any breath of wind in order to pull away from their rivals.

Now we had to bring the spinnaker down, and the sock jammed at the top of the mast. So we dropped this huge sail in billowing folds of blue and white all over the foredeck, then stuffed it down the forward hatch, seawater and all. (It was full of seawater because it fell overboard, and it didn't really matter that we soaked the V berth mattress as it was already covered in black Sikaflex stains.)

Our glorious moment of catching everyone up was short-lived and, once again, we were pottering along on our own, with only four or five boats behind us. Ahead loomed the 'gate' with the large committee yacht standing guard to starboard, and a fat orange marker buoy to port. We had to get through the 'gate' but there was very little wind, and a certain amount of adverse current.

The committee boat became a total magnet for *Deusa,* and she drifted closer and closer to it. It was embarrassing because we knew the people on the boat, and Tara's minder, Phil, was also there.

"Oh, hello Tara," said Phil, "what are you doing so close to the committee boat?"

And off she went into barks of delight at seeing an old friend. Not only were we getting close to being pinned to the committee boat, we were making a huge noise about it, too. Finally, a friendly puff of wind drew us away from this awkward encounter, Tara barking farewells to Phil as we slowly left the scene.

The Phang Na area had spectacular scenery, full of sheer, white-cliffed, limestone islands, topped with lush vegetation and hollow with caves and interesting weather sculptures. We were sailing so slowly we had lots of time to study all this dazzling nature.

In the evening after the race, the organizers threw a party and prize-giving on a huge, wooden junk that must have been at least forty metres long, with two deck levels and enough space to entertain a thousand people. Free beer and free food were gulped down by the hot and hungry sailors who had been sitting in the tropical sun all day, with hardly a breeze to cool them.

The next day there was a race around a small group of islands: not such a long distance, and trickier with all the sail changes. This time we got our act together at the start line, and as soon as we were through we tacked and headed off up the bay into the wind. Several tacks were needed to get to the first buoy, and at some point after the third or fourth tack we discovered that Tara was no longer on board.

"Robert, where's Tara?" I shouted up to the cockpit, while I was making coffee down below.

"I don't know, isn't she with you?"

"No, she's not down here, I've looked around and no dog."

Climbing back up with the coffee, I called her name a few times just in case she had tucked herself into a corner on the aft deck.

"She's not here, she's not down below, I think she's fallen overboard."

We couldn't believe it. Tara hadn't fallen overboard for more than two years, and it was then normally after she had seen dolphins and barked so much she lost her balance and we would see her fall. This time, without a murmur, she had vanished. When had she disappeared? How far back down the bay? Was she still swimming after us, or had the strong north setting current swept her away?

I felt a cold, sick chill in the pit of my stomach, and a helpless shiver of panic.

"What do we do; how are we going to begin to look for her?"

Robert looked as devastated as I felt.

"I'm going to call the committee boat to tell them what's happened and cancel us out of the race. You stay on *Deusa* and motor back along our GPS path, and I'll put the dinghy in the water and go in large circles on our track."

What a truly terrible feeling to lose an animal overboard. People had warned us about this when we discussed having a dog on board. Be prepared for heartache, they said: it can happen so quickly and for no apparent reason. It must have been all those sail changes and manoeuvres as we raced up the bay. Oh, dear God, we should have shut her away in the cabin while we were doing this stupid race.

✂✃

Now it was a question of searching back and forth across the bay, hoping to spot the small, black triangle of her head in the water. Luckily, it was another calm day, so there was hardly any wave action, only a ripple on the water. The committee was most shocked at the news, and Phil organised a dinghy and two people to help us look. Robert checked around any small, rocky islets in the bay that she might have swum to. Every coconut, every twig, beer bottle, floating debris, could have been Tara. I steered *Deusa* back along our route, scanning the water with my powerful binoculars, motoring towards any object that looked like a dog's head. There was a painful lump in my throat; I wanted to cry and had to fight back the tears as I searched the sea.

We searched for more than three hours and couldn't find her. Jumbled thoughts swirled through our minds. What a way to die. Imagine if it was a person we couldn't find. We must offer a reward and get someone to translate it into Thai. If she survived and was picked up by a fisherman, would she have a happy life in a Thai fishing village? I sometimes wished we didn't have a dog on board: be careful what you wish for. We'd have to stay in the area until we found her or her body. And if the current was so strong, how would we find her body, possibly swept out to sea and eaten by sharks?

What if she had crawled into a cave in one of those craggy little islands, and slowly starved to death? What if she was flicked off by the roller furling when we tacked, and was hurt? But, wait a minute, there was a moment when she could have been flicked overboard by the falling staysail as it fluttered to the deck, still billowing with vestiges of the wind. We had sewed netting all along the lifelines to avoid precisely this, but the knock must have been too strong and over she went. She might have even been trying to bite the sail to help bring it down to the deck.

The race committee advised the boats behind us that we had lost our dog overboard and to keep an eye out for her. Our friend, Phil, on the committee boat was very worried, too, as he had grown fond of the tough little terrier who had stayed in his house.

All the other competitors had sailed on. We were alone in the bay, motoring back and forth, the committee boat was lifting its anchor to accompany the race to the day's finish line.

Suddenly, the radio crackled into life.

"*Deusa, Deusa* this is the committee boat, your dog has been found on a beach by one of the multi-hulls that has finished the race."

We were far away, high up in the bay continuing our search, so Phil went to the beach in a dinghy to pick her up. Tara was overjoyed to see him – and to take a ride on the committee boat!

Overcome with emotion, we gathered up Tara, who was overjoyed to see us, but didn't want to get into our dinghy, preferring to stay on the committee boat where Phil had been feeding her barbecued sausage. She wasn't tired by her long swim; she wasn't panicked at being abandoned: she was amused at her adventure! These Jack Russells are very tough little souls, much tougher than Robert or me, who still felt very shaky and tearful.

Piecing the story together, we deduced that Tara must have gone overboard when we tacked a second time, and swum across the current to try and catch us up. Seeing that it was hopeless, this clever little dog turned around and headed for the nearest piece of land that she could glimpse from her lowly position in the water. At some moment a tourist paddling past in a kayak, saw her and gave her a lift to the beach. According to some onlookers, she ran and hid amongst the rocks for fifteen minutes or so, maybe to draw breath, having been in the water for nearly three hours. She then came out to play along the shallows, trying to catch tiny fish, as if nothing had happened.

When we joined the regatta we thought it would be a good opportunity to meet some of the cruisers who would be around for the next year. We didn't have it in mind that our dog would make us instantly famous. The experience served to remind us that we were laden with books and provisions, and that we were far too heavy for light-wind regatta sailing. We needed a lot more practice in nimble tacking and sail changes.

We also learnt that Tara stayed down below during competitions ...

fourteen

Langkawi, Malaysia

A couple of years passed and it was time to haul *Deusa* out of the water once again, look at the hull, the prop shaft, wear and tear on the anodes, and generally carry out repair and maintenance work on our floating home. This was a regular occurrence; it was not unusual to have to check over a yacht every two years or so. The anti-fouling paint that prevented barnacles adhering to the hull would often require another coat, and the bearings in the prop shaft could become worn and need replacing.

We always hated this dangerous time of being on the hard – when more accidents happen in which people are seriously hurt falling off their boats on to the hard – but it was necessary. Our venue of choice was Rebak Marina on the island of Langkawi in Malaysia, as it had a reputation for careful haul-out, good workmanship, and a pleasant community of people, some of whom lived permanently in the marina on the floating pontoons in the yacht basin. A bar and restaurant ashore made for sociable get-togethers, laundry facilities helped with the washing load, and quite a large area offered walks to a restless dog.

The bicycles that we had bought in Australia were still on board *Deusa,* and gave me a brilliant idea. If I could get Tara to run alongside me as I biked around the island, we would both get exercise, and I could do the distance on the bike that would stretch Tara's legs. Good thought ... only I hadn't planned on meeting water monitors, enormous lizards who grow up to one-and-a-half metres in length, run very fast, and swim even faster.

Tara and I began training on our bike ride expeditions around the haul-out facilities, weaving in and out of the boats as they stood on their cradles on the concrete platform. Tara's lead was about ten metres long, which gave her the liberty to run ahead or to one side without being too confined. We had a few upsets and spills, but on the whole we got along fine ... until, that is, we set out along an island path amongst the scrub bush and stunted trees of the island. A lovely sunny day with a light cool breeze, Tara and I cruising along in harmony with nature and our surroundings when, suddenly, we came upon one of the island residents, a monitor lizard, dozing on the sunny path in the warm sand.

Up shot the lizard with a hiss; off shot Tara with a bark, and I plunged helplessly into the thick bushes, my bicycle skidding wildly in the thick sand as I was unseated by whipping branches. The lizard escaped. Tara and the bicycle came to a halt in the undergrowth, and I spent some time untangling them before walking back to the yard with as much dignity as I could muster. That was the last of the bike excursions – on foot was a lot safer.

As usual, we had the problem of climbing up and down the ladder with Tara when doing boat maintenance on the hard, and we decided it would be safer to haul her up and down in her fold-up travelling carrier made of tough plastic, with its good, strong carrying handle, using a pulley attached to our mizzen boom. All we had to do was put Tara in the carrier, close the door, snap a shackle onto the handle, and gently lower her to the ground where one of us met her on arrival and let her out. This worked absolutely fine for about a week. It was such a relief for us not to be on the wobbly ladder with her tucked under one arm, while we clung on with our free hand as we clambered up or down.

Then, one morning, we prepared to leave the boat, placing Tara in her carrier, snapping on the pulley mechanism, and starting to lower her. Abruptly, the handle broke, and Tara dropped head first onto the hard concrete below. I let out a scream of horror and rushed over to get her out of the carrier. There she was, lying stiffly, with her eyes rolled back and blood oozing from her mouth.

"Oh, Robert, Robert, come down here quickly, it looks like she's dead." It was such an awful sight that I burst into tears.

"We've gone and killed our dog," I sobbed as the Muslim Malay yard workers gathered round and stared in silence. Muslims don't care for dogs, and they wouldn't be brokenhearted over this one.

Robert carefully eased Tara out of her death trap, laid her on a towel in the shade, and noticed that she was still breathing. We didn't know whether her back or legs might be broken ... and was the blood in her mouth from a deep internal haemorrhage or had she bitten her tongue? I sat beside her, crying, and stroking her head, talking to her all the while, saying how sorry I was to hurt her.

A friend had recently fallen from her boat, breaking her arm in several places, which only reconfirmed to us how dangerous boatyards were. Now, here was our dog, dying because we thought we were so clever putting her in a cage, instead of carrying her.

After about half-an-hour Tara opened her eyes and licked my hand. Her gaze was misty and out of focus, but there was no more blood coming from her mouth. Then she sat up and stared around in bewilderment, as if she didn't know where she was. It was when she stood up that I knew there were no broken bones, and that she was just severely concussed.

It was miraculous: by the evening she was as chirpy as ever and enjoyed her dinner. It was just the best feeling in the world: our beloved companion was going to be all right. We never tried the carrier again.

&)C&

Langkawi and surrounding islands made for very attractive cruising grounds, and many of the small islands were uninhabited, so we could let Tara run free on these. One particular island was a favourite place for day visitors to stop off in their boats, have a swim and a barbecue. To give Tara a good run, she and I would head for a corner of the beach in the dinghy, where I would drop her off, then drive to the other end with Tara racing along the sand to catch me up. Two or three runs up and down was good exercise for her, after which she'd get bored, and look for crabs and fish along the water's edge

This particular day there were several people ashore, and I could see wisps of smoke rising from the barbecue area.

"They won't worry about Tara," I thought, "I'll just drop her off here, speed away, and she'll follow me on the beach."

What I didn't know was that somebody had brought their Red Setter with them, who was sitting quietly amongst the party. At that time Tara had no manners when it came to meeting other dogs, and she flew at this poor animal, teeth bared and eyes flashing. Chaos reigned: the dog fled, pursued by Tara, beers were knocked out of hands, and everyone was shouting.

I rammed the dinghy onto the beach, leapt out, and ran after my dog through the thick sand, calling her name, tripping on tree roots and falling flat on my face in front of the hysterical visitors, gulping down mouthfuls of sand.

"Control your dog," shouted the Red Setter owner, as Tara snapped at the long feathery tail streaming out behind the dog running in desperate circles.

"I'm trying to catch her," I choked, spitting out sand and leaves.

At this moment the Red Setter plunged into the sea, and began swimming frantically for the boats, with Tara in hot pursuit. The Setter's owner leapt in and scooped up his large, wet dog, staggering ashore to the hilarity of the lunchtime crowd. But Tara wasn't giving up, and as the dog's long tail dangled in the water, she seized it. By now I had caught up, grabbed her, forced open her jaws and pulled out the red-gold tail ...

Bundling her into the dinghy, I ferried her back to *Deusa* in disgrace, then returned ashore to apologise to everyone – the dog owner in particular – for spoiling their party. What humiliation. How could such a small dog terrorize such a big dog? The people onshore were really quite amused by the incident, the Red Setter had only injured dignity, and the whole scene had been good entertainment, as far as they were concerned.

From then on I was very careful to properly check out the beach before letting go of Tara, though once, on the same beach, I learnt a very different lesson.

ഇന്ദ

Tara loved to chase monkeys, and there were a lot of macaques in Malaysia, on both islands and mainland. These bold monkeys would come and steal from tourists, grabbing food at picnics, and even the hot meat on barbecues. This particular day there were no people ashore;

it was very quiet, so I took a book and lazed in the dinghy by the shore, while Tara explored the beach. She had run inland towards the forest and dense bush, when a troop of macaques came down to the water's edge, and were watching me as I ate potato chips from a rustling packet. They were concentrating avidly on the food, all facing towards me, when Tara came shooting out of the bushes to see a row of monkey bottoms all lined up for her to pounce on. Not missing a chance like that, she charged into the midst of them with a yelp of excitement, biting left and right.

The macaques fled up the nearby trees leaning out over the water, but one big monkey remained, and was in the water, dragging Tara down. Who was drowning who I'll never know: all I could see was Tara's white tail and rump sticking up out of the water; the rest of her submerged. I think the monkey was trying to drown her. Frantically paddling over to her, I grabbed her tail, hauling her into the dinghy. The monkey crawled along the sand underwater to a submerged branch, pulling itself out to sit in a sodden, shivering bundle.

The monkey didn't seem to be bleeding, but Tara had a nasty gash across her throat, and was splattering blood all over the dinghy. Hurrying back to *Deusa*, I rinsed her off in fresh water, towelled her dry, and checked the bite. The monkey's sharp teeth had slashed her throat just below the jaw line, a nasty, deep cut some 4cm long. Our friend Jan on *Yawarra*, anchored nearby, was a nurse.

"*Yawarra*, *Yawarra*, this is *Deusa*, *Deusa*. Please come over and look at Tara. She's been bitten by a monkey; it looks quite bad."

"I'll be right over," responded Jan.

We thought we could close the wound with butterfly plasters but Jan felt it was too deep, and had sliced through several layers of skin down to the throat muscles. Tara let us examine her wound without any fuss, so the shock was still keeping the pain at bay, and she wasn't aware of the long, red wound under her chin.

Now the challenge was to find a vet to stitch her up in a Muslim country where government vets don't touch dogs. What a perfect nightmare! Someone suggested calling an English lady, Norelle, who lived on Langkawi and owned the Bon Ton restaurant. She rescued animals, and had many dogs and cats at her home, so she might have a solution. We had met her previously, and knew that she got a vet from Singapore to fly up to Langkawi once a month to tend to the sick animals. We had her phone number so gave her a call, explaining the situation. Norelle was marvellous, and immediately came up with a solution.

"Bring the dog to the jetty near my house. It belongs to an hotel but I'm sure they won't mind. I'll meet you there with my car and take you to the restaurant. There's a vet working at the crocodile farm: Rita's an Indian and a Hindu, so no problem with dogs. I've a couple of rooms where the Singapore vet does her operating so I'll drop you there and fetch her."

We headed for the jetty on *Deusa*, dropping anchor in the small, sheltered bay, and Robert ran me ashore in the dinghy, with Tara

TARA

wrapped in a towel to keep her warm. Even though it was a hot day, she was still wet and shivery with shock. So were we!

Norelle arrived, gathered us both up and carried us away to her restaurant. Robert stayed with the boat, and I took the hand-held VHF so I could call him when I got back. It was now about 4pm, and it was after 10pm that night when I got back. The vet was busy operating on a crocodile that had been in a fight, and wasn't immediately available, so Tara and I sat for hours and hours in the small clinic, waiting for her to arrive, Tara hardly moving, while I became more and more anxious.

"Hello, Rosemary, I'm Rita," said the pretty young vet, her white coat covering her blue jeans and T shirt, "let's see what we've got here."

She stroked Tara gently and examined her open wound, still oozing blood.

"It's a deep gash," she explained, "you can see that the monkey's teeth have cut through the skin and the internal muscle that runs up her throat. I'm going to have to give her a general anaesthetic to sew her up."

"Oh, no," I thought, remembering Tara and the botched spaying job in Thailand; her blank stare and staggering gait.

Tara was extremely hard to knock out (unless dropped on her head from five or more metres, that is) and we already had the experience of trying to tranquillize her when she was chipped in Fiji.

Now, here we were again, with some doubt as to how much anaesthetic she'd need. I told Rita the story of the chip and the spaying. She picked up Tara to judge her weight, and give the correct dose. After half-an-hour Tara was still awake, wondering why she had to be shut in this room with all its nasty medicinal smells. Rita didn't want to overdose and maybe kill her, but she couldn't stitch her up in her present state. So she gave her another half dose, and this did the trick.

I was the vet's assistant, holding the pliers to pull the needle through the tough skin; the scissors to cut each piece of thread; the cotton wool to mop up the blood. Rita said sewing up crocodiles was a tough business, but Tara's thick skin was nearly as bad. Altogether she had sixteen stitches: eight inside in the muscle, and eight outside in the skin.

Even though Tara's rabies shots were up-to-date, Rita gave her another for good measure, plus a handful of antibiotics for the next few days, and instructions for her to stay out of the sea. Not such an easy task with this water baby ...

Finally, we were driven back to the jetty and I called Robert on the VHF to collect us. He had been worried that we were taking so long, but with only one mobile phone there was no way I could call him.

Tara was a healthy dog, and the wound soon healed – thank goodness. We were so lucky to have found Norelle who looked after us, and the vet, Rita, who did an excellent job.

⁂

The Andaman Islands lie below Burma but belong to India, so visas from India were necessary in order to visit, and it was a three-day sail, stopping at the Surin Islands off Thailand on the way. It was our first time

continued page 161

I hear what you're saying, but that certainly doesn't look anything like a mouse to me!

The life raft on the cabin roof was another good vantage point from which to survey the world.

Let's go! Tara and Robert deciding when to go ashore for an adventure!

Whilst carrying out repairs and maintenance on Deusa, we rented a house in Phuket.

The dog - later named Ocean - we rescued at sea in Borneo, dripping dry in the dinghy. Ocean had a very sweet personality and was delighted - and relieved - to be on board.

While in Thailand we bought a truck, which was most useful for moving stuff on and off the boat.

Our travels took us to some of the most remote and beautiful tropical islands in the world.

Hole in the Wall was one of the most secluded and peaceful anchorages, away from all bad weather.

Our yacht, Deusa, sailing in Kuah harbour, Langkawi, past the big concrete Brahminy Kite.

Tara loved to travel, and here she is guarding the luggage – or maybe making sure she doesn't get left behind! – as we prepare to depart on a trip to Northern Thailand.

We stayed with our friends Richard, Angkhana, and their dog, Benny, in Northern Thailand.

Deusa is a tiny dot on a vast, blue Madagascan ocean ...

Please, Captain Robert, may I take the helm?

There's nothing quite as comfortable on deck as a coiled hose!

Tara and I waiting for a visitor. She is on a lead in order to keep control of the anticipated over-enthusiastic welcome.

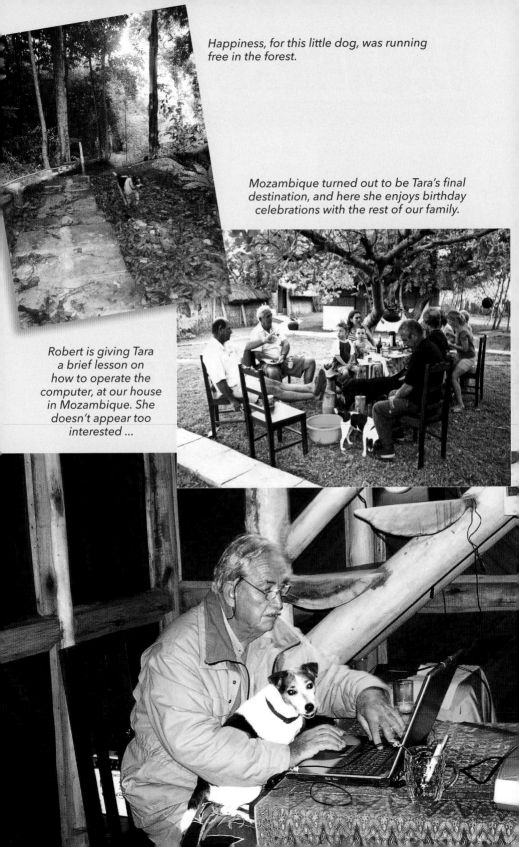

Happiness, for this little dog, was running free in the forest.

Mozambique turned out to be Tara's final destination, and here she enjoys birthday celebrations with the rest of our family.

Robert is giving Tara a brief lesson on how to operate the computer, at our house in Mozambique. She doesn't appear too interested ...

☆星期日 A11

有見過我的愛犬嗎？

航海家尋墜海狗

報導 陳愛娣

（亞羅士打一日訊）「你有見過我的愛犬嗎？」

愛狗墜海失蹤，洋人航海家沿著海岸線駕車，由霹靂紅土坎南下至瓜拉雪蘭莪漁村，見到漁夫就問：「你有見過我的愛犬嗎？」

這對來自英國的退休夫婦羅拔（六十一歲）與羅絲瑪麗（五十六歲），與迷你獵犬為伴，揚帆航海，環遊世界過著悠閒生活。

不料，最近他們的愛犬從船上跌落海裡失蹤，令他們擔心得茶飯不思。

他們相信，愛犬已經游上岸，故

據說，達拉在船上見過鯨魚及鯊魚，雖然經常下水游泳，不過，在見到大魚時，就不敢貿然下水。

十月廿九日，羅拔的船來到馬六甲海峽距離巴生港口卅海里處，達拉不知何故跌進海裡。當時，他們正要航向東馬。

羅拔夫婦在兩小時後，始發現愛犬失蹤，且許久都沒有游上船。夫婦倆心急如焚，在海上嘗試尋找，不過始終無法尋獲。

尋找途中，他們遇到在該處捕魚的漁船，不過由於本地漁夫都不懂英文，因此雙方無法溝通。

張貼尋狗啓事

為此，羅拔夫婦倆把船航入雪蘭

國際帆船俱樂部，協助尋找愛犬下落。

這對夫婦今日特別通過「中國報」，發出請求，希望公眾相助，尤其是巴生港口一帶的人民，如果見到這隻迷你獵犬，致電聯絡他們，獎賞是三百零吉。

羅拔與羅斯瑪麗指出，「達拉」獵犬與他們在海上共處七年，是一隻迷你小狗，擅長游泳。

他們表示，退休後，他們夫婦過著悠閒生活，帶著這隻可愛的獵犬，乘帆船環遊世界。

「我們是乘帆船從巴納馬運河，來到東南亞，而這隻愛犬與我們相依為命，分別橫渡過太平洋、法屬波利尼尼亞、斐濟、所羅門群島、

■可愛的「達拉」，與主人航海了七年，深受主人寵愛。

A Chinese newspaper printed a story about Tara becoming lost overboard, and the reward that we offered.

We made a poster in English and Malay, offering a reward to whoever found Tara, after we lost her overboard.

HILANG DI LAUT DEKAT
LOST overboard at SEA between
Kampong Karang (03:22N : 101.07 East)
And
Kampong Passir Panjang (03:35N -100.55East)
REWARD GANJARANRM 300.00
Small DOG answering to the NAME of TARA
ANJIG kecil NAMA TARA
KEPADA YANG MENEMUL TOLONG HUBANAL SAYA DINO
When found please contact one of the following
Robert & Rosemary Forrester H/P Tel 012-489-1704
Royal Langkawi Yacht Club (Shikin) 04-966-4078
John Ferguson H/P Tel 012-31-16058
Royal Selangor Yacht Club 03-31686964

in an Indian country, and we were enchanted by the lovely ladies in their colourful saris, the spicy food; the friendly people. With so many small islands and interesting anchorages to explore, a month's visa was not enough, but the authorities were not prepared to extend our time there.

On the way back we stopped at the Similan Islands of Thailand, south of the Surin Islands, arriving as the sun was setting at Koh Similan. We dropped the sails, fired up the motor, and approached the anchorage crowded with dive boats. Once the anchor was set, we began to tidy up the deck, fold away the staysail, and pour an evening whisky.

But where was Tara? Had she jumped down below to take a quick nap on the sofa? Was she tucked in a storage space in the forepeak – where had she gone? We called and looked but couldn't find her anywhere.

Oh, no, we had lost our dog again. How could that be possible? That same horrible, sinking feeling made me break out in a cold sweat.

Once again we thought through our actions of the last hour, and the only thing that came to mind was that I had dropped the staysail to the deck as we arrived at the anchorage. Tara was beside me, and she must have been knocked overboard by the heavy sail. Even though the safety nets were in good repair, if she had been standing on her hind legs to grab at the sail as it came down, it could have flicked her over the net. I was standing one side of the sail, she the other, so I didn't see her.

Immediately, we pulled up the anchor and motored into the twilight on our GPS track, straining our eyes to try and spot a small dog's head in the inky sea. It grew darker and darker, and soon it was impossible to see, so we returned to the harbour, heavy-hearted, dropped the anchor, and went ashore in our dinghy to talk to the tourists in the dive resort.

"Please look out for a small black-and-white dog," we told everyone we met. "She was on our boat when we were a mile away from the island, but now we can't find her. We think she fell off when we dropped our sails. She's very friendly and answers to the name of Tara. She's an excellent swimmer and will paddle towards the island."

The manager of the resort – a sunburnt foreigner with an American accent – came over to see if he could help.

"You should talk to the dive masters and boat captains as well. They visit various reefs for the scuba diving; she might have landed up on another island."

Having spoken to as many people as possible, we began walking along the beach and the rocks in the dark, each with a flashlight, calling Tara's name. Not a sign of our darling dog. I went one way and Robert the other.

Then I lost Robert. One minute I could see his torch twinkling about half a kilometre away from me, and hear his voice calling; the next, silence. No torchlight, no voice. Oh, dear God, I prayed, let Robert be all right. Let me find him in the dark. I can't lose both Robert and Tara.

I stopped calling Tara and started calling Robert, and faintly, from the direction where I'd last seen the torchlight, I heard a call for help.

With my heart pounding, I ran to the dinghy, dragging it into the water. Starting the motor, I made my way towards the sound of Robert's voice, telling him to keep shouting so I could find him. And find him I did, caught amongst rocks, cut by sharp oyster shells, and unable to scramble up to the path.

I edged the dinghy as close as I could and he waded out and clambered onto the little boat, all cut and bloody. We motored back to *Deusa*, and Robert told me how he had been swimming along the rocky shore with the torch calling Tara, when a wave caught him and washed him into a ravine, dragging him across oysters and barnacles. He was worried about being dragged out by the next surge so hoisted himself onto a rock, and shouted for me to bring the dinghy and rescue him. We were both very depressed and despondent: our dog lost and Robert hurt.

Back on deck I washed Robert's wounds with peroxide, stopped the bleeding, and bound them. We then had a stiff whisky to steady our shattered nerves, and made a plan for the next day, as by now it was pitch dark, and there was no point going out again that night.

At the first glimmer of daylight we were up and away, armed with a Thermos of coffee and sandwiches, to continue the search for poor little Tara. Binoculars in hand we scoured the beach, the rocks, the countryside, calling her name until we were hoarse.

"Let's take a break and have some coffee," I suggested, fishing in our picnic basket for the mugs and Thermos. I handed Robert a steaming cup but he soon handed it back again, as it had no sugar and tasted bitter. In my distress I'd obviously forgotten to stir in the sugar when I poured the coffee into the jug.

I rummaged around in the picnic basket in case there was a bottle of sugar, but couldn't find any, so we headed back to *Deusa*, deciding that we would print out a picture of Tara with a reward notice and get the sugar at the same time.

Robert had printed the reward notice, ready to hand out to the tourists, the lodge, the dive masters, and the boat captains, and we were about to get back into the dinghy to continue our search – this time with coffee and sugar – when the radio crackled and someone called *"Deusa! Deusa!"*

We both leapt for the handset, just about colliding in mid-air, but Robert was faster.

"Yes, this is *Deusa*."

"We are dive boat *Coral Seeker*, and we've found your dog. She's okay. We're anchored off Island No 9 if you want to come and pick her up."

"Oh, thank goodness, that's wonderful news!! Which side of the island are you anchored?"

"We're on the south-east tip – you can't miss us."

"We'll be there right now, thank you so, so much. You've no idea what a relief it is to get your call."

It took us fifteen minutes to get to Island No 9 and find the boat. Overcome by emotion, we could hardly speak as we took Tara from the dive boat and thanked the captain profusely, handing him a bottle of whisky and the reward we had offered. Robert had tears in his eyes, and kept wiping them away so others wouldn't see how upset he was.

They told us that they spotted Tara standing on a rock, barking her head off as the dive boat cruised past. The current must have washed her past our island (No 10) and carried her to island No 9, where she scrambled ashore and spent the night. The captain had slowed his boat and was wondering how to pick her up, but the next minute she had leapt into the water as a big wave surged up the rock, and started swimming valiantly to her rescuers. They fished her out of the water, dried her off, and called us.

Was she affected by her night on the rocks? Not a bit of it. Tara was as bright and happy as ever, ready for the next adventure. And us? We were exhausted and emotionally drained, hoarse with shouting her name, stiff with clambering over rocks and gullies, bruised and battered. We decided to stay another day at Island No 10 and recuperate, while Tara raced up and down the deck, barking at the dive boats as they moved to and fro with their passengers. You had to admire her.

～ Borneo ～

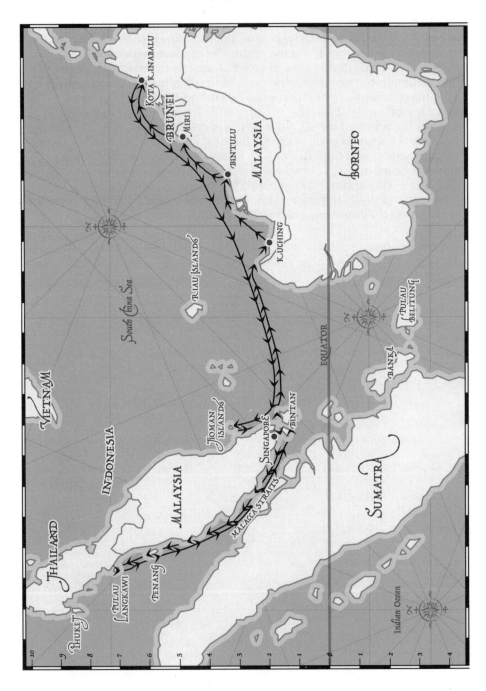

fifteen

Borneo

One of our great ambitions while living in South East Asia was to visit the island of Borneo, lying to the east of Malaysia and Thailand. This meant sailing via the Malacca Straits, considered dangerous for piracy, so we sailed during the day only, and anchored near the shore at night.

Local fishermen staked long bamboo fences into the shallow waters, creating fish traps with narrow exits where they strung their nets. These were good places to anchor as other boats travelling at night would avoid the traps, and therefore not see us. People were surprised that we weren't worried about the pirates, but they were after the big ships carrying valuable cargo, not small yachts with little to steal – and a Jack Russell to contend with.

At the time we were travelling through the Straits, the big ships were rigged with jets all along their decks, that rained down a heavy waterfall of salt water all along the hull, preventing pirates from clambering aboard. There must have been chinks in this armour, though, because ships were still seized and sailed up a river on the Indonesian island of Sumatra, where all the cargo was removed. The crew were usually locked up in a small room on board when the pirates took over, and only freed at the end of the operation.

Passing through Singapore was a great and nail-biting adventure: avoiding the endless stream of cargo ships, watching out for harbour police, keeping our eye on the port and starboard channel markers, telling Tara to "shut up that incessant barking or you go down below." It took us nearly a day to weave our way through the maze of markers and cargo ships to our evening anchorage, ready to start early next morning for Borneo. After three days and nights of sailing at daybreak we reached the point of Tayong Datuk in Sarawak: the sea was pewter and silver, there were ribbons of pink and grey cloud in the morning sky, and scarves of mist streamed from the distant mountains. A magical arrival at an island I have dreamt of visiting ever since I was a child.

We found a safe and protected area to anchor in, then went to visit the Ranger Station on the nearby island of Pulau Dalang Tabong.

80C3

"Welcome to our island," the two smartly-uniformed men greeted us in good English, "it's good you've come to see us. We were going to come out to your boat to tell you about the green-backed turtles. This is a nature reserve, and one of our jobs is to protect them when they come ashore to lay their eggs at this time of year."

"Oh, fantastic," we both exclaimed, "can we come and watch them?"

"Yes, that is possible. Come around 2am, but you must be very careful not to disturb them. Don't shine your torches on them and be very quiet. And, by the way, please don't bring your dog, we can see it running around on your boat, and it's not allowed on shore."

So at 2am we shook ourselves out of bed, left Tara to look after the ship, and chugged over to the beach in our dinghy. Borneo was not cold, and even at this hour we were barefoot, in T-shirts and shorts. We waited and waited on the moonlit beach, tiny waves sighing onto the sand, tall palms silhouetted against the night sky, rustling quietly behind us. We watched the stars swing through the heavens, the moon slide towards the horizon, but, alas, no turtles. "Maybe another night," said the rangers, but we needed to move on to the anchorage of Santubong where we had arranged to meet up with our friends, Bob and Eli, and their two boys on their catamaran *Cathouse*. This was the best anchorage at which to leave the boats and visit the capital of Sarawak, Kuching (meaning 'cat' in Malay), where we could buy provisions before moving on up the coast.

ଓଓଓ

The story of the White Rajahs of Sarawak is a fascinating one. James Brooke, an English adventurer, arrived in Borneo on his sailing ship *Royalist* in the early 1840s, and helped the Sultan of Brunei to chase pirates out of his kingdom. As a big 'thank you' from the Sultan, James was given Sarawak, and he, his nephew, and grand-nephew, went on to govern the country until 1946, when the Brooke family handed over Sarawak to Britain.

After several days of shopping and looking around Kuching, we sailed on up the coast to the Kuala Poloh river. Borneo is full of wide, brown rivers, navigable for long distances into the hinterland, where all the beautiful forests were being hacked down and logs floated out to waiting ships on the coast. Having read a lot about these rivers, we felt we should at least try one, circumnavigating the island of Palau Bruit.

It was dangerous anchoring in these fast-flowing rivers, as all sorts of strange stuff wrapped itself around our anchor chain and thudded against the hull, including fair-sized logs which could do considerable damage. Every now and then along the river we could see little encampments with flimsy wood jetties, half-hidden in the deep green foliage of the palms and mangroves. Surprisingly little traffic used the river: mostly small fishing boats and fast outboard motor boats, one or two ferries, and a couple of barges.

The next morning the fast-flowing current swished us out of Muara Lassa river back into the open ocean after our brief exploration of the Borneo waterways. About four miles offshore, Robert was preparing a fishing line, and I was down below making bread; I heard him call out.

"Come and look at this, there's something swimming in the sea; it could be an otter."

I ran up on deck, binoculars in hand, always curious to know what was around us. Initially, it looked like there was a coconut husk floating in the water, but with the binoculars I could definitely make out a head and ears, and a 'V' of ripples as the animal moved through the water.

"It's a dog, I can see it clearly now."

We dropped the sails, started the motor, and turned towards the dark little bobbing head. I took over the helm while Robert lowered the dinghy into the water and started the outboard, heading for the dog.

"Watch out," I shouted, as he hauled the dripping, snapping dog into the dinghy, "she might have rabies; don't let her bite you."

But the dog was so exhausted she just flopped at his feet, immobile, as he motored back to where I was turning _Deusa_ in a slow circle. Arriving at the stern of the boat, the dog stood, wagged her long tail forlornly, and licked Robert's bare feet. A bitch, about seven months old, she was black, with golden legs and eyebrows, and double Tara's size.

Tara was incensed at us picking up another dog, screaming her rage from the aft deck at the new arrival, sitting in the dinghy sopping wet and shivering. Now what?

"Put Tara down below," decided Robert, "we're going to have to make a plan for the new guest."

Tara was bundled below with a squawk of disgust, and we continued on our way, leaving the dog in the dinghy, towed behind _Deusa_, giving her a little food and water, while we pondered our predicament.

Over a cup of tea Robert came up with a plan. We would build a barrier on the aft deck, separating the two dogs, until we got to the nearby port of Bintulu, where we would try and find a home for our latest crew member. We certainly didn't want two dogs on board: one was quite enough, and she was hostile to other dogs, unaccustomed to her own kind due to her isolation on _Deusa_.

With consummate skill - and odd bits and pieces - Robert built a blockade and invited our visitor on board, with our resident dog complaining loudly from below. Our new dog was the most gentle soul; obviously someone's pet. She must have fallen into the river or from a fishing boat, and was swimming for her life, out at sea, when we found her.

We imagined her, a child's pet, playing on the jetty by a house, losing her balance and tumbling into the murky water. But even in that swift current she could have swum ashore and scrambled out onto the muddy bank. No, it was more likely that she was on a fishing boat, learning to be a guard dog, and, like Tara, had lost her balance. The people of Borneo were a mixture of Animist, Muslim, Christian, Hindu, and Buddhist, and she definitely belonged to someone, because she was so friendly.

The next day we arrived in Bintulu and spotted our friends on _Cathouse_ anchored in the corner of the busy port reserved for yachts. Bob and his kids rowed over to welcome us.

"Have we got a surprise for you," we called to Bob, "we've got a dog for your boys."

TARA

"Oh, no you haven't!" replied Bob adamantly, "I've got two cats on board and I'm certainly not having a dog as well."

"Oh, come on Dad – look, she's such a cute dog," the boys begged.

They began to scramble up the stern ladder, and the dog growled and barked at them, as if she was guarding our boat. What a surprising animal: she'd only been with us 24 hours and was already looking after us. Tara was on the foredeck, studiously ignoring the interloper, and pretending there were more important things to do, such as watch the water traffic.

꿍ᙏᛣ

What were we going to do with our new dog? Sarawak was largely Muslim, but maybe we would find someone to take her. There wasn't such a thing as the SPCA in South East Asia, and there weren't that many foreigners around who would adopt her. She spent another night with us, secure on the back deck, enjoying any food we gave her, licking our hands to say 'thank you.' She was such a nice dog, and we really hoped we could find a good home for her.

The next morning we loaded her into the dinghy and took her to where the tug boats were stationed, ready to escort the big ships in and out of the harbour. Approaching them, we caught a seaman's attention, and asked him if he would like a dog. He looked most surprised.

"I'm a Muslim," he said, "but let me see if I can find a Christian."

He disappeared into the depths of the tugboat, and we sat anxiously waiting to see who would appear. The door opened and a Chinaman appeared, speaking to us in perfect English.

"Yes, how can I help you?"

We lifted up our new-found dog.

"Would you like a guard dog? We found her in the sea off Palau Bruit, and think she must have fallen off a fishing boat. Look what big feet she has, she's going to grow into a big dog, and look how pretty her markings are. Black body, golden legs and eyebrows, nice curly tail, she'll be a good dog for you."

Our sales pitch done we sat and waited, holding our breath. The Chinaman thought a while, stroking his chin and then he nodded his head.

"I'll take her," he said, "put her on the deck."

"Now that you have a dog," said Robert, "what will you call her?"

Oh, clever Robert. If you name an animal you are less likely to eat it! He was thinking of the Chinese taste for dog meat.

The Chinaman looked at Robert, looked at the dog, and said, "I'll call her 'Ocean' as that is where she came from."

We were delighted, shook his hand, wished Ocean a good life, and returned to *Deusa* with happy hearts. We were so relieved and so was Tara, who took back control of the aft deck and told us never to do that again. Later, we learnt that the Chinese have a superstition about dogs found at sea: they are considered very good luck, and the Chinese are always looking for good luck!

Our travels took us up the Borneo coastline to Kota Kinabalu, but soon it was time to return to mainland Malaysia as Robert had a Regatta (yacht race) to organise for the Royal Langkawi Yacht Club, which promised to be a big affair with over a hundred boats participating. The Prince, Tunku Abdullah (son of Tuanku Abdul Rahman, the first king of Malaysia), was not only the owner of the Yacht Club where the races would be held, but also patron of the Regatta. He was the most charming and educated man, and a pleasure to work with.

 ❧☙

We anchored at the Ranger Station by the point where we had first arrived in Borneo a month ago, and went ashore to greet the rangers, and ask about green-backed turtles. Sadly for us, they had laid their eggs and left, so we decided we should leave, too, and headed out into a gloomy evening sky, heavy with clouds and squall lines. Not the kind of weather I wanted to start a journey in, and I got the familiar tight knot in my stomach and dry mouth, but Robert felt we should press on, as time was running short and we had a good strong boat.

It was a three-day sail back to Singapore, and we soon ran into rough weather with 30 knot (35mph) squalls and a lot of rain making it an uncomfortable sail, just as I had feared. On the second day out, Robert began feeling very ill, with vomiting, diarrhoea, and a high temperature. I gave him something for the nausea and the headache, and we decided to carry on to Singapore, as there was no point in turning back. He spent the next 24 hours in bed, which provided good practice for me to manage the boat on my own. Thank goodness the weather had calmed right down: the moon was out, glimmering a silver path on the dark sea, and the knot in my stomach had loosened its grip.

After my initial anxieties, I was surprised I was able to stay awake for 24 hours, as I normally felt very tired after just a six-hour watch, longing to fall into my warm and comfortable bed. We had often practised this exercise in case of just such an emergency, and I also knew I could call on Robert if things went really wrong. Fortunately, we had a smooth passage, and *Deusa* looked after us kindly, carrying us gently on the ocean. Tara divided her time between keeping Robert company in the cabin, and keeping watch with me on deck.

When we finally got into Raffles Marina in Singapore I went straight up to the office, exhausted and worried about Robert.

"Hello, I'm Rosemary from the sailing yacht *Deusa*," I greeted the friendly Chinese lady on duty, "we've just arrived from Borneo and need to check in to Singapore. But first, do you have a doctor that we could call; my husband is very sick."

"I'm sorry, no doctor here," she smiled apologetically, "maybe you speak with Mr Gee. He works in our staff dispensary; he might have some medicine for you."

Well, it was certainly worth a try, so I walked down to the dispensary,

TARA

tucked under the marina office stairs. Mr Gee was a Sikh; a splendid, sturdy-looking man in his white turban, bushy black beard, and wearing the required adornments of his religion, which are known as the five Ks. The steel bracelet (Kara), the small dagger (Kirpan), the wooden comb (Kanghe), the long underpants (which I couldn't see) (Kashhera), and the long hair (Keshi) bound up in the turban.

Mr Gee gave me some pills, and said he would call in to see Robert later. Hurrying back to where *Deusa* was tied up to the dock, I was met by Tara, who welcomed me on board.

"How's Robert, my dear dog, are you taking care of him?"

She gave me her doggy grin, and scampered to the companionway, leaping down the stairs as I followed her.

There was Robert, lying propped up on pillows, looking wan and pale. Tara bounced onto the bed to announce my arrival. I dosed Robert with the medicine, telling him to possibly expect a visit from Mr Gee, then returned to the marina office to check in with Customs and Immigration.

Imagine my total surprise on returning to our boat an hour later to find Robert sitting in the cockpit with Mr Gee, who had one hand on Robert's stomach and the other on his brow, eyes closed, and muttering under his breath. It was the first time I had ever come across the ancient art of Reiki, an energy therapy from Japan using a technique known as hands-on healing that transfers universal energy through the palms. I was totally fascinated. From being a very sick Robert lying in the cabin with a high fever, this was an altogether different Robert, looking bemused and cheerful.

Well, either the shock of receiving a cuddle from a stranger, or the relief of getting into harbour, put Robert right, and from that moment on he was cured. I was so impressed by Reiki that I tried to find out about some courses, but we really didn't have the time to stop in Singapore, as we had a commitment with the Regatta in Langkawi.

കൗൽ

Moving on up the coast of Malaysia, we stopped in Port Dickson and Port Klang, visiting people who were interested in participating in the yacht race. From Port Klang it was a day's sail to the harbour of Lumut (meaning moss or seaweed in Malay) in a river mouth on the mainland, off Pangkor Island. It was during this part of the journey that we lost Tara overboard, but it was much more serious than the previous times. Much, much, more serious. We were a full seven miles offshore when she disappeared.

I had been down below making bread, and had seen her when I came up on deck with tea and biscuits at 10am. She joined us to see what we were eating, and discover whether we might offer her some to taste. Sometime after that she must have fallen overboard, because Robert and I met again at 1.30pm for lunch, when it was my watch. As always, Tara would join us for a meal, sitting beside Robert in the cockpit, or lying under his chair if we were on the back deck.

A lot of fishing boats were in the area, and we had to weave amongst them to avoid becoming tangled in the long nets they dragged. Tara barked madly at these boats, standing right on the anchor stock at the bow, warning them to come no closer. The Asian fishing fleet had many superstitions, one of which was about bad spirits who chased away the fish. If it was possible to charge another vessel, and turn away at the last minute, the bad spirits would lose their balance and tumble onto the other boat.

We often had them coming straight at us as if they would ram us amidships. Initially, we'd take evasive action and turn away, with them in hot pursuit. We soon realised, however, that if we maintained our course they'd finally veer away. A daunting moment for the faint-hearted, and, of course, noisy Tara loved every minute of it, barking herself off her feet as the fishing boat loomed close. It must have been one of those extra energetic barks, or the wave rocking *Deusa*, that tipped her overboard.

She was gone, and really gone this time. No friendly island to swim to. No canoeist to haul her on board. No race committee to send out a VHF alert about a lost dog. No friendly dive boat captain to pluck her off the rocks. Here we were in the middle of the Malacca Straits, surrounded by fishermen trying to earn a daily living, worried about us getting in their way, and not interested in a lost little dog. We imagined these were Malay Muslim fishermen, and only later discovered that the majority were Chinese.

My heart started beating very fast, and I felt quite sick. My vision blurred, and I sat down with a thump, my head in my hands, trying not to cry.

"She's gone, Robert, she's not here. She's not down below; she's not on deck."

Robert looked grim and didn't say a word. He was thinking fast about what action to take.

Calculating that she had been gone for three hours, we backtracked on our GPS route, scanning the water for her small, dark head. We approached fishing boats, shouting to them that we had lost our dog. From the little Malay we had learnt we could say "Angin putih kechil" (small white dog) but "lost overboard" was beyond us.

The roar of their powerful motors, the slap of the sea against the hull, and the wind in the rigging muffled our words. They didn't understand us, and didn't want us near them, shaking their heads and waving their hands in a desperate effort to chase us away in case we became entangled in the great big nets being dragged behind them, often in tandem with two boats, one on each end, a balloon of net between them.

After backtracking some 8 nautical miles (ten land miles), we realised it was an impossible task, and we were getting nowhere. We slumped in the cockpit in despair, both of us gazing at the sea, willing her little head to appear, bobbing amongst the waves. The sparkling blue ocean became an immense and hostile body of water that had swallowed up our beloved Tara.

We had to get help: we simply would not find her like this in the middle of the Malacca Straits. We had to sail on up to Lumut, make

TARA

posters with Tara's picture, with details in English and Malay, hire a car and drive down the coast, visiting all the small fishing villages where she might swim ashore, handing out the poster and tacking it up on trees and notice boards.

But would she make it all the way to the low-lying shore, hardly visible to us, let alone a small dog at sea level, water splashing in her eyes, the current pulling her on down the channel? How would she know which way was the shore: she might frantically swim towards one fishing boat after another, desperately looking to be rescued.

It was a very dejected captain and crew of *Deusa* who arrived in Lumut at 2am in pouring rain and wind directly on our bow, making for a horrible, bumpy passage, with us feeling totally wiped out, wet, and miserable. The weather fitted our mood – dark clouds, dark night, and rain, rain, rain. How on earth were we going to find Tara in this great stretch of water with a muddy, swampy coastline and a large Muslim population, which would sooner kill a dog than rescue him or her?

After a restless four hours of sleep we headed for the Lumut marina office and asked where we could hire a car.

"Oh no, captain, sir, there're no cars for hire around here, this is only a small village, you know. We don't have much tourism, no need for car hire." The young, round-faced Malay girl with her hijab (headscarf) pinned tightly under her chin, shrugged her shoulders: she couldn't help.

Now what? How do we get back down the coast by road to visit all the tiny villages along the river inlets that might have seen a dog: a small, black-and-white dog with a blue collar?

With the help of Fatima, the girl in the marina office, we translated the wording for our poster into Malay alongside the English, then trudged back to *Deusa* to print it on the printer we carried on board. The heading was 'REWARD – LOST DOG' with a picture of Tara below, and a description of where we thought she went overboard, plus a note of the reward.

"What on earth are we going to do about transport?" Robert looked at me with troubled eyes as we sat in the cockpit. "It's ridiculous that a town of this size doesn't have a car hire company. What would a tourist do if he arrived here?"

"I don't think tourists come here, what's there to see? It's Pangkor Island they'd visit, there's much more to see and do over there, and it's got an airport." I replied.

Someone climbed off the neighbouring boat and wandered towards us.

"Hi, my name is Louis and I'm looking after the boat next to you. I couldn't help overhearing your conversation, and it sounds like you need a car. I've got a 40-year-old Mercedes, and if you want to borrow it, you're welcome. I don't know if it will take you very far. I only use it to drive into the village and back."

This wonderful man, with his Chinese face and American accent, dangled the keys in front of us, and we snatched them in desperation and relief. At least it was wheels, and we could travel down the coast distributing our flyer to all the villages. Action was better than no action.

It certainly was an old car that had seen better days: once a cheerful yellow, this was now a faded custard-colour. But, hey, don't mock the car: the engine started, the gears worked, and we rolled into a nearby petrol station to fill up with fuel.

Thus began our search for Tara. With a glimmer of hope in our hearts and a flask of coffee beside us on the torn seat, we set off on our journey of 110 miles back towards Port Klang, exploring every little turning and side road heading towards the sea, sometimes leading through dense palm oil forests; sometimes through tall sour grass. At times, it was a dead-end track to a small rural house with a few scrawny chickens scuffling in a dusty yard; sometimes it was a miserable riverside village of impoverished stilt houses, crouched on the edge of foul-smelling muddy banks and rotting vegetation.

Surly, wrinkled fishermen worked at mending their nets. Women hung out laundry, and washed pans in the filthy waterway where the fishing boats were tethered. Small, naked children played and poked sticks at crabs scuttling for cover. No-one spoke Malay or English, and we realised that a lot of them were Chinese, who spoke neither language that our the poster used.

Our Malay was minimal but our Chinese was zero. With much sign language, we waved our poster around, and asked to pin it up in small shops, boat yards, markets, and garages. We kept on imagining that Tara, by some miracle, had struggled ashore in this hostile muddy environment, exhausted by her long swim, very thirsty, very hungry, very lost.

By the end of the day we were exhausted and depressed, our earlier energetic burst draining away in hopelessness at the situation. How could we find her in the miles and miles of inhospitable lowland, amongst people who wouldn't care if a dog crawled out of the sea, wet and shivering and exhausted, and would probably kick her away as just another scavenging cur?

In silence and gloom, wrapped in our own thoughts, we drove the trusty old Mercedes back to Lumut and handed the keys to Louis, telling him there was at least half a tank of fuel in the vehicle, and that she went very well. Then we climbed onto *Deusa*, poured ourselves a stiff whisky, and wondered what to do next. Finally, weariness overtook us and we climbed into our lonely bed in the aft cabin, without our beloved dog. It was a heartbreaking moment.

Next morning, while making coffee, Robert turned to me and said, "I have an idea. Let's call our newspaper friends. I've been awake most of the night worrying about Tara: we have to find her."

I shrugged my shoulders and sipped the hot coffee, hoping it would ease the tight feeling in my chest, and the constant desire to cry.

"I'm going to phone Eric. Do you remember Eric, the guy from *The Star* newspaper, who we took sailing on *Deusa* in the Langkawi harbour?" Robert asked.

Whilst we were in Langkawi several months earlier, we'd made friends with the press and photographers who were promoting the Royal

TARA

Langkawi Regatta, and had even taken them sailing around the bay by the yacht club. They'd met Tara and taken photos of her with us, as they were most amused at meeting a dog on a boat.

"I'm going to remind him of his visit on board, and ask him if he could write an article on Tara. He'll remember her, and he has several photos of her on record. Can you find his card and I'll go across to the marina office right now and see if I can get hold of him?"

Robert has a wonderful spirit – he doesn't give up – and, while he looked for his wallet, I found Eric's card and handed it to him.

"Good luck, it's well worth a try, and nothing is going to happen while we sit here doing nothing and feeling so miserable." I sighed and sat down. I had no energy, and everything was an effort, even looking for the card. Robert gave me a hug and a kiss and left the boat with a look of determination in his eyes.

He had been gone about an hour-and-a-half before I heard his footfall on the deck above me. I had collapsed in a huddle of misery on the bed, all rolled up in a ball, trying to calm my mind and stop it imagining all the dreadful things that could have happened to Tara.

"Come up and sit on deck, Rosemary, it's much nicer outside. No use moping down there. I know how you feel but it's not going to bring Tara back. Let me tell you what I've found out."

I put the kettle on for a comforting cup of tea, then joined Robert in the cockpit. His eyes were sparkling with success.

"I got hold of Eric, he remembered us and said he would look for Tara's photos and write an article. He also said that his girlfriend, Miss Chin, was the editor of the *China Press* newspaper, and he would ask her to do an article in Chinese, as so many people along the coast are Chinese-speakers, having emigrated to Malaysia many years ago."

"Oh, well done, Robert," I said, giving him a hug, "I'm so glad you thought of Eric, at least we are doing something towards finding her. The Chinese newspaper's a good idea."

The kettle began to whistle and I went below, feeling a little more cheerful.

৪০৫৪

Losing Tara had delayed our journey northwards, and, as we felt we had done everything we could in Lumut to try and find her, decided to continue our journey to Langkawi, keeping in touch with the newspaper people by cell phone. Leaving the marina, we anchored out in the waterway to make an early start the next morning. Both of us still felt emotionally exhausted and devastated, which is probably why Robert woke up the next morning feeling sick with 'flu symptoms. It was a rainy, miserable day, and we decided not to travel, but stay where we were.

On Sunday morning, four long days after Tara had disappeared, we had just finished breakfast, sitting below in our cosy saloon out of the rain dripping into the cockpit, when the phone rang.

"Hello, is Mr Robert Forrester there, please?" said a Chinese-accented voice in English. I passed the phone to Robert.

174

"Hello, Mr Forrester, this is Miss Chin from the *China Press* newspaper. We think we have found your dog."

Robert nearly dropped the phone, and stared, wide-eyed with astonishment, at the little instrument that had been clasped to his ear.

"Can you hear me, Mr Forrester?" came the tinny enquiry.

"Yes, yes," stammered Robert, "please go ahead, I can hear you very well."

"It seems a dog has been rescued by a fisherman from the village of Sekinchin, and now you must go there to make sure it is the right dog. I'll send an interpreter, and you can meet up with her at the fuel station on the highway, just before the turn-off to the village."

"Oh, my God, I don't believe it, that's wonderful news, it's a miracle. Thank you, oh, thank you so much, Miss Chin." Robert was ecstatic and couldn't believe his ears, but Miss Chin was more pragmatic, and told him not to get his hopes up too much until he had been to the village.

"Let's get the anchor up, Rosemary, and we'll go back into Lumut and borrow that old Mercedes again. I don't think we drove as far as Sekinchin. I've looked it up, and it's about 68 miles from here."

Robert and I looked at each other, and I know that both of us were praying: dear God, let it be Tara they have found. Even not knowing for sure, it gave us something to pin our hopes on, and lightened our heavy hearts.

Returning to the marina as fast as we could, we slotted back into the berth we had vacated only the night before, and went to look for Louis and his old Mercedes. But Louis was nowhere to be found, and nor was his car. Local people told us that he was so delighted that the car had managed to travel many miles beyond Lumut, he had taken off the very next day on a long journey, with the tank of petrol we'd provided. No car, and no possibility of car hire in this small town ...

"So, what do we do now?" I asked Robert, my heart sinking back down again at the thought of Tara in some fisherman's hovel, with no way of getting there to rescue her. We threw ideas back and forth to each other across the cockpit, and it seemed our guardian angels heard us.

"Hi, I'm Steve," said our friendly saviour, as he strolled over from a big, old, wooden yacht near us. "I couldn't help overhearing you've lost your dog and need a car in order to meet someone down the coast. Here are the keys to my old Mercedes; she doesn't look up to much but she's still a runner."

He dangled the keys in front of our incredulous eyes. Thanking him profusely, we grabbed them and headed for the car park.

"Do they only have old Mercedes in Lumut?" Robert asked to no-one in particular as we found the car and climbed in. This vehicle was a lot older and more dilapidated than Louis', with gaping rust holes in the floorboards and windows that wouldn't shut, but it was painted a shiny white, and looked good at first glance.

We didn't say much to each other as we headed back down the now-familiar highway, with its tall stands of oil palms and open pastures. We were both praying silently, willing the dog to be Tara. It started to rain, and the water splashed in through the floorboards, sprayed in through the windows, poured in at the windscreen, but we didn't care. It was wheels, and it was getting us to our destination.

We had phoned Miss Chin to let her know we were on our way, and after what seemed like an age, we spotted the service station where we were to meet the interpreter and a photographer. Climbing out, wet and stiff, we walked over to the only other car in the courtyard.

"Hello, we're Robert and Rosemary Forrester from the yacht *Deusa*, are you waiting for us?" asked Robert, extending a damp hand.

"Oh, yes, so pleased you are here," said a young and pretty Chinese girl in smart jeans and a T-shirt, "my name is Miss Wang, and this is my photographer, Mr Chin Lee. Now, if you will follow us we will lead you to the house. We have already been there and the family is expecting you."

There was the strangest feeling of breathless excitement and fear for both of us: excitement of finding Tara again; fear that it wouldn't be her.

With our hearts pounding and our mouths dry, we followed the press car as it wound through the many houses of this small riverine village, finally arriving at a quite substantial house with a neat fence and tiled garage. Would Tara be there? Would she be sick and dying; nearly drowned? Would it even be her? Perhaps it was a dog like Ocean who we had rescued in Borneo. The suspense on that short drive was almost intolerable.

We stepped out of the car, and there, in the garage, stood Tara, a great, big chain attached to her collar and fastened to the wall, a bowl of dog biscuit and water beside her. It was her. It was our dog. It wasn't a dream, an illusion, a ghost. There was our beloved companion, looking as fit and bright-eyed as ever.

"Oh, Tara," I sobbed, bursting into tears with all the stress, "you survived. You clever, clever dog, you made it, you're alive!"

Robert turned away, mopping his eyes. Men of his generation don't cry.

Tara yelped with joy at seeing us, and the Chinese family hurried out of their house to greet us. She was let off her chain and bounded towards us, delighted to be reunited with her family, jumping around us as if to say, "Where were you? I waited and waited and you never came."

Inside their immaculate Chinese home, the family invited us to sit on one of the sofas in the living room, and the man of the house explained how they had found Tara. He was a rugged, sun- and wind-burnt man in his forties, his many children in an excited flock around him. His wife, a gentle, quiet lady, served us fresh lemonade. Tara rushed from Robert to me and back again, wildly excited at the reunion, licking and licking us in sheer ecstasy.

Mr Heng Lai Hong began to speak in Chinese, and Miss Wang interpreted for us.

"I was returning home on Wednesday evening around 6pm after a good day's fishing, when I saw something in the water."

Robert and I looked at each other and nodded. Fishermen are very sharp-eyed: they are always looking for shoals of fish breaking the surface, or leaping dolphins in a feeding frenzy.

"So I turned my boat around and motored towards this strange thing bobbing in the sea, and then I saw it was a small dog; half submerged, paddling frantically in the choppy sea."

Once again we glanced at each other. This was a big, heavy fishing boat, weighing at least 20 tons with many crew on board to handle the nets, and we often saw them at work.

"We Chinese are superstitious folk," he continued, "and I saw this as good luck for me and my family, and for my boat as well. I slowed the boat down, and one of my crew members said he would jump in to pick up the dog. But I said, no, I would do it, the good luck belongs to me, so I took off my clothes and jumped in to get the dog. My boat is too high off the water, at least a metre and a half (five feet) from the deck, and my crew couldn't reach. As it was they had to haul me back on board. The dog was shivering and shaking and vomiting water, so I wrapped her in my jacket and headed for home."

Just think. Tara had fallen overboard on Wednesday, at around 10 or 11am, and Mr Heng had picked her up at 6pm that same evening, which meant she had been in the water, swimming, for at least seven or eight hours. We humans can float, but dogs can't, they have to keep paddling, so their noses stay out of the water. Tara must have paddled for hours and hours. How did she do it? What incredible determination kept Tara alive and swimming? We'll never know; she believed she would live, and didn't gave up.

"When I got home with this pretty little black-and-white dog, my young children were delighted, and immediately set about making her comfortable. We went out and bought special dog biscuits, a water bowl, and a chain to tie her up."

We had seen the chain when we arrived. It was big enough to secure a Great Dane, and it dangled from Tara's neck as if she was a dangerous prisoner, likely to escape.

"We are very happy with the dog," said Mr Heng, "and we are not going to give her back. We rescued her and she will stay with us. She is our good luck." Tara had now been in his house four days.

We couldn't believe our ears. Why had he told the press that he had rescued her, if he had no intention of giving her to us? Our joy at seeing her was now clouded by the horror of a fight to get her back.

I was so upset I went outside to play with Tara on the verandah; I couldn't stomach the thought of not taking her with us, and Robert was looking totally furious.

Well, it turned out that the neighbours also knew about the dog, the newspaper article, the reward, and were going to let the press know so they could claim the money. Mr Heng was a successful man and a leader of his community. He couldn't have someone else telling tales on him, so he let Miss Chin of *China Press* know that he had the dog.

Miss Wang continued with the translation.

"Why did I tell the newspaper? I told the newspaper because I felt sorry for the foreigners, maybe they worried about their dog. I wanted them to know that she was alive and well."

He spread his strong, brown fisherman's hands and shrugged his shoulders. The children crowded, wide-eyed, around him.

Robert became even more annoyed.

"You'll never be able to keep my dog. All I have to do is call and she'll come to me." Robert obviously wasn't thinking of the heavy chain that would tie her up for the rest of her life.

Tara's rescuers were enchanted by this pretty little black-and-white dog with the brown face, sparkling eyes and shiny black nose, and didn't yet know what a determined and strong-minded character lay behind the charm. One of the kids in the family would sooner or later tease her, pull her ears or tail, and get bitten, and then she would be cast out of the home to fend for herself. It was a terrible scenario.

The Chinese fisherman made it clear he didn't want the money, he wanted Tara. Our Malaysian friends had suggested the reward should be the equivalent of US$100 in the local currency, ringgit. Robert felt this was too little, and so had made the amount US$200, which they felt was too much, considering the local culture.

Robert said he felt a terrible, cold anger rise up in him. With all the emotional strain of losing Tara, then finding her, it became unbearable, and it was all he could do to control this wave of fury. He vowed to himself that he would not leave the house until he had Tara, but when he looked at the large crowd gathering at the outside gate, he knew he had little chance of escape. He would be had up for dog theft.

"Anyone in your position as leader in your community, would not want the reward," Robert said through gritted teeth. "he would ask that it be donated to a local charity."

The interpreter looked sideways at Robert and proceeded to speak to Mr Heng in an entirely different tone to that which Robert had used. Her body language was much more placating, whereas Robert was bristling with rage.

Miss Wang turned back to Robert after the fisherman had spoken.

"If you are prepared to increase your reward to US$400, Mr Heng might be interested."

Robert gave an inward sigh of huge relief; it was – after all – all to do with money. The door was not closed; it was now a matter of bargaining.

Back and forth went the conversation, the interpreter turning from one man to the other, the children watching wide-eyed on the sidelines, until they finally came to a figure of US$300, which satisfied Tara's rescuer. Naturally, we would pay whatever it took, but we had to appear unconcerned and cool about the whole deal. For this very reason I stayed outside, and just held my breath, tears streaming down my cheeks, because I couldn't do 'cool' as well as Robert.

The interpreter explained to Robert. "This is where East is East and West is West, and you two will never understand each other. Now that you have reached agreement, give each other a hug as new-found friends, and a big smile for the cameraman."

This was the last thing that Robert wanted to do.

"New-found friends be damned: the bastard didn't want to give me back my dog!" he muttered to himself, grudgingly shaking Mr Hang's extended hand.

The large crowd at the gate pointed and stared, intrigued by our presence and the little black-and-white dog causing such a furore. It was time to leave before things became heated. We were hugely outnumbered: foreigners in a strange land, worried about a dog – the lowest form of life here in Malaysia. But we knew about the good luck that dogs at sea bring to those Chinese who find them. After all, we rescued one in Borneo, and now we had experience of the 'good luck' superstition again. Someone else had rescued our dog, and we had finally got her back. Was that not a miracle? I'm inclined to believe in miracles, and I felt that Robert willed Tara to live, concentrating so hard on finding her that he brought her back to us. Call me superstitious, but I do believe in the power of the mind when faced with incredible odds.

Driving back to the marina, Tara ecstatically bounced around in the car, enchanted to be going for a trip, seemingly none the worse for wear after her 8-hour ordeal in the sea. Incredible, but true!

Our emotions were in tatters. The rollercoaster ride of the trauma of losing Tara, the joy of finding her, and negotiating with the Chinaman, was pouring over us in waves of exhaustion.

"Do you realise," asked Robert, his hands firmly on the steering wheel of the old Mercedes as we pottered back up the highway to Lumut, "that when Tara fell overboard she must have swum from one fishing boat after another, hoping it was *Deusa*? She obviously fell off amongst the boats, which is why Mr Heng found her, but if he hadn't, I reckon she would have drowned by nightfall. Have you thought that while she was in the water she might not have been able to pee or poo?"

I started to cry again, even though Tara was sitting in my lap, licking my hands. It was all too much, and I couldn't bear to think about it, even though her warm body lay across my legs.

Back at the marina we were met by a welcome committee of yachting friends, all hugging us and congratulating us on finding Tara. They all piled onto *Deusa* and drank our whisky and our wine, cuddled the happy dog, and told their own stories of remarkable rescues.

A couple of days later an article about Tara's rescue was published in the English-speaking and Chinese-speaking newspapers. We were described as rich foreigners arriving in a white Mercedes at the humble village of the Chinese fisherman. No mention of the fact that the Mercedes was thirty years old, and held together by rust ...

&OCB

Robert had an amazing time running the Royal Langkawi Regatta in Malaysia, and it was most successful, attracting racing boats and cruisers from around South East Asia. We stayed in the yacht club marina, and enjoyed getting to know the beautiful island of Langkawi and the friendly Malaysian people, but now it was time to visit family in England and America, and check on our house in Brazil.

The yacht club said we could leave *Deusa* in the marina, but the big question was, who would look after Tara??

We had a good friend called Richard, living in the north-east of Thailand, over by Cambodia, and he very kindly offered to take her while we travelled. Richard worked with malaria control along the Thai border, and at one time had received a grant from the Bill and Melinda Gates Foundation that helped with his research.

Getting Tara to Richard required quite a lot of planning, as we were in Malaysia The first thing to do was sail *Deusa* to Thailand, the neighbouring country, where we had spent some time previously. Leaving *Deusa* in a marina in Phuket, we would look for a car to drive Tara to Richard.

We finally hired a really beat-up old Toyota Corolla, and set off on a two-day journey up the narrow peninsular of Thailand, around Bangkok, then out west to Kanthararom. Somewhere in her short life Tara had picked up bad memories of people in dark glasses and uniforms, and Thai policemen fitted this description exactly. Every time we came to a road block or traffic control and were approached by an official, she would go off into paroxysms of barking, deafening us to whatever the policeman was trying to say to us.

"Good morning, officer," Robert would say, rolling down the car window; then, "I'm sorry, officer, I can't hear a word you're saying. You want to see what?"

The policeman, bulging stomach straining at his skintight brown uniform, would try and peer into the car as I wrestled Tara to the floor, covering her eyes so she couldn't see the sinister figure at the window. The racket was often so bad that the policeman would wave us on with a tired sigh, stopping the next car instead. It was times like these that I risked being bitten by Tara, who, very angry and frustrated at being restrained, might decide who better to bite than the person lying on top of her?

Any animal – cat, dog, chicken, cow, elephant – we passed on our journey, was greeted by a chorus of barks, Tara furiously biting at the car's upholstery, just as she did the jib sail on *Deusa*. It was a real challenge to ensure she didn't rip the rental car to pieces!

While we spent time in Asia I had tried to study the Thai language, and could ask for the ladies toilet, a hotel room, and where the next town was. Understanding the answers I received was quite a different matter, however, and we both watched for hand signals as a local person explained where to go. The journey took two days, so we needed to stop the night somewhere along the way in a dog-friendly hotel. Unlike the Muslims, Thais like dogs, so most hotels greeted us with a smile and a nod when we showed them Tara tucked under an arm.

We think the Thais liked dogs because, in the Buddhist philosophy of re-incarnation, bad monks come back as dogs. We met so many stray dogs in the Buddhist temples because people were always dropping unwanted puppies over the temple walls, not wanting to be cruel to a past-life monk.

Richard owned a lovely white, poodle-type dog called Benny, a gentle soul who liked everyone. Benny was prepared to like Tara, but she wasn't having any of it, alighting from the car snapping and snarling. However, Richard knew just what to do to introduce them.

"Come," he said, "we'll walk the dogs on their leads outside the property. Just ignore them. They pick up our agitation, but if we walk and chat quite naturally, they'll get used to each other."

This was a very good lesson for both Tara and us. We learned how to introduce strange dogs to each other, and Tara learned how to get on with her own kind. It was about time, too, as her hostile attitude didn't win friends for any of us. She would be well cared for in this household where Richard's Thai companion, Angkhana, looked after the animals. When we waved goodbye a few days later, we never thought it would be so long before we came back.

Now we had to sail *Deusa* back to Malaysia as the Langkawi Yacht Club was letting us stay there for free because of the Regatta. Our air tickets to England meant we departed from Kuala Lumpur, so once *Deusa* was carefully tucked up in her berth, we took a local flight from Langkawi to Kuala Lumpur to begin our long journey.

୫୯୪୫

We left Malaysia at the end of March, and it was November before we returned to pick up Tara, reversing the whole process of sailing *Deusa* back up to Thailand from Malaysia.

Robert discovered that he could fly to Kanthararom and return with Tara by train, rather than rent a car. The airline didn't allow dogs on board but, strangely enough, the train did, and took Robert as far as Bangkok, from where he could catch a bus to Phuket, where I and *Deusa* awaited him.

Richard collected Robert from the airport, taking him back to the house where he was met by an ecstatic and very plump Tara. Angkhana had spoiled her rotten, feeding her morsels of chicken breast in case she felt sad and homesick. So, Tara, being a clever soul, often looked sad and woeful, growing fatter and fatter as a result.

The train stopped right in Kanthararom, and Robert got a bunk in the sleeping car, amongst a group of foreign backpackers and Thais travelling to Bangkok. He chose an upper berth as he didn't want anyone else scrambling over him if he was in the lower berth, and thought that Tara would be more controllable in the upper berth, from where she would not be tempted to jump down and go exploring.

Robert never enjoyed ethnic travel, so made sure he was as comfortable as possible. A half jack of whisky, bottle of soda and a glass were stowed in his carry bag, and all he needed was ice to make his evening as perfect as possible. Richard took him to the train station, stopping for a bag of ice en route, which Robert tucked into his holdall.

The train chugged out of the station. Robert waved goodbye to Richard, then settled down for the overnight journey to Bangkok. The train stopped at many little villages and towns on its journey westward and, at every opportunity, Robert took Tara for a walk and a pee. The step from the railway carriage to the cinders and sleepers of the railway track was quite high, and Robert had to lift Tara down and back up again. There was nothing as civilised as a railway platform; passengers scrambled on and off wherever the train stopped, and no warning

TARA

whistle let passengers know when the train was about to move on again, gathering speed as it chuffed up the track.

Robert had never travelled on a Thai train, so imagining that there would be niceties such as these meant he and Tara were in for a big surprise.

The first time they got out to stretch their legs, they nearly got left behind, meaning Robert had to run alongside the train, trying to leap onto the high step and into the carriage with his dog tucked underneath his arm. Locals thronged the windows, encouraging him to run faster, willing hands reaching out to grasp him as he hurled himself and Tara through the door.

One of the friendly Thai train guards took pity on him after this, and each time Robert got off the train, he warned him when it was time for the train to leave.

"Hurry up, Sir, hurry up! No time for walking. No time for dog. Train leaving soon, soon."

At least Robert was able to buy a couple of chicken satays and a bowl of noodles at one stop so that he and Tara could share a meal. The backpackers and Thai passengers in Robert's carriage regarded Tara with a certain amount of suspicion, especially after the ice began to melt and spread in a big puddle across the floor. Robert tried to rub it away with his shoe, but puddles don't disappear, they spread. Some people asked if our dog had peed so he showed them the melting bag of ice and his whisky glass.

The sleeper car had little privacy curtains to each bunk, but it wasn't easy for large Robert to change into a T-shirt and shorts for the night in the limited space available. He just took off his slacks and shoes, placed them in one corner of the bunk, tucked Tara up in the other corner, and fell asleep to the rocking motion of the train, plunging through the tropical night.

The next morning the pair caught a bus to Phuket, and Robert bought two tickets so Tara would have a seat to herself. When the late arrivals hurried on board, a grossly overweight and sweaty Thai lady pushed Tara off the seat, and plonked herself down beside Robert with a sigh of relief, wriggling her swollen feet out of her tight shoes. Smiling at Robert, she opened a packet of greasy delicacies, popping pieces into her mouth, oil dribbling down her wobbling double chins. Robert rescued Tara from the floor, deciding not to make a fuss and wave his extra ticket in the woman's face. He spoke no Thai – and she was bigger than him.

Deusa was in the Yacht Haven marina on the northern side of Phuket, and Robert asked the bus driver to drop him off there.

"No, no, cannot," said the bus driver, who spoke some English, "that village very bad, very dangerous, bad people, make trouble. You get off here, main road."

So Robert and Tara got off the bus and walked through the 'dangerous' village down to the boat where I was delighted to see them, throwing my arms around Robert, and picking up Tara for a big, big hug. We had missed her terribly over the past eight months, but had kept in touch with Richard and Angkhana by phone. Tara had continued to get on with Benny, so it was probably a nice change for her not to be at sea, and learning to play with another pooch.

What the bus driver had said was quite true, actually, as the village had a most dubious reputation, and some very strange folk were seen walking around in Middle Eastern Muslim dress, their women heavily shrouded in black, with slits in their heavy veils that allowed limited vision. This kind of dress was unusual for Thailand: its Muslim minority did not dress in the severe style of Saudi Arabia.

I quite often walked with Tara through the village to the rubber plantation nearby, so that she could stretch her legs and run free. I always carried a stick with me in case we met a snake. There are at least eighteen different kinds of poisonous snake in Malaysia, though their bite isn't fatal, just very painful, and makes one feel awfully ill. The snakes would rather get out of our way, however, so we didn't meet any in our rambles.

One day, I was confronted by a man wearing a shirt bearing the image of Osama bin Laden. He proudly pointed to his hero, as if challenging me to comment. I greeted him politely in my few words of Thai, and walked on ...

sixteen

Tsunami!

At Christmas we needed to book *Deusa* into Rebak Marina in Malaysia for an underwater clean and paint job in early January, spending the Christmas period in a very nice anchorage outside Telaga Marina on Langkawi Island. The anchorage was sheltered from ocean swell and changeable weather systems by two man-made islands, built to protect the marina's entrance channel, and ideal for dogs to romp and explore on, as they were small enough to be able to keep Tara in sight.

Tara loved to run free on the islands, and while she explored, I gathered rubbish that had floated ashore with the tides – old shoes, plastic bottles, broken dolls, Styrofoam containers, beer cans. It's horrific what people toss into the sea, which invariably ends up on some distant shore. My problem was, what to do with the rubbish once I'd collected it? Dig a hole and bury it above the high water mark? Start a fire and burn it? Carry it back to the municipal rubbish dump on the island? As burning rubbish affected the ozone layer, burying it in a really deep hole was probably the best answer, because the municipal rubbish dump was likely to set fire to it in any case.

On December 26 – Boxing Day – Robert was down below at the computer, and Tara and I were sitting on deck, enjoying the cool breeze (Malaysia, as I've said before, can be very hot in summer). I glanced towards the shore, wondering whether I should take Tara for a walk.

"Hey, Robert," I called, "the tide is really far out today, is it spring tides?"

Robert glanced up at our tide clock on the bulkhead.

"Don't be ridiculous, it's high tide, you don't know what you're talking about." he replied.

"Oh, I do, too!" I answered back, "Come and see for yourself, it's as low as I've ever seen it."

Robert muttered and mumbled something about people who, having lived on a boat for so many years, still couldn't tell high tide from low tide, but, arriving on deck, he was equally amazed.

At this moment, friends on a nearby boat made a general announcement on Channel 16, the calling channel on VHF radio that all yachts use to speak with each other.

"Look at the waves breaking on the island behind us. There's something very wrong; the waves never break there."

Our caller was right – waves didn't break on those rocks; they were very sheltered. We looked at the gap between the two artificial islands, and saw a curling green wave breaking in the opening where there should have been calm water. I watched it with fascination, sitting quite still in the cockpit, almost as if it were a mirage that would vanish if I moved. The wave was so beautiful as it curved gracefully through the gap, catching the sunlight glowing through the clear, emerald wall of water.

Robert was not fascinated, however, and immediately saw the danger of it catching us on the stern, and tossing us onto the beach. Our boat weighed 18 tons – a lot of boat to move in a hurry – but Robert didn't think twice: he leapt down below and started the motor, slamming the gear into reverse. The anchor stretched out away from the beach as the three metre high wave crashed into us, violently rocking the boat and covering us in sprays of saltwater, but with the motor racing and the anchor holding firm, we didn't change position.

"What the hell was that?" we asked each other, looking around to see how the other boats in the anchorage had faired.

A trimaran (a main hull and two outrigger hulls) called *Cream* was washed high on the island, right by the tree line, and other boats had dragged their anchors, and were struggling to reposition themselves. But the strangest sight of all was the boats in the marina. We could only see their masts from our position outside, but all of a sudden they began twirling around like so many toys in a funfair park: a merry-go-round of yachts. The wave had surged into the channel and filled the marina with rushing, swirling water, ripping the boats from their moorings. There was nowhere for the water to escape except back through the same channel, and as it ran back out to sea, the boats were sucked with it.

We watched in horror as boat after boat was spat out of the marina, to drift, out of control, towards the rocks and beaches of the artificial islands. Some boats were swept right past the islands, and directly out to sea. Where were their owners? As it was Christmas, it was likely they had gone to visit family, leaving their floating homes in the safe waters of Telaga Marina. All of the boats drifting past us were closed and locked for the holiday season, with no-one on board, and no-one taking care of them. Not knowing, of course, that this was the devastating Boxing Day tsunami that swept away so many lives in South East Asia and beyond, we didn't stop to think.

"Come on, Rosemary, put Tara down below, we've got to rescue these boats before they go out to sea. *Deusa's* anchor is holding so I think we're all right."

Robert was already in the dinghy, starting the motor, and I scrambled down the stern ladder to join him. First of all we tried to guide the loose boats away from the rocks of the islands, using the bow of our dinghy and our powerful outboard motor.

Once the boats had drifted free of the islands, Robert would put me on a drifting boat to drop the anchor. All the boats were different, with different anchoring mechanisms to *Deusa*, and I battled to figure out how they worked. Robert stayed in the dinghy, keeping each boat from moving too far out to sea, and helping me with the anchors. Thank goodness it was a very shallow area in which the boats were drifting, so we didn't have to put out too much anchor chain to secure them, moving from one boat to the next to stop them going too far.

Others were doing the same thing, and I know we saved seven boats. The water was very agitated, and, unaware of it, three waves swept into the marina and surged out again, so the currents we were battling against were enormous. Robert was nearly sucked under a catamaran while trying to help me drop the anchor. The boat stopped moving as the anchor bit, but the current swept Robert and the dinghy right between the pontoons. He could have been severely injured if he hadn't managed to race the dinghy motor and escape. In all this panic we had neglected to put on our life jackets: we never appreciated that this was a tsunami, and very dangerous, and it was foolish of us not to have worn the jackets.

When we got back to *Deusa* we found a fishing boat entangled alongside us with no-one on board. Our anchor still held securely, and Tara barked frantically from inside the cabin, telling us something was very wrong. The fishing boats doubled as rustic homes when they were offshore for several days. Pieces of old tin strapped to a makeshift roof acted as shelter from sun and rain. Bits of metal stuck out from the deck for tying on fishing poles, or hoisting lights for squid fishing at night. None of this did any good to our topsides, scraping alongside and wedging tightly against us. Local fishing boats don't have anchors, so once we had got it away, Robert took one of our spare anchors, and a length of rope, and anchored the boat some distance from us.

As things began to calm down, those of us in the anchorage decided it was not safe to stay near the shore, in case more tidal waves roared in, so we lifted our anchors and moved about a mile offshore to re-anchor. What saved Malaysia from much greater damage from the tsunami was the very shallow seabed surrounding Langkawi. Phuket, in Thailand, with its mountainous profile and deep seas, was devastated by the tidal waves, and thousands of people lost their lives – more than was ever announced officially, because the illegal migrants from Burma, who were seeking work in more prosperous Thailand, were not taken into account. As the sea receded on the beaches of Phuket, Burmese workers on the construction sites ran down to the beach, fascinated by the disappearing water, and the small fish and molluscs they could gather up for an evening meal. Sadly, they never had that meal, as they were swept away by more in-rushing water that claimed their lives. Never officially recorded in Thailand, they were unknown, and simply vanished.

Normally, the tide changes every six hours and twenty minutes, but the night of the tsunami it sloshed to and fro like an erratic washing machine, carrying with it bits of broken jetty, sunken fishing boats, and logs. During that troubled and sleepless night we kept in touch with each other by VHF radio, advising of floating debris and deadly hazards passing by us. The restless sea was a disturbing phenomena, and our subconscious senses knew something was very wrong. We listened to commercial radio as well, in case there were reports of further waves, but we knew we were safest on *Deusa*, some distance off-shore, on a very level seabed that did not shelve up. Close to shore the tidal wave would rear up in the shallows, and flood onto the land, casting everything before it. No, the safe place was on the ocean, away from the land. Ships many miles away would not even have felt the surge of the tsunami as it rushed towards Thailand and Malaysia, Sri Lanka, and beyond.

Daylight brought some relief because at least we could see what was going on. An unbelievable amount of rubbish floated and bobbed around us, with the sea still surging in strange patterns. News began filtering in: thousands of lives lost in Phuket, Phi Phi Don Island wiped out; so many tourists drowned. Amazingly enough, only one person died in Langkawi, though several people died in Penang further down the coast. The tsunami was not nearly as strong in Malaysia; in Thailand it was much worse.

The next days were spent helping to localise boats. Our friend, Richard, ran an SSB (Single Sideband) radio net giving an update on which boats were damaged, lost, sunk, saved. Messages arrived from all over the world, from people looking for friends and family, including ours. As soon as we could, we phoned or emailed to let them know that we were fine.

One yacht we were unable to help was a concrete boat called *Ike Rere*, whose owners were away in New Zealand, visiting family. The yacht was swept out of the marina, and drifted onto rocks on the island near us while we were anchoring other boats; attempting to pull it off the rocks with our dinghy and motor had proved futile. The more the sea swirled back and forth, the more the vessel was ground onto the rocks, wearing a great hole in the hull where water flooded in. By the time the owners returned, the inside of their boat was a total mess of tumbled provisions, sodden books and charts, and wet bedclothes. They spent days cleaning up, and a tug boat finally dragged them free of the rocks. They patched the hole as best they could, and took her off to be hauled out for repairs.

The trimaran *Cream*, jettisoned to the tree line of the island, was an interesting rescue mission. Several strong poles were laid close to each other on the beach, and slathered with thick, white grease. About twenty men – including Robert – heaved and grunted, shifting the trimaran onto the first greased pole. Inch-by-inch, they shuffled her down the beach, bringing forward the slippery poles from the stern, once the boat had rolled over them. The tide was out by the time the greasy, grubby crowd got the trimaran to the edge of the lapping water. It was New Year's Eve, and we all gathered together by the stranded boat with drinks and snacks to welcome in 2005. A great cheer rose as the incoming tide lifted *Cream*, and floated her clear.

ജൈ

Rebak Marina, only a few nautical miles from Telaga, where we had booked in *Deusa* for a haul-out, was also completely devastated. Boats broke away from the concrete docks and swirled out to sea, some with the dock still attached to the boat, potted plants and children's' bicycles balancing precariously on the cracked concrete. Rebak was more of a residential marina, with people living on their boats for years at a time.

All the damaged boats there needed repairs, which created a long queue for haul-out onto the hard, where they could be worked on. Some had been holed and were slowly sinking, so these had priority. Nasty fights broke out amongst desperate owners, and one night we were woken around midnight by our VHF radio.

"Mayday! Mayday! Help! Help! We're being attacked. Come quickly – help! Help!"

I leapt out of bed and grabbed the handset.

"Where are you? Give me your co-ordinates so we can send help."

We imagined it was a ship at sea being attacked by pirates, so were very surprised when we heard the answer.

"We're on the hardstand in Rebak, and someone is trying to knock our boat off its supports!"

With all the nervous energy created by the tsunami, tempers were running high. One boat had jumped the queue, whilst another boat, in dire need, was still sitting in the water. The owner, having drunk too much at the bar, had decided to knock the invading boat off its supports, and grabbing a sledgehammer lying under the boat, proceeded to first knock down the stern ladder, and then attacked the supports keeping the boat upright and safe in the yard. The terrified owners were woken by the smashing and banging of his hammer, the infuriated man raging at them for taking his place. The wife made the Mayday call. When we learned that they were actually safely in the marina, we decided that someone there – either the night guard or a fellow yachtsman – would sort out the problem, and they did. One of the angry man's buddies calmed him down, and took him back to the bar to drown his sorrows, whilst persuading him not to knock down boats belonging to others.

In Telaga Marina, a couple who owned a trimaran had decided to go for a walk to the nearby shops, and this saved their lives, as their fragile boat was mown down in the merry-go-round, and sank without trace. A friend of ours who had her boat in the marina, was away for the day, and when she came back, all she could see of it was the mast. She eventually managed to re-float the boat by pumping air into flotation bladders that divers installed inside the boat in the murky depths of the marina.

∞

After we hauled *Deusa* from the water and repainted her hull in Rebak Marina in Malaysia,we moved on up to Thailand, stopping en route at Phi Phi Don in Thailand, almost a month after the tsunami. We moved a lot between Malaysia and Thailand, as it was pleasant sailing, they were neighbours, and we kept having to renew our tourist visas when in one place for too long.

The devastation on Phi Phi Don was shocking. This had been a bustling tourist destination, with little bars and restaurants, shops selling tourist junk, dive shops, DVD shops, and internet cafés. Now, it was just a pile of rubble, with the strange, sweet, terrible smell of death about it.

Buildings had collapsed as the tidal wave rushed in, trapping Thais and tourists alike. Volunteers had come from all over the world to help clean up the reefs and beaches.

Extraordinary stories of survival were told. A friend's son snorkelling nearby was lifted two storeys with the wave and deposited on the second floor of the Phi Phi Don Hotel that, thankfully, remained standing: another friend on Phuket island was washed into a basement garage, his shoulder broken as he slammed against a wall, realising that he would drown as the water rose to the roof. All he could think of were his twin children and wife somewhere on the island at a children's party. He knew he was going to die, and felt so sad at the thought that he would never see them again, but then the water began to drain out of the basement, taking him with it, Clutching at a pole as he swirled past it saved his life, and his wife and children were safe inland.

Another man we met told us how he was sitting in his living room with his mother, wife and children, looking out at the beautiful view of the ocean through the large glass window. Next minute, the wave exploded against the glass, roaring through the house as foaming tumbling water. He survived ... but he never saw his family again.

People were washed far inland, then sucked back out with the receding water, managing to cling to a palm tree, the roof of a house, anything solid that wouldn't give way under the huge weight of water and debris.

Our friend, Hans, a single-handed sailor, had just left Langkawi in his little wooden boat *Tumblehome*, and was anchored at Teritao, the next island north, belonging to Thailand. When the tidal wave struck, it rolled his boat over and over onto the beach. Hans was asleep on board, and crawled out in a state of shock, not knowing what had hit him. As he did so, the Thai National Parks guards arrested him. According to them, he had come ashore illegally without checking into Thailand! They marched him off to immigration officials on the mainland. Thank goodness he wasn't injured; just extremely indignant that he had been bundled off like a criminal. We later heard that he wanted to sell his boat. He was a tired old man, and this was the final straw for him.

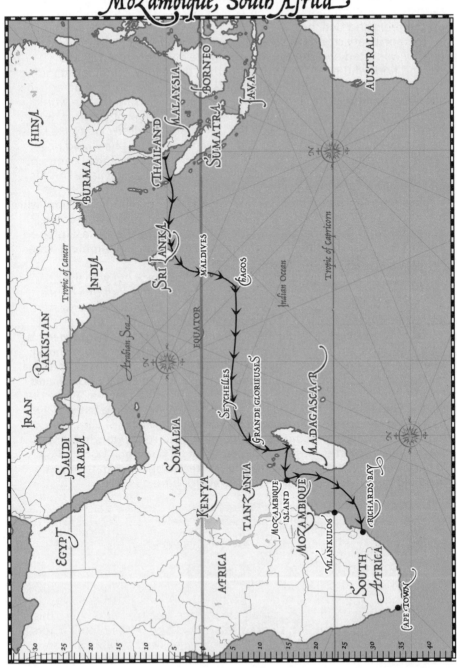

seventeen

Across the Indian Ocean

When Tara began passing blood in her urine we knew something was wrong. Initially, we thought it was a bladder infection, so gave her antibiotics, which cleared it up for a while but then it came back again. We were preparing to leave Asia for Africa: a long journey across the Indian Ocean, stopping at the Maldives, Chagos, Seychelles, and Madagascar, finally arriving at Africa on the Mozambique coast.

Because Tara peed on deck, we found tiny little white bits like grains of sand, now and then, and realised something was not right, but what, we didn't know. It would take her a long time to pee as she squatted and strained, and then out would plop a little stone. How very painful for her, yet she never whimpered or complained. Having asked around, no-one could recommend a reliable vet, so after our one bad experience in Thailand, we reluctantly decided to wait until we got to Africa to see a vet. We also knew that Tara's condition was a chronic, and not an acute one, and felt confident that she wouldn't get much worse.

In February we finally said goodbye to South East Asia, having stocked the boat with provisions for the Indian Ocean crossing.

Our first stop was Sri Lanka - a journey of approximately 1400 nautical miles. One of Robert's nieces had married a Sri Lankan doctor, Stuart, and we thought it would be fun to meet our new extended family. Galle harbour was not a very comfortable anchorage, with a lot of swell coming in around the harbour mouth. We had to drop anchor, then back up to a rocky wall, tying a stern line ashore. It involved a lot of rock and roll and discomfort, so we spent more time ashore than on board.

Each evening a line of floats was dragged across the harbour mouth to close it off and underwater mines were set off during the night to deter the Tamil Tigers, who were interested in sabotaging the nearby naval base. The deafening thwack of the exploding mines really bothered us, and hurt Tara's ears, setting her off on a barking frenzy.

"Dearly beloved Tara," I explained, kneeling down beside her, "this horrible noise is bothering all of us but it's to keep out the Tamil Tigers. They swim underwater and attach limpet mines to navy boat hulls to blow them up."

Tara replied that it was her duty to warn us of any strange noise, and this one was particularly strange. She didn't care about tigers - they were just big cats, weren't they?

TARA

Once we'd made sure that *Deusa* was safe and secure, we hired a cheerful Sri Lankan called Ramsey, together with his car, to take us up to Kandi to meet Stuart's father, Carlo and his cousin, Claudia. Poor Tara couldn't go for more than an hour without needing to pee, so it was a stop/start journey as we let her out to relieve herself on the verge of the road. The drive along the coast towards Colombo was dismal, with ruin and destruction from the tsunami fifteen months ago everywhere. It was estimated that 35,000 people died in Sri Lanka. When we checked in with Customs and Immigration at Galle harbour, they showed us the high water mark in their offices from the tidal wave, at least two metres up the wall. Their building withstood the flood, but so many other more fragile houses around the harbour were washed away, or had all their windows and doors smashed, leaving just empty, hollow shells.

Carlo very kindly asked us to a delicious Sri Lankan meal in his house, and Claudia put us up for the night. It was very difficult to cope with Tara's problems, as Claudia's own dogs were shut in the garden, so I couldn't take her out every hour to pee.

This very clean little dog, who never had an accident down below on *Deusa*, had to pee on the bedroom floor, and felt very embarrassed about it. We had a towel for mopping up pee, but our situation wasn't easy for any of us.

80C3

The next port of call was Gan in the Maldives. Tara was not allowed on shore here as this was a strictly Muslim country of many islands. However, people wanted to come out and visit us, as they could hear her barking in the anchorage, and were fascinated to know there was a dog on board. Children were particularly curious to see a dog at close range, as there were no dogs on the islands. When people came out to the boat, we put Tara down below so they could gaze at her from a distance, and therefore did not offend their local imam or mosque. But they still got into trouble, and when I ferried them back to land, they were told most severely by immigration that they were forbidden to visit us.

Our SSB radio that we used for emails, weather reports and communications was giving trouble, so we decided to buy a new one before setting off for Chagos, the group of islands below the Maldives. This meant waiting in harbour for several days while it was sent by air to Gan. During this time Robert did repairs and maintenance, and one necessary job was to grease the quadrant, the steering mechanism that linked to the rudder, which lay under the boards behind our bed in the aft cabin.

This also happened to be the platform that Tara slept on, and from where she gazed out of the aft portholes. With one bound she'd leap onto the bed, the second bound taking her onto her favourite spot, watching the traffic passing our stern. No-one had thought to close the cabin door, and, of course, Tara came tearing in to check out a passing boat. The boards covering the quadrant had been removed, and the next moment she plunged into a dark hole full of cogs and cables, scrabbling back out in alarm, smeared in black grease from nose to tail, which she then spread across the bed cover, the carpets, the sofa, and the cushions, as she hurried back the way she had come.

"Oh, my God, Tara, where have you been?" I shouted, grabbing at her, as she skidded past, smearing more grease around. "Bloody hell, Robert, look what you've done, Tara's covered in grease!"

"I did not cover Tara in grease," he shouted back, "she nearly knocked me over as I was working on the quadrant; then fell into the hole. It's her silly fault, and who left the door open, anyway?"

It took a lot of soap and scrubbing to clean up both Tara and the boat, with Robert and I just about speaking again by the time we turned in.

෴

The weather was good, and it was time to move on to Chagos where there were no religious restraints; no local residents to point a finger or complain; no clerics to berate the young folk who wanted to visit us.

In fact, nobody lived on the Chagos Archipelago at all, except for Americans at the naval base on Diego Garcia. As part of an agreement between Britain and the United States in the early 1970s, a British naval base on the largest island, Diego Garcia, was handed over to the Americans, and all the Ilois (as the local residents were known) had to be removed; not only from Diego Garcia, but the surrounding islands as well, where we were anchored. No wonder there were no people. The visiting yachts had to get special permission from BIOT (British Indian Ocean Territory) to anchor on these adjacent islands, and were expressly forbidden to venture anywhere near Diego Garcia.

The original inhabitants of the islands, a mixture of African, South India and Malay, had been there for 150 years, brought in by the French from Mauritius and the Seychelles. They harvested the coconuts, living a simple island life, with a clinic, a church, and a weekly ferry boat to take them back to Mauritius or the Seychelles for provisions. The people were summarily evacuated, allowed to take just one suitcase, and no possessions, furniture, or pets, and dropped on Seychelles and Mauritius, with the promise of homes and jobs. In fact, they were abandoned at the docks to integrate into the poverty and lowlife of the islands. All-in-all, a disgraceful tale.

These people – who once had a life and dignity – were pitched into misery. We later met a man in the Seychelles who was sent out to Chagos to euthanize all the pet dogs and cats who had been abandoned when the Ilois left. He enticed the animals into the coconut sheds with scraps of meat, closed the doors and gassed them, then set fire to the bodies. There were even donkeys that had to be caught and killed, though we believed that two escaped and still lived there.

Chagos was a strange place. The only visitors were yachting folk on their travels between Africa and Asia, stopping off for several months at a time, living off the provisions they had brought with them, trading with each other, and fishing. There is possibly no other place on earth that is totally uninhabited, and we were the only living souls on the islands.

TARA

Well, not on the islands, exactly, as we were anchored *by* the islands, living on our boats, and visiting the land each day.

Walking through the forest of coconut palms, we came across the ruins of people's homes; a broken-down chapel, a clinic with a tree growing through the shattered roof, the crumbling remains of copra sheds, and a graveyard with tumbled, moss-covered headstones. It was a lonely, sad, abandoned little village. Just before we arrived, a group of Ilois had visited Chagos to lay a memorial stone on each island, commemorating their presence and the dead who were buried there.

Tara, Robert and I all ate fish and rice, and each day we'd go out in the dinghy with several lures trailing behind us, hoping to catch something for dinner in the wide, blue ocean. Skipjack tuna was what we caught most of the time, and I'd bottle some for the onward journey, cooking the rest for our meals while at anchor. We became very adept at preserving fish, and, besides bottling it with the help of a pressure cooker and Kilner jars, we also dried it to make fish jerky, pickled and curried it. When it was fresh out of the sea we would eat it raw with Wasabi mustard (a green horseradish mix very popular with the Japanese), which was absolutely delicious.

A nice little island right near to where we'd anchored was great for Tara and I to explore, and each day we'd go ashore by canoe to investigate the island, look for shells and beachcomb to see what gifts the ocean had left. Tara spent happy hours fishing in the shallows, running back and forth in the little waves, chasing tiny fish. She had endless energy and kept going all day, but we found that with her ongoing bladder infection, she became very cold and shaky by the time I took her back to the boat.

One day, a small, black-tipped shark had the misfortune to check out Tara's white legs flashing by in the shallows. Cruising for a closer look, the shark didn't realise it had come up against a formidable adversary, who drove it onto the beach, bit it through the back of the head and killed it. Tara was so pleased with herself, and carried around this 40cm-long shark for the rest of the time we were at the beach, giving it a sharp shake every now and then.

"Tara, would you like to take the shark back to the boat and show Robert?" I asked her.

She looked at me quizzically, her head on one side, the dead shark dangling out of her mouth. I walked towards the dinghy and she ran ahead, leaping over the side of the little boat, the shark still clamped in her jaws.

Returning to *Deusa*, I called to Robert, who was working down below on maintenance.

"Look what Tara has brought you from the beach. Would you like it for lunch?"

He climbed out into the cockpit, and walked to the back deck to peer over the railing. "My goodness, Tara, a baby black-tipped shark, how on earth did you catch that?"

I explained while Tara looked up at Robert with great pride, wagging her stubby little white tail.

"So, what are you going to do with it, do you want to bring it onto *Deusa*?"

Tara wagged her tail some more: she loved the sound of Robert's rich baritone voice.

"Robert, she won't get out of the dinghy without it. And what's more, I'm not going to pick her up: you know what she's like with fish and me. You'd better come down here and get fish and dog onto the boat."

After a while Tara became bored with her fish, so when she wasn't looking, I surreptitiously tossed it overboard.

ଞଠଊଷ

Every now and then the *Pacific Marlin* – the patrol boat of the British Indian Ocean Territories – would come round to check up on us and collect the monthly fee that everyone paid to be there. They were very welcome visitors as they gave marvellous parties, inviting us on board their ship for a barbecue feast of steak, pork chops, bacon, chicken, noodles, rice, potato salad, and chocolate cake and ice-cream (what luxury). As you can imagine, we had long ago run out of these delicacies, and were living off fish, rice and bean sprouts. Starving for a meat fix, we all leapt into our dinghies, hurrying over to our benefactors for a banquet of a lifetime, bringing back bones for Tara to gnaw on to her heart's content.

At any one time there were only about thirty-five yachts in the anchorage, as there were other small islands we had permission to visit, so we spread out amongst these. Even though we knew all of the others in the anchorage, this was a good time for us to get together and exchange news and views, or else we'd visit each other's boats for a sundowner or a snack, or else meet on the beach for a game of beach volley ball or 'boules' (balls), also known as petanque, which originated from France in the early 1900s.

ଞଠଊଷ

This paradise spot had been fine for a couple of months, but once again it was time to lift anchor and catch the fair winds towards Africa. Next stop, the Seychelles Islands: a 7-day sail westward. The fishing across the Seychelles Banks was fantastic, and we caught eight fish in two hours. Tara remained constantly restrained so that she couldn't attack the fish, me, or generally get in the way.

"Stop, stop!" I called across to Robert over the noise of the wind and sea as he reeled in yet another flapping fish. "We can't handle this much fish; there's no space in the fridge. It's too rough for me to do any cooking or preserving down below in the galley."

"Don't worry," Robert shouted back, "we know lots of boats in the harbour, and everyone loves to get a fish or two."

"But I'm not going to clean them," I yelled back against the wind, brandishing a bloody knife which I was already gutting a fish with. "If you want to give fish away, they go guts and all."

TARA

The cleaning operation on the heaving back deck had to be the worst part of the whole operation: filleting the fish, throwing the carcases back into the ocean, dipping the bucket into the sea on a long rope, and sluicing down the bloody deck. Luckily, we were only a few hours away from the harbour at Victoria, the capital of Mahé (the principal island of the Seychelles group). The extra fish wouldn't spoil, and even with giving it away we still managed to bottle twenty jars for future fish pies and Tara dinners.

The drive shaft to the propeller was very slightly bent, which gave rise to bad vibration when we ran the motor. We couldn't carry on to Africa with this problem, so Robert found a boat yard that could haul out *Deusa*, remove the shaft and straighten it. Consequently, we didn't see much of the Seychelles, but at least managed to do the necessary repairs. It was a messy job; the yard had to remove the shaft through the saloon, first lifting out the engine and leaving it dangling in the air over the cockpit. I took up all the carpets as the yard was filthy dirty, and any time Tara and I went for a walk, we had to clean our feet very well before going down below.

To add to the muck and dirt, we had to move out of the back cabin because the quadrant under the boards behind our bed, which Robert had recently greased, was leaking where the steering mechanism went through the hull to the rudder. The fibreglass was quite sodden, and had to be ground out and repacked with fresh resin. The fine fibreglass dust flew everywhere, covering us and the inside of the boat in a choking grey coat. This wasn't a happy time for any of us, and we couldn't wait for it all to be finished. At least there was a nearby artificial island where Tara could run free, and where we looked for cowry shells, dug from the ocean bed for the landfill. This was the only light relief in an otherwise dismal stay in the Seychelles.

Once the repairs were done it was time to provision *Deusa* for our journey to Madagascar, and fill up with diesel and water, cooking gas and petrol for the dinghy. This passage of approximately 1100 nautical miles was known to be rough, taking us around the north of Madagascar and down to the island of Nosy Be, a favourite spot for yachts.

En route we caught a massive fish, a short-billed spearfish, of about one-and-a-half metres in length, and weighing 25 kilos. It took a huge effort to get it aboard, both of us struggling to heave it over the stern railing, where it flopped onto the aft deck. What a big fish to fillet, but we needed fresh fish, and there was nothing for it but to squat down with a sharp knife and cut it up as quickly as possible while the deck heaved in the rough sea.

Around this time we realised that Tara could no longer hold her pee. Robert had dropped his waterproof jacket on the saloon floor when his watch was finished and Tara peed on it. She normally always asked to go out, so I picked her up to put her on deck and was bitten sharply on the hand.

"Ow! You little bugger," I cursed her. "What did you do that for, look at my hand? Look at the blood you've drawn!"

Tara hung her head in shame and went to sit on her bed under the dodger. I felt very bad for shouting at her – she must have been in a lot of pain to bite me. I stroked her head and told her how sorry I was for getting cross, and would be more careful next time not to hurt her when I picked her up.

The next day, when Robert picked her up, she bit him in the face. Something was very wrong. She quite often gave me a nip if she didn't want to do something, but Robert was her beloved pack leader whom she respected. We didn't know it at the time, and only found out from a vet in South Africa later, that her bladder was full of stones, Poor girl, she must have been in a great deal of discomfort, but never made a fuss. We think the stones were caused by the great strain to her bladder when she fell overboard in the Malacca Straits and probably didn't pee for eight hours. A bitch squats to pee, of course, and Tara was unable to assume that position in the water, so may not have emptied her bladder at all.

Apart from the antibiotics that we had on board for Tara, we were very hesitant to give her any other medication, such as painkillers or anti-inflammatories, because they could be fatal to canines.

The passage to Madagascar was one of the roughest we had experienced in a long time, and one night, during my watch, there was a sharp crack as something crashed to the deck. I leapt into the air with shock, peering into the dark to see what it was. It was a very black night, however, and I couldn't see a thing, so rushed below to shake Robert as he lay sleeping peacefully in the aft cabin.

"Wake up! Wake up! Something's fallen from the main mast and I can't see what it is."

He woke immediately, flung on some clothes, and was soon on deck with our powerful torch. Coiled like a silver snake at the foot of the mast, lay the port shroud (the left side rigging wire that supported the mast, and a very important part of the rig), sheared off at the gooseneck fitting where it slotted into the mast.

Robert thought for a bit. I sat nervously by, feeling most unhappy at this latest development in the middle of the night.

"What we'll do is use the running back stay (a moveable rigging wire used as an extra brace to the mast when the staysail was up) as a support for the mast, reef the sails, and look on the chart for the nearest island to stop and do repairs." he announced.

We slowed *Deusa* by reefing the sails, both of us on deck with the spreader lights turned on – powerful beams attached to the main mast that illuminated the entire deck so we could see what we were doing. Once the yacht was moving more calmly through the ocean, Robert went forward and adjusted the running back stay to take the place of our broken shroud. Turning off the spreader lights, Robert went below to study charts of the area.

TARA

Closest land was the French island of La Glorieuse, a military outpost, and not a good place to stop. But two little islands just off the main island looked like they'd provide enough shelter to stop and decide what to do, so we changed course and headed for these, anchoring behind the larger island (noted as Ile de Lys on the chart). Exhausted from the rough trip, we dropped anchor, hung out our wet clothes, and caught up on much-needed sleep.

Our yacht was very strongly rigged, and the next morning Robert studied the situation more thoroughly, deciding we could borrow a forward stay (another support wire of the main mast) and place it where the shroud had broken.

"Unfortunately for you, my love, you're going to have to go up the mast and slot the gooseneck fitting of the forward stay into the place where the other one broke off. I'd gladly do it, but you won't be able to hoist my heavy weight up the mast." Robert told me.

This was, unfortunately, quite true; I always did any mast work for just this reason. I didn't have the strength to winch big Robert up the mast, and was only excused this duty when we had another man on board, who could wind the winch to hoist Robert aloft.

It took the best part of two hours to achieve this, with the boat rocking in the strong wind and the fitting extremely difficult to slot into the mast. When we first started sailing I didn't feel too happy up the mast, but got used to it in time, although it was never my favourite occupation, even though you could take great photos from the top!

"This is really difficult," I shouted down to Robert, standing below me. "I'm being bashed against the mast with every roll of *Deusa*, and this gooseneck is a really fiddly thing."

My language became coarser and coarser as I struggled with the gooseneck, but finally it hooked into position, and Robert lowered me back to the deck, my legs shaking and my ribs bruised. I crumpled into Robert's arms as I landed, and he gave me a big bear hug – carefully, because of my painful ribs. Tara simply looked at me as if to say – what on earth were you doing up there? The new rig wasn't quite long enough, so Robert extended it to the deck fitting with a turnbuckle, and now we felt much more confident about continuing this very rough passage with the high winds and waves that we would have to face. Inwardly, I was absolutely dreading this next stage of our journey, and couldn't help letting Robert see how fearful I was.

The island was full of Terns and other seabirds, and we thought of putting the dinghy in the water and going ashore, but we could hear the military base on La Glorieuse calling us on channel 16 of the VHF, asking us to identify ourselves. We therefore decided to lay low, not go ashore, and not speak to them!

The next morning, early, we lifted the anchor and departed, sailing past the main island.

The VHF crackled, and a strongly-accented French voice came through.

"White boat, white boat, please identify yourself!"

"What shall I do," I asked Robert, "do you want me to reply to them?"

"Yes, why not? I'm sure they've no powerboat to come and check us out."

So I returned the call, answering their questions about our boat name, how many people there were on board, and where were we going. Their English was dreadful; my French even worse!

Our friends, Margi and Gerard, who visited us in Panama, had landed on La Glorieuse a year before. They spoke French, and could communicate with the base, but the base was very unfriendly and told them to leave immediately. The military base had wanted to do the same to us when we sheltered behind their small island for two days, so thank goodness it had no boat.

❧◌❧

By now we realised that Tara could no longer stay down below with her leaking bladder, so we made her as comfortable as we could, up in her day bed, with lots of small washable rags that we put under her like nappies. She was embarrassed about this, but in a strange way she knew that we were only trying to help. Being such a clean dog she was horrified at losing control. Even when it was rough and raining, she had to stay up on deck under the dodger, where she was sheltered from the bad weather. While we were sailing there was always one of us on watch, so we could keep an eye on her when she got out of her day bed. Of course, we were very worried about her falling overboard again, but she was much less active now with her sore tummy. We needed to get her to a vet as soon as possible, and the most likely place to find one was in South Africa.

At last, after a most challenging passage of twelve days, we made landfall in Madagascar at the island of Sakatia. Dropping anchor with a sigh of relief, we went below to collapse on our comfortable bed to catch up again on much-needed sleep, but no sooner had we nodded off than we heard Tara's familiar bark, warning us someone was approaching *Deusa*. Reluctantly, we hauled our sleepy selves up on deck to see who it was.

A friendly, next-door yacht owner stood holding onto the toe rail, with Tara barking in his face.

"Sorry about that," I said, leading Tara away, "please come on board."

"No, I won't thanks, I'm just going ashore. But I thought you should know, you may not take your dog ashore on this beach – it's fadi."

"Fadi? What's fadi?" I asked, "I've never heard of it." I imagined some horrid disease that decimated dogs.

"Fadi is local custom, and it is all through Madagascar. You must find out what the particular fadi is on each island and, wherever you stop, ask questions, otherwise it's quite a hassle."

Our well-wisher waved a hand and set off for the beach, Tara rushing up to the bow to bark him goodbye.

We discovered later that a yacht had taken their dog ashore on this very same beach. That evening, there was a ceremony on the beach, with much beating of drums, dancing and chanting, but they presumed it was a local ritual. No-one said anything, but next morning they woke to find a severed goat's head, eyes rolled back and tongue sticking out, oozing blood and buzzing with flies, lying on their foredeck. Shocked and horrified, they went ashore to find out what it was all about. Apparently, the dog had offended the gods by walking on the beach, so they had to do a purification ritual, and place the goat's head on the boat as an appeasement.

We didn't fancy dead goat on *Deusa* so paid close attention to local customs.

₧∓

Madagascar was a fascinating mixture of races from distant lands. The great, red island was only populated some 2000 years ago, initially from Indonesia and Malaysia, with other ethnic groups moving in after that. They were extremely polite and non-confrontational, very like the people of Asia, and as a Westerner one could be offensive without meaning to be.

Fadi is where one can go seriously wrong, without knowing it. You mustn't whistle on certain beaches; not sit under a particular shady tree on another, or swim in a cool and inviting waterfall in yet another destination.

Tara was now feeling much more cheerful, as we were mostly at anchor and not doing long passages in rough conditions. Her bladder was still leaking, but whenever we were able to take her ashore on non-fadi beaches, she ran around, overjoyed, leapt into the sea for a swim, and searched for small fish to chase along the shoreline. She still shivered a lot when back on board, so we would rinse her down and towel her dry so that she was comfortable.

We were anchored off one particular island where a big celebration was going on. Drumming, dancing and singing filled the air; many people crowding into the small village by the beach. Leaving Tara on board, I put my canoe in the water and paddled over to see what was going on, but was met by hostile stares and people waving me away.

"Guess what?" I said to Robert on my return, "there's a fascinating ritual going on here, but I'm not welcome. I was told that it's a ritual for the dead, performed every five to seven years in all the villages and towns around Madagascar."

Robert put down his mug of tea and looked with more interest at the small village hidden amongst the coconut grove from where all the noise was coming.

"Relatives come from near and far to exhume their dead loved ones," I continued, "and parade them through the village in their burial shrouds. Then they wrap the bodies in clean white cloths, and write their names in felt tip pen on the new wraps, so everyone knows whose body is whose."

"Ugh, I'm not sure I'd like to carry a smelly old dead body around, singing and dancing for hours and hours," said Robert with a look of disgust, wrinkling his nose.

"Finally, they are returned to their tombs for several years until the next big party," I went on to explain, very pleased with myself for finding out this information. "They don't like tourists seeing this religious, traditional event, so no wonder I wasn't welcome! They drink lots of cheap rum, strong Malagasy rum, and the party was getting louder and louder as I left."

And speaking of cheap rum, we bought ten litres of lethal rocket fuel rum, cut it with 90% water, spiced it with vanilla pods, cinnamon bark and raisins, and left it to mature for several months. Robert made a very fancy label on the computer and stuck it on the bottles. The name was 'Revo Gnah' (Hang Over spelt backwards), and though it tasted smooth and sweet, it had knock-out potency, and was a great success amongst our friends.

Madagascar split from Africa millions of years ago, and has an amazing array of fauna and flora not found anywhere else in the world. We wanted to see lemurs and, as we couldn't leave the boat for more than a few hours, due to Tara's worsening bladder problem, we sailed over to Nosy Komba, the next-door island to Nosy Be, where lemurs are guaranteed. It was a popular stop for tourists and the village of Ampangorina had a great artisan market of woodwork, ceramics, tablecloths, bedspreads, and T shirts – in fact, all the things to gladden a tourist's heart and empty his wallet.

Patrick, our cheerful, sunburnt Malagasy guide, with his French-accented English, said he would take us to where the lemurs lived, up a nearby hill. (French is the official language of Madagascar and everyone learns it at school.)

"The lemurs you will see here are called Black Lemurs. Their Latin name is *Eulemur Macaco*."

"Oh, does that mean they are monkeys?" I asked Patrick. "We come from Brazil, and 'macaco' means 'monkey' in Portuguese."

Patrick flashed a smile full of brilliant white teeth. "Yes Madam, that is true. The lemur is related to the monkey, and, like the monkey, they are very destructive. They raid our gardens, eat our crops, steal our fruit … and the farmers kill them."

"That's terrible," said Robert as we stopped to buy bananas for the lemurs. "Isn't there any way you can protect them?"

"That is why tourism is so important for the lemurs. We try and convince the farmers that tourists bring income to the island; that maybe they should build a small hotel or restaurant, so that they, too, can benefit from the visitors."

"Yes, that makes good sense: do you think it's working?" Robert asked Patrick as we arrived at the lemur feeding station.

And there they were, gambolling through the trees, leaping onto our shoulders, and delicately nibbling at a proffered banana. What pretty animals: the males with very dark fur and bright orange eyes; the ladies a rich chestnut with white ear and cheek tufts. Their long, black fingers clutched our hands, and their silky fur tickled our necks. We were enchanted. How could the local people kill these attractive creatures?

଼ଔ

TARA

Ampangorina had a public laundry area where water ran over great slabs of concrete, and local ladies brought their clothes for a good scrub. Being aware of local superstitions, I went to speak to the women.

"Bonjour, Mesdames, good morning ladies," I greeted them, "could I possibly come and wash my clothes here with you?"

An older woman in a floral sarong and grey hair knotted at the nape of her wrinkled neck, nodded to me.

"Pas de probleme. Voila, you ici, next to me." And she slapped the wet concrete near her.

However, when I returned with my bundle of clothes, all the best spots were taken, and I was relegated to the end of the slab where the dirty water ran off.

The alternative to sharing the dirty laundry water with the village ladies involved a short sail to a nearby beach opposite Nosy Komba Island, where a cool stream burbled down through the forest and over rocks onto the sand. It was a good place to collect clean water for our tanks, and take the laundry buckets with our dirty clothes.

Tara came, too, as there was no-one living on the beach to offend while she rummaged through the leaves on the forest floor and dipped in the stream. One day, however, we were surprised by a National Parks guard, dressed in camouflage uniform, with a smart green beret pulled down over his brow. He had discovered us by the stream, and it was Tara who gave us away; we were hidden from sight in the forest, but she rushed out and barked at him – of course!

"You can't stay here," said the guard, looking quite fierce, "this is National Parks land and you have to get special permission to visit this area, and you certainly cannot have a dog on shore."

"I'm so sorry," said Robert, putting on his most apologetic face, "my name is Robert and this is my wife, Rosemary, and our little dog, Tara. We didn't know we weren't allowed to visit your beautiful forest. Please could we take some water for our tanks, and we won't come back again?"

The guard let down his defences a bit. "My name is Gerard and we try and protect what little we have left of our natural forests. Some people sneak in here to cut down trees – I thought you might be doing that."

Gerard decided we weren't about to destroy the forest or the stream, and when we asked him back to *Deusa*, he was delighted. He saw yachts anchored around the islands all the time, but had never been invited on board one. Here was a floating home, better equipped than his house on land, and he was fascinated. After this encounter, we had no further problems with collecting water and doing our laundry by the pretty stream in the forest.

∞∞

Moving on down the coast, we stopped at many enchanting anchorages, and always looked out for other species of lemur. We were told of a 2000 year old baobab tree; was this possible?

We knew of a huge baobab in South Africa estimated to be 1275 years old, but 2000 years? That had to be a record. The baobab's Latin name is Adansonia, after Michel Adansonia, a French naturalist, and examples can grow up to 30 metres (98 feet) tall, with a diameter of 11 metres (36 feet). A pretty big tree!

So, when we got to Morumba Bay, we set off in the dinghy with instructions for how to find this magical tree. Many nautical miles and litres of gasoline later, we had not found the fabled tree.

"Oh, you've gone quite the wrong way," said a sailing friend, "head for that island over there to the left."

He waved an arm casually towards a whole group of islands. "Curve around to the back of the island and you'll see a small sandy landing. Pull the dinghy up the beach and walk about a hundred metres into the bush, and there you will find this amazing tree."

"Come on, Tara," we said, "we're off to find a mystery tree. You enjoy a dinghy ride, let's go, let's go!"

As always Tara was enchanted to be a passenger, her front legs propped up on the bouncing bow of the dinghy. We insisted she kept her back legs on the floor of the dinghy with only her front legs dangling over the front. The waves and bumps could topple her overboard, and the outboard motor would slice her in two. There were quite a few tussles with this command, and her wilful nature insisted she stand with all four paws on the bow, ready to throw herself into the water at any excuse: a darting fish, a piece of seaweed, a suspicious underwater shadow. My goodness, the things this sharp-eyed dog could see.

We found the elusive tree, tucked around a corner on a small, insignificant beach, only a humble path leading to its magnificent presence. We had met baobabs in Southern Africa, but this fine example beat them all. With its huge girth and stubby arms reaching into the blue sky, it was a majestic and ancient tree; a tree to be respected and revered. Local people had left offerings at the foot of the tree, and requests for solutions to the problems of life.

The baobabs of Madagascar are spectacular: so many different types and so many wonderful shapes. They grow on rugged and impossible terrain – no soil, no nourishment – they cling to craggy cliffs with determination, creating ancient and weird shapes on the skyline.

ഇരിരു

We were lounging in the cockpit reading our books and enjoying the late afternoon sunshine, when Robert suddenly sat up straight, dropping his book on the floor.

"Look over there by the beach, there's something moving through the trees. Have a look through your binoculars, it could be a lemur."

At the word 'lemur,' I leapt up, throwing my book aside. I was determined to see more lemurs, and grabbed my binos lying on the table beside me

"Where? Where? I can't see a thing," I said, frantically searching along the shoreline.

"Calm down, love," said Robert, "you're making enough noise to frighten them away, and just now you'll set off Tara."

TARA

As it was, Tara was peering intently at the island, quite sure that we had seen something of great importance that we needed to tell her about.

Suddenly, they flashed into view, Coquerel's sifakas: shy, beautiful, wild lemurs with white, furry bodies, and dark brown patches on their legs, chests and thighs. We were enchanted.

"Let's go ashore and see if we can get a photo." I suggested to Robert.

"We can certainly try," he replied, "but Tara should stay on board."

Motoring quietly in the dinghy to the shore, we pulled it up on the sand and crept through the rough undergrowth, in an effort to capture the lemurs on camera. Tara was disgusted at not being invited to join the party, but dogs are not known for creeping silently through the bush. The lemurs were very suspicious of us, and kept moving away as we inched forward. After an hour or so, we managed to photograph them and returned to the boat, scratched and prickled by the dense brush, eager to see on the computer how our pictures had turned out.

ജ്ഞ

Trading was always a good challenge for our French on Madagascar. We had a lot of clothes to trade for fish, bananas, paw-paws – even a live chicken – although I wasn't able to kill and pluck the bird. Canoes paddled up to our stern, greeted by a volley of barks. I would seize Tara and peer into the canoe to see what was on offer: a stalk of bananas, some wild honey, a dozen lemons, or a fresh fish. It was always a lucky dip – what would the land and the ocean offer us? Strangely enough, plastic bottles had trade value, so a bunch of bananas could equal two one-litre plastic bottles and a T-shirt. A fish might have a trade value of a fishing line and several hooks.

My French was elementary, but the traders understood, and we had a lot of laughs together. *Their* French was a patois, and we got on well with hand gestures and words. They didn't care about my pronunciation, and trade was the name of the game. This was much more fun than trying to learn French at school!

eighteen

Mozambique and South Africa

Next stop, Mozambique. The winds were right, and we needed to head for Africa as our window of good weather and winds would soon close. Our landfall was Mozambique Island: once an important outpost of the Portuguese colonists, and now fallen into disrepair, but still with some fine old buildings along the waterfront.

Taking the dinghy ashore to check in, we were met by a crowd of youths, offering to look after the dinghy, take us to the Port Captain, take us to the market, the fort, the ancient ruins – anywhere, in fact, as long as we would pay them. Lucky for us we spoke Portuguese, having lived in Brazil for many years, so we soon sorted out who would look after the dinghy, and who would be our guide.

This was an old and dilapidated town in ruin and neglect, but now declared a World Heritage Site. Individuals had bought and renovated old houses, and, bit by bit, it could all come together. The civil war was devastating to Mozambique, and even though it had been over for a good many years, families still squatted in abandoned houses without roofs, lighting cooking fires in the once-elegant living rooms, and keeping a few goats to wander in and out of the corridors and dusty rooms.

Tara was uncomfortable on the sea passages, but cheered up once we got into a calm anchorage or harbour. She still loved going for a dinghy ride and a walk, to see and smell all the exciting things of a new destination. Even though we needed to get on down to South Africa as soon as possible to find a vet, we chose to hop along the coast of Mozambique because of the adverse weather in this region, which constantly affected sailing conditions.

It was a long and sometimes uncomfortable journey, especially when we had to duck into the river leading up to the town of Quelimane. Our steering cable broke as we came into the river mouth, and we had to steer with the emergency rudder, fighting against a four-knot current. It was a scary and unpleasant experience, with one of us calling out the directions from the GPS plotter on the computer down below in the saloon, and the other hand-steering from the aft deck. The sandbanks in the river had moved considerably since the last chart was updated, and at one moment we ran hard aground where it should have been deep water. Tara was jolted out of her basket, and glared angrily at us for being so careless. Robert and I glared at each other for the same reason.

"You gave me the wrong directions," muttered Robert.

"I jolly well did not. You heard me wrong!"

This wasn't going to get us out of the situation, as the current swung us more and more towards the river bank. Luckily, with the power of our strong motor, we managed to reverse off the bank, and found a channel that took us on up to the port.

The port was filled with a fleet of Chinese fishing boats, harvesting the ocean off the coast. We anchored amongst them; there was nowhere else to go. It was a worry that, with the turn of the tide we would swing into each other, depending on how much anchor chain they had out. The river had very swift currents of up to 4 knots, with only an hour of slack at the top and bottom of the tides; this made getting in and out of the dinghy very tricky when we wanted to go to shore. A violent storm was blowing along the coast, and the ham radio network told us to stay in harbour for at least a week while it passed.

The first night we were woken by a thump against the hull at 2am, and thought we had been hit by a passing log. Then Tara, up on deck, went off like a rocket, barking fit to burst. Rubbing the sleep out of our eyes, we arrived on deck to see two lads in a dugout canoe, clinging to the side of the yacht, near to where the outboard motor was stored on the stern railing.

"What are you doing here?" Robert asked them in Portuguese.

"Oh, just fishing," they replied, letting go and drifting away into the darkness.

We stumbled back to bed, and next morning, when we were ready to put the dinghy and outboard motor into the water, we discovered something interesting.

"The little buggers," said Robert, "they were in the process of stealing our dinghy motor when we woke up. Look at this, they've undone the bolts holding the motor onto the support and cut through the security webbing."

They obviously didn't realise how heavy the motor was, or that we had a watchdog on board. If they had dropped the motor into their little wooden canoe, they would have sunk to the bottom of the river, canoe, motor, and all.

Now that we had the dinghy and motor set up, we went ashore to check in, leaving Tara guarding the boat. Mozambique requires yachts to check in at every harbour where they stop.

The sleepy ladies in rumpled, white uniforms, slumped at their desks in Immigration, insisted we pay a fee. We had already been confronted by Immigration at Mozambique Island with the same request. At that time – and after some discussion – they decided we were a private yacht and didn't have to pay anything.

But here we were again being told to pay.

"Please show me the regulation that says, as a private yacht, we have to pay?" Robert asked the plump and sweaty staff in his best Portuguese.

"Um momento, por favor," said the more senior-looking woman, reaching for some dusty files.

There was much thumbing of manuals, shaking of heads and clicking of tongues before they finally agreed that there was nothing to pay. No wonder so many yachts hesitated to sail along the Mozambique coast, given the difficulty with officials on the take. Not for the first time were we very glad we could speak their language.

𝕤𝕠𝕔𝕤

Sailing on down the coast, our next stop was in the Bazaruto Archipelago at Santa Carolina Island, where we had spent our honeymoon 38 years previously – a long time ago when we still lived in Rhodesia/Zimbabwe: how about that?! In those days there was a smart hotel, a fishing boat, and snorkelling – fun things to do on the island – but now it was all gone; the hotel abandoned and crumbling into the sea where the waves had eaten away the foundations. A couple of cyclones hadn't helped, either. The only occupants on the island were a National Parks warden and a caretaker.

The Bazaruto Archipelago of five islands, of which Santa Carolina is one, is the largest marine park in Africa, and, amongst others things, protects some of the last dugongs –a marine mammal of the order *Sirenia* - on the east coast of Africa. Walking along the clean and sea-swept beach with Tara the next morning, we were met by the irate warden, dressed in drab brown uniform, with a National Parks badge stitched to his breast pocket.

"Hey, you!" he called arrogantly in Portuguese. "What are you doing here? Where's your entrance ticket?"

"Bom dia, Senhor," I said, hanging on to Tara, who was eyeing him suspiciously, "we came here by sailboat and didn't know about an entrance ticket."

"Everyone knows they have to pay an entrance fee. You must pay a fine right now, otherwise I shall report you to the authorities." He glared at me as if I was a threat to national security.

At this moment, Diego Ernesto, the island's caretaker, arrived, rescuing Tara and me from being locked up and deported.

"Look," he said to the officious guard, "that's their boat over there. They haven't been to Vilanculos yet, so of course they couldn't buy a ticket from the Parks office. They can pay me and I'll radio the mainland to let them know."

The fellow calmed down and wandered back to his dilapidated shack on the beach. Diego Ernesto offered to take us on a tour of the island, so I went back to *Deusa* to pick up Robert.

"I've met a charming Mozambican, and he says he will show us around the island." I told him.

Back on shore, Diego Ernesto was waiting for us.

"Come and look over here by the tall trees. Do you see these crumbling ruins? They used to be old houses, where the slaves were kept, chained to the walls, and fattened up for the long sea voyage to Brazil."

"Do you know, Diego," said Robert, "the nearby town where we lived in Brazil once had a slave market long ago; maybe the same poor slaves that were captive here, arrived in the town of Santa Cruz to be sold."

It was a sobering thought, one of suffering and anguish for thousands of people, and we talked about it with Diego as we walked up the old abandoned airstrip, where he wanted to show us another landmark.

"Look at these two graves, side by side, one large and one small. This is where the governor's wife and tiny baby are buried. Her name was Carolina, and the island is called after her." He pulled up some weeds growing tall by the gravestones. What a lonely and far-away place to die in childbirth.

Diego Ernesto was an educated man, an historian who ran a cultural programme on the local radio when he went back to Vilanculos on the mainland. Funnily enough, we met him again a year later when we went there by road to set up a dive centre, but that's a whole other story.

From Santa Carolina we sailed on to Inhambane, our point of check out, before heading for South Africa and Richards Bay, where we hoped to find a vet for Tara. She was such a brave little girl, putting up with rough seas and discomfort, always prepared to be cheerful and welcome a walk along a sandy beach when we stopped.

Once again we were challenged by Immigration when we went to check out of Mozambique.

"Where is your piece of paper saying 'Tourist Visa?' demanded the short, fat man behind the imposing wooden counter of the Immigration office. Hundreds of people milled around us, trying desperately to catch the eye of indifferent officials, sheltered from the irritated crowd by glass and wood barriers.

"We don't have a piece of paper," we argued. "The visa's stamped in our passports. Have a look, right there under the Mozambican entry stamp."

It was hot and dusty, and we had been standing there for hours, trying to check out. Why was it all so difficult? It took several conferences with other officials, obviously higher up the authority chain, for us to finally be stamped out of the country and sent on our way. Once again, we thanked our lucky stars we spoke the language.

ജഇൽ

And so we continued south, heading for Richards Bay some three days' sail away, with our one thought in mind: find a cure for Tara. What a pleasure to check in to South Africa in comparison to the challenges of Mozambique. As soon as we could we went to look for a vet.

Several people in the marina had dogs, and they told us there was a good veterinary practice in Meerensee, a small village near Richards Bay.

Hiring a car, I drove over there, with Tara sitting on a pile of towels on the back seat because of her leaking bladder, promising her we were going to find a solution to all her troubles.

At the clinic we met Stella Hitchens, a young and friendly vet with a mop of curly hair.

"I need to take an x-ray of Tara's bladder, but meanwhile we must stop this pain and infection. I'll give you a course of antibiotics and anti-inflammatories for her: if you'll just sit in the waiting room while I take the x-ray, we can find out exactly what the problem is."

Tara gave me a baleful stare as she was led away by Stella.

Twenty minutes later a relieved Tara was delivered to my side, and Stella showed me the x-rays.

"No wonder poor Tara was suffering such a lot of pain," said Stella, " look at this." She held the x-rays up to the light. "All these lumps you can see are struvites, a type of calcium deposit that builds up into pyramid-shaped stones in the bladder. The only solution is to operate, but there could be complications."

I looked at Stella, very worried about what she was going to say next. Tara couldn't carry on in this condition; it was a miserable existence for her. What if they operated and she died? She was now 11 years old, and still had a lot of living to do as a well dog.

"With big stones like these," Stella continued, stroking Tara's floppy ears, "the bladder wall could be compromised, and, if that's the case, we might have to insert a catheter to bypass the bladder."

"Thank you, Stella," I said, very shakily, "I need to speak to my husband, Robert, before we make a final decision, but we know she can't go on like this."

Back on *Deusa* with Tara curled up between us in the cockpit, I told Robert the outcome of our visit.

Robert looked horrified. "What if she dies on the operating table? She's been with us for such a long time; it would be like losing our best friend. But, you know, there's no alternative, she must have the op."

So, feeling very sad and with heavy hearts, we phoned Stella and Tara was booked in to the veterinary clinic in two weeks' time. Stella wanted the anti-biotics to control the infection before she operated. This meant that we would have only fourteen more days of Tara's companionship and love before we sent her off, perhaps never to return again.

෧෬

We waited around anxiously on the day she was operated on, wondering if our marvellous little dog would face this ultimate challenge in her long life. She had survived so many dramas, never given up against all odds, and was always ready to take on whatever life threw at her.

"You know," said Robert as he gazed sadly into his coffee cup, sitting on *Deusa* waiting for Stella to call us, "we've got to face the fact that Tara isn't going to live forever. She's not young anymore, and this operation might just be too much for her."

I sighed and put my arm around his broad shoulders. "Tara has been the best dog we've ever had. She's lived so close to us for so long. I once had a Spaniel when I was a child, and he lived to be eighteen, but a lot of the time I was away at school, so it wasn't the same relationship."

"I've had several dogs as I grew up, and I was particularly fond of one of them. He was called Dr Banda, and he was very, very clever. But not as clever as Tara; I don't think I've ever met a dog with as much intelligence as her." Robert stopped gazing into his coffee cup and threw the dregs overboard.

At last the phone rang and Robert leapt to answer it, putting it on loudspeaker so we could both hear the conversation.

"You'll be very happy to know that the operation has been successful." Stella's voice came through clearly. "Tara has come round from the anaesthetic and has already drunk some water. The bladder wall was not too compromised, and I didn't have to put in a bypass to the urethra."

I burst into tears of relief, Robert looked away, mopping his eyes; he could hardly speak.

"Thank you so much, Stella, that's the best news we've heard for ages. We've been sitting here biting our nails and drinking coffee, afraid to answer the phone when it rang, in case it was bad news."

"No, the news is very good, but I think you should let her rest for at least 48 hours before you come and visit her. I don't want her getting too excited just yet."

As soon as she had recuperated and we were allowed to see her, we rushed over to the clinic to find our beloved Tara, standing wagging her tail at us in her cosy kennel, a row of black stitches in her pink tummy

Stella handed us a jar with five enormous triangular stones, and a whole handful of smaller ones. These stones had to be the cause of her shivering and shaking after swimming: they got cold and took a long time to warm up again.

"I think she should stay here for a few days, so I can observe her," recommended Stella, "I don't want her bouncing around your boat and tearing out the stitches."

Once again this extraordinary little dog had overcome amazing odds, better than we had dared to hope. Stella looked after her very well, giving her love and attention and taking her for gentle walks, which was amazing dedication, considering she was a hard-working vet.

ഇന്‍ങ്ങ

When we first arrived in Richards Bay, and before Tara went for her operation, we stayed in the Tuzi Gazi marina, as this was the check-in point, and where, unbeknownst to us, a vicious Boxer dog lived on a catamaran in the marina. I was walking back to *Deusa* with Tara and a bag of groceries one day, when the Boxer flew off his boat and grabbed Tara by the throat.

"Help! Help! Someone help me!" I screamed at the top of my voice, having learnt in Brazil to make as much noise as possible if attacked.

Several men ran to my rescue, chucking the two dogs into the water, which made the Boxer let go. Tara was bleeding from the mouth and the ear, and I had dropped my groceries all over the dock. I was absolutely furious: a dog like that should be tied up and not allowed to terrorize the dock. When I got back to the boat, with Tara dripping blood, I told Robert what had happened to us.

He leapt off *Deusa* and marched over to the offending boat, calling the owner.

"Listen here," he said, "you can't have a dog like that loose on the dock, you must make sure he can't jump off your boat. He's bitten my dog and you will have to pay the vet's bills."

"Fuck off!" shouted the red-faced, burly man. "I'll let my dog do what he bloody well likes, and don't come here giving me orders. I'm going to fight you, just you watch out."

He was a newcomer to yachting, and obviously didn't know much about the unwritten laws of good manners in marinas. I wasn't too happy about Robert being challenged to a fight; this was brawling bar talk. Luckily, it was all bravado, and after causing more trouble in the marina, he and the dog were asked to leave. Tara's wounds were superficial, and she didn't have to be stitched, just cleaned up with antiseptic. She had bitten her tongue and her ear had a little split in it, but nothing too serious, thank heavens, as she was already suffering quite enough pain and discomfort.

From that time on, I always carried Tara out of the marina until I got beyond the security gate and couldn't be attacked. Thank goodness she was a carrying size, and I could easily tuck her under my arm. However, we decided this was not the place to stay and found a much nicer marina, the Zululand Yacht Club, with pleasant grounds to walk Tara, and friendly people.

⟡⟡⟡

Our nephew and niece-in-law, Kyle and Nicole, wanted to start a dive centre in Mozambique, as they were both PADI dive instructors and taught scuba diving in Harare. It seemed a good idea for us to go into a partnership with them, and set up a business in Vilanculos: we thought we knew the Brazilian/Portuguese rules and regulations for setting up a business, and they had all the necessary knowledge for teaching scuba diving and taking clients out onto the reefs.

"What do you think about living in Mozambique for a while, love?" Robert asked me over a cup of coffee, sitting on *Deusa*.

"It could be fun - a new adventure - but what about *Deusa*?" I asked, wondering whether we could leave her at the marina in Richards Bay. "How long do you think we'd go for?"

"To set up a new business and get it running smoothly takes a minimum of three years. Maybe we should think of selling *Deusa* and go back to living on land? We're not getting any younger, you know."

What a thought. Sell our beloved yacht, which had been our home for the past twenty years, had looked after us through thick and thin, shown us what a beautiful world we live in. A dreadful idea, but a practical one, nevertheless, and we finally decided it was for the best. But what a hard decision: we talked about it long into the night with Tara sitting between us in the cockpit. Did we really want to give up this free and adventurous lifestyle, wandering in the world where our fancy and the wind took us? The South African coastline was not the most hospitable to sail along, but perhaps we could go back to the Caribbean where we had spent many happy years.

TARA

The reality of growing older was a very serious consideration. We were still both fit and well, and it was easy to sail in fair weather. But what about the foul – I hated it and wouldn't be sorry not to face another storm again. Robert was always the adventurer, but agreed that some of the challenges we had faced were no fun.

There was something else we had to consider. On our yacht we could change our anchorage as we pleased. If the neighbouring yacht was doing trombone practice at night – well, we could move. But being on land was an entirely different kettle of fish! What if we landed up with the neighbours from hell? We couldn't just pick up the anchor and sail away, but that is the risk we took.

We advertised *Deusa* for sale on several websites, and when we had an offer, we knew that this was what we wanted. The buyer asked for the boat to be delivered to Cape Town, and we decided to sail her there, without thinking that perhaps it would be a good idea to ask for a deposit first ...

Tara needed to go into kennels for the time it would take us to get to the Cape, because it would not be a pleasant journey for her, and we certainly were not looking forward to it. We contacted Tannie Rina, the lovely lady with all the small dogs, and booked in Tara for a month. How long would it take us? We didn't know, because sailing the South African coastline – with its high winds and even higher waves – was very tricky. Many ships had been lost along this treacherous route: it wasn't called the 'wild coast' for nothing. I persuaded myself that this would be my swan song – one way or another ...

As we expected, rough weather and hostile seas ensured it was not a nice passage, but we finally made it, only to be told that *Deusa* was not exactly what the prospective buyer was looking for, so no sale! Stupid us! Now we had a boat in Cape Town, a dog in Richards Bay, and the possibility of a business in Vilanculos, Mozambique: great!

In Richards Bay we had bought a car, so a friend very kindly drove it down to Cape Town for us, a journey of 1200 miles, so we could return to Richards Bay, pick up our precious dog, and drive on up to Mozambique to start a new life. We said goodbye to our beloved *Deusa*, who had carried us so many thousands of miles, and left her in a safe marina in Cape Town. Patting her on the bow, we told her to be a good ship, and headed back by road to get Tara.

"Have you heard that, once you take a dog into Mozambique, you can't bring it back to South Africa again?" I asked Robert.

"Yes, I believe so, but I also know that many people come and go from Mozambique to Zimbabwe, taking their dogs with them, so that border can't be a problem."

Mozambique has a huge rabies problem, which is why, once a dog enters the country, he or she may not return to South Africa. However, as we had family in Zimbabwe, we could always go and visit them, taking Tara out of Mozambique, then go from Zimbabwe to South Africa, as here there was no border quarantine control concerning dogs. What we needed now was a permit from the Mozambique Embassy to allow Tara to travel to its country, and this all took time.

Luckily, we *had* time as we were staying with Pete and Stella Hitchins in Richards Bay, not having *Deusa* to live on any more. They had become very good friends to us, and it was Stella who operated on Tara to take out the bladder stones, then cared for her so well while we were away. Using their house as a base, we were able to get Tara's permit and ready ourselves for a new life in Vilanculos.

Tara was delighted to see us when we picked her up from Tannie Rina. She was in very good health, and had made friends with all the other little dogs in the house.

"Now, Tara dog, listen very carefully," Robert told her, "we are setting off on a long drive, and will be going through a border post. Don't bark at anyone, even if they are wearing dark glasses and look like policemen. They mightn't take kindly to little dogs barking at them, and turn us back."

Tara laughed in Robert's face and wagged her tail furiously. She was so pleased to be back with her family, and leapt around the car, bouncing from the back seat to the front seat and back again.

When we got to the South African border with Mozambique, a stern quarantine official confronted us.

"Do you know that if you take this dog into Mozambique, she will never come back?" she scowled at us.

"Yes, we understand," we nodded.

"If you come back here with the dog, we will take her off you and destroy her."

"Yes, we understand" we repeated, fingers crossed behind our backs. The quarantine officials were really fierce.

೮Ω೮ೞ

And so began our lives in Mozambique, believing that we knew all the answers to any problems with Portuguese bureaucracy, having lived for some time in Brazil. What we had not considered was the African overlay. This was a whole new learning experience, as well as a challenge to cut through the muddle of red tape, open a new business, and obtain all the documents we needed to operate.

Fortunately, there was a self-catering chalet for us to move into at the lodge where the dive centre would be established. Coming off a boat, we had no furniture; only a picnic basket of cutlery and crockery, one dog bed, and one dog. The chalets were furnished and very nice, built in a shady garden, overlooking the ocean.

Robert's first job was to rebuild the old dive centre that had been abandoned some time ago, which meant tearing off the old roof and rotten beams, replacing them with new beams and new thatch. This was harvested some distance away, and arrived by sailing dhow - very traditional. Mozambique must be one of the few places in the world where traditional sailing dhows are still used for everyday commerce, and it was very pleasing to see them sail out to sea on the morning breeze, returning late in the day with the evening current. What a good thing we could speak Portuguese as it made things a lot easier working with the local people. We had to get everything ready as quickly as possible, as our family from Zimbabwe would be arriving in a month or so with boats and equipment to start the business.

Living with Tara on land was quite a different experience, too.

"What do you think is going on in Tara's little head?" Robert asked me one evening as we sat on the verandah of the chalet, gazing out at the golden sea, touched with the sun's last rays.

"She must be very puzzled that she now lives at floor level. She really only met our knees at eye level when we took her off *Deusa* for a walk, otherwise she'd be sitting on the settee with us in the saloon, or above us in the cockpit in her day bed."

"Yes, and even at night she was above us on her bed by the aft portholes – she must be very confused."

Tara slept next to us on her own bed in the bedroom, though she didn't have her own personal mosquito net. We could hear her snapping and shaking her head all night as the mosquitoes nibbled her ears, so we bought her a small net to go over her bed. But it didn't do the trick, and we realised that we were also getting mosquitoes inside our net tucked round the bed, however careful we were. Mozambique has malaria, so it was very important not to get bitten, yet here we were with red dots all over us each morning.

The windows of the room were mosquito-proofed, and we sprayed the whole area before going to bed, but *still* the pesky blighters flooded in. Then we checked the floor. This was slatted, and the chalet was built at least half a metre off the ground for coolness ... but also for mosquitoes to hide in the darkness during the day. At night they rose in their thousands, following the scent of our carbon dioxide breath as it drifted tantalizingly down through the floor planks. No wonder we were being eaten alive! The only solution was reed mats, made by the local ladies, and sold in the marketplace. Four for us and one for Tara: finally, we all got a good night's sleep!

Many mangy, ravenous dogs lived on the beaches around Vilanculos, and wandered into the resort looking for scraps. This was another danger: Mozambique has a lot of rabies, and no-one owned these feral dogs. An impossible thing to control, they were too wild to capture and vaccinate. Anyone bitten by a dog was rushed off to hospital for a course of injections, whether or not the dog was rabid. Many people died of rabies each year, and a horrid death it was, too.

Part of the reason for deciding to take on the project of helping to set up the scuba diving school in Mozambique was that Kyle was the son of Robert's brother, Michael, and Robert wanted to support him and his family on a new venture, and get them out of a crumbling Zimbabwe. The family arrived with three children, two dogs and four cats. One of the dogs, Noel, was a large, black bitch with the markings of a Doberman inherited from her dubious bloodline. She was definitely an Alpha female, and soon had all the beach dogs under control, seeing them off the property with a few smart nips.

Noel loved going down to the sea to help launch the dive boats, and would get involved in the local football games amongst the fishermen's kids. Only she did not play fair, and once bit someone who got in the way.

A delegation from the football match marched up to the dive centre.

"Your dog has bitten me on the foot," said a tall, gangly youth, in Portuguese. "You must take me to the hospital for an anti-rabies injection, and I want compensation for being bitten."

Robert was called in to translate. Money was handed out, and the victim taken to the hospital. All our animals were vaccinated and we had to take proof of this to the doctor on duty, whenever someone was bitten.

Unfortunately, this became a way for unscrupulous locals to make money. Anyone who stumbled on a rock or was scratched by a stick would appear at the dive centre, claiming that Noel had bitten him, demanding compensation, and to be driven to hospital for the antidote. Noel had to be kept off the beach at all costs, so for a while remained tied up at the dive centre. However, she soon learned to chew through the toughest rope, and sneak back down to the beach for another game of football.

She'd also chase the taxi trucks, crowded with people perched along the sides of the open back, squashed into the middle, clinging desperately to the cab roof. And this is how she nearly got killed, as one annoyed citizen swung a machete at her, slicing her across the head, narrowly missing her eye. It was a deep wound down to the skull, and, as there was no vet in Vilanculos, Noel lay forlornly under the dive centre table for many days with a terrible headache. Being a healthy dog, she eventually recovered, but never chased another vehicle. In fact, she was so badly affected by the accident that she was never the same dog again, preferring to stay close to home and not romp on the beach. It was a tough lesson for her to learn, but we had no more problems with paying out compensation.

Tara was now an old lady of twelve, who didn't enjoy the beach or swimming any more, preferring to stay close by Robert wherever he was. Because she had stayed with Tannie Rina, she had become much more accustomed to other dogs, and didn't bother about them. Fortunately, she and Noel tolerated each other, and the family cats stood their ground when Tara tried to chase them – there is nothing more boring than a cat who refuses to run.

Tara did make one friend in Mozambique, and that was Brum, a handsome, brown beach dog with a docked tail, who used to come and sleep on our veranda. The cleaning staff hated him because he was a biter, and any time they saw him they would whack him with a broom or chase him away with a bucket of water. Of course, the more aggressive they were to him, the more aggressive he became to them. The lodge visitors took pity on him, and would often feed him morsels from their meals.

One day we noticed that Brum was missing but thought nothing of it; he was a free dog and nobody owned him, after all. Our family's girls, Savannah and Sabrina, were down on the beach at low tide looking for shells, when one of them noticed something strange in the mangroves.

TARA

· "There's something in the mangroves," Sabrina called to her elder sister, "I'm going to check it out."

Getting closer she saw it was a dog tied up with wire, amongst the roots of the trees, his head all bloody, with cuts on his body.

"Hey, Savannah, come and help me. It's a dog and he looks pretty bad; someone has beaten him up."

The two girls recognised Brum, tied up and left to drown with the rising tide.

Because he knew the girls, Brum let them untie him and carry him up to our house in the lodge, where we laid him on a bed on the veranda and tried to clean him up. He was very damaged – blinded in one eye, and cut across the head and shoulders, as if he had been slashed by a knife. Why his attackers didn't kill him there and then is a mystery, but maybe they thought he would suffer a slower death by drowning in the rising sea. People can be so unbelievably cruel.

Coincidentally, one of the guests staying at the lodge was a vet who came down from Zimbabwe every year and looked after the local animals, setting up his veterinary practice at the back of his chalet. The white folk would bring their pets to be neutered, spayed, vaccinated, and generally treated for any problems they were unable to fix. We carried Brum over to him wrapped in a blanket.

"I don't think I can save this dog's eye," he said, "it looks like he has been hit with a rock. I'm going to anaesthetise, him and while he's under, I'll castrate him as I see he's got canine VD. Look at these warts: I'll cut them out, too."

Brum came back to our veranda half-conscious, with a bandage around his head and wound medicine dabbed everywhere. The vet couldn't save the eye so stitched it closed. Being a strong dog, Brum soon recovered, but didn't wander too far from our veranda where he got a good meal once a day, eating side by side with Tara.

ಬಿಲ್

A couple of months later we moved down the beach about a kilometre away and Brum stayed at the lodge, which was his territory. But not for long. Noel, having recovered from her head wound, bullied him horribly, so he found his way over to us and was adopted by our night watchman, Sergio. We still fed Brum together with Tara, but he spent his days with Sergio on the beach where he was building a fishing boat. When Sergio came to work in the evening, Brum was a companion to him through the long, lonely hours of the night. It was interesting that Brum and Sergio formed this bond after Brum had been so cruelly treated by local Mozambicans.

After the vet returned to Zimbabwe, unfortunately, Tara developed a tumour by one of her nipples. At first it was just a small bump, but grew larger and larger by the month. Another vet arrived in town and we took her over to see him. "I don't have the right equipment with me to cut out the tumour," he said, "and it could be very risky, she might bleed to death. You're better off leaving it alone."

It was the risk we took in coming to Mozambique, both for ourselves and our dog. The local hospital had been trashed by Cyclone Flavio a couple of years ago, and was still in total disrepair, with one doctor taking care of a population of 30,000 people. The nursing staff were good at sewing on fingers, hacked off while opening coconuts, pulling thorns from feet, and curing malaria. Within half-an-hour of a blood test they had a result, and dosed the sick person with a host of pills at no cost. All of this medication was provided by the Bill and Melinda Gates Foundation.

A number of times we took our family's kids for tests. Anyone with a headache – which can be symptomatic of malaria – was bundled into the car and rushed to hospital, because Mozambican malaria is falciparum and extremely dangerous. After a while, they learnt not to admit to headaches anymore because the finger prick test was painful!

One family member, Archie, got so sick with malaria he was hospitalised in the emergency sector on a urine-stained bed, with a drip in his arm. We went to rescue him and, as we were driving back through 'thieves alley,' we checked that the doors of our vehicle were firmly locked. Robert was driving, and Archie was sitting next to him, hallucinating and muttering all sorts of strange things. I was in the back seat leaning forward, talking to Archie and telling him everything was alright. I glanced over my shoulder and saw a woolly head right next to me, its owner throwing our tools and other possessions out of the back door onto the sand road. Obviously, the rear door lock hadn't engaged, and one of the rogues and bandits who rob unsuspecting motorists on this small stretch of road had opened the back door and jumped in.

"Stop, stop," I yelled to Robert, "there's someone in the car stealing our stuff."

The vehicle skidded to a stop and, amazingly, Archie recovered his sanity, leaping out of the vehicle in hot pursuit of the shadowy figures melting into the bushes surrounding the bamboo huts by the track. Robert and I rushed after Archie and hauled him back to the car where he collapsed in a heap, muttering strange incantations.

The thief had tossed all of our tools onto the road and an accomplice had gathered them up.

"Oh, bloody hell," swore Robert, "those tools came off *Deusa* and were old, as well as useful, friends."

Several days later, someone broke into a boat anchored in the bay. He was surprised by the night watchman before he managed to steal the radio, battery, fishing rod, and other bits and pieces, foolishly left on board. Several tools were found on board and taken to the boat owner who was staying at the lodge. He didn't recognise any of them and brought them over to the dive centre, telling us about the attempted robbery. Robert took one look at the tools, wrapped in a greasy cloth, and exclaimed, "They're mine, I've known these tools for years, and they were swiped from my car the other night!" He was so pleased to have his tools back where they belonged.

Foreign residents had always to be one step ahead of the local petty crime squad. Friends of ours had a riding school, and riding hats and bits of saddlery would go missing, only to turn up somewhere for sale, dangling on sticks along some dusty path, and they bought them back again. You did have to ask who would be wanting riding equipment in darkest Mozambique besides them?

We bought fuel for running the boats out to the reef, and initially got it in 25-litre containers tucked into the open back of a Toyota Land Cruiser. The kids used to ride in the back with the cans. One day, having filled up with 400 litres of gasoline, Kyle was driving slowly past the crowded market street when a skinny local lad reached a long arm over the side of the vehicle, seized a full can, hauled it up and away, and vanished into the swirling mass of humanity.

"Dad! Dad! Stop! Stop!" yelled the kids, thumping on the cab roof. "Someone is stealing the fuel."

Of course, by the time Kyle came to a stop, the thief was nowhere to be seen amongst the milling crowd, so he went straight to the police station to report the crime.

The overweight and grumpy policeman, the buttons of his uniform straining across his distended stomach, leaned back in his chair, and drummed his gold-ringed fingers on the coffee-stained desk.

"There is nothing we can do about it," he said, "you will just have to drive faster."

"How can I," said Kyle, "there're people everywhere; I might knock down someone."

"That's your problem," said the policeman, now bored with the conversation, fiddling with his cell phone.

From then on we collected fuel in 250-litre drums strapped securely into the back of the vehicle.

Another favourite trick was for the thief to stand near a vehicle as it was parking, and as the driver got out and pressed the central locking button, flick open the back door so that the locking pin didn't connect. The driver would walk away, happy in the knowledge that the vehicle was locked, while street lads opened the unlocked door and helped themselves to whatever was inside.

I got caught like this when I was buying provisions for the dive centre, and lost two crates of Coca-Cola. Amazingly enough, I got them back, though, because the Tourist Board had organised Tourist Police, local lads in uniform who spoke a bit of English, and helped bewildered tourists lost in the maze of the market, or in the complications of the Portuguese language. These uniformed kids knew me, because I had taken their photos and made them name badges to wear with their smart, blue outfits, so they came to my rescue, pursuing the thief to his shack where he had stashed the drink.

ಬುಡಿ

The lodge where we lived was right next door to the residential houses belonging to the Teachers Training College just a short distance up the road. The Mozambique government had built seven of these Teachers Training Colleges throughout the country, and one was up the road from us. We heard that six Cuban teachers were living there and teaching at the college, and as we had sailed to Cuba and enjoyed it so much, we looked them up.

It was just the best thing we did. These charming people, three men and three women, really brightened our lives while we lived in Vilanculos, always having parties, playing music, dancing, and generally having fun. We communicated in a kind of Portuguese/Spanish language mix, and often had them over for a meal or cup of coffee.

At one time we had to move out of the lodge, and, as the Cubans were going back home over the Christmas holidays, we stayed in one of their houses for a month, whilst looking for a house to rent. It was quite an experience, and we had to keep Tara firmly under control as there were pigs, cats, chickens, goats, and guinea-fowl, wandering around outside the front door. With no fence to keep in a dog, just an open tract of land with an outer wall circling the twenty or so houses of the teaching staff, Tara arrived at and departed the house on a lead, and could only be liberated once we reached the dive centre in the lodge grounds.

One day, when I wasn't looking, Tara slipped out of the door. Next minute, I heard a tremendous cackling and flapping of wings as fifty guinea-fowl took to the air in a flurry of black-and-white spots, with a black-and-white dog joyfully tearing after them. One bird did not become airborne quick enough, and Tara locked her jaws onto its tail feathers, dragging it into the dirt where she began to maul it. We battled to get it away from her, carrying the limp and stunned bird to the owner's house.

"Is Vicente home," Robert asked his puzzled wife, "I need to speak to him." Just then, Vicente appeared behind her.

"I'm terribly sorry, Vicente; our dog chased and caught one of your guinea-fowls." Robert looked most remorseful, holding out the limp bird. "Please let me pay you for it."

"Oh, don't worry," said Vicente, taking the speckled body and laying it on the ground by his feet, "I've got lots of guinea-fowl, and this one will recover, it's just fainted from shock."

Tall, slim Vicente was a most interesting man, who spoke Russian, English, Portuguese, and Chitswa, the local dialect. He had spent time in Siberia studying IT. As the first president of Mozambique after independence in 1974, Samora Machel sent young people to the Communist block to study, returning to Mozambique as qualified engineers, electricians, mariners, and IT experts, to help the country's people. Vicente taught computer technology to the students at the Teachers Training College. He kept us entertained with some of his hilarious experiences amongst Russians who had never met a black person. One lady proposed marriage as she found him so exotic.

When the Cubans returned from their holidays we moved to the house where Brum joined us. It had a baobab tree, and a lovely wild garden, and looked across the sea to the distant islands. We'd watch the dhows sail out to fish in the early morning, returning with the afternoon breeze.

The fishermen used a path near our house, and we often bought a

TARA

fresh fish for dinner. No-one knew how much the fish weighed, and as we didn't have a scale, Robert rigged up an ingenious invention: a plank of wood with a rope through the middle looped over the branch of a tree. On one end was a hook to dangle the fish, and on the other, an empty bucket into which he poured litres of water until a balance was reached. The fishermen understood it, we understood it, and a fair price was reached.

A very handsome, tiger-striped tom cat adopted us in our new house. Part African wild cat, part domestic moggy, he was very unpredictable, liking to be stroked, but suddenly striking out with a fistful of claws. He and Tara had the same dinner menu of fish and rice, though she ate on the front veranda, and he ate at the back door. If I didn't put his food down quick enough he would bite me in the leg. I was intrigued to tame this feral cat, but it was a painful experience. He had no fear of Tara, and when she barked at him, he merely glared at her, turning his back and strolling away, his striped tail in the air.

In the winter months green vegetables were in short supply. I had read in our tree book that young baobab leaves were tasty, so, as soon as they started to sprout, I harvested a bowlful and cooked them like spinach. Robert was most suspicious initially, but admitted it was better than tinned peas. I asked our gardener, Jordao, if he had ever eaten baobab leaves.

He looked at me in disgust.

"I will never ever eat baobab leaves again. As a child in the civil war, we were starving, and my mother made us kids eat baobab leaves. We hated them but they helped keep us alive."

The war was more than thirty years ago, but for the Mozambicans it is still a bitter memory of hardship and death.

Jordao knew a lot about plants and trees, their curative and magical powers, as his father was a herbalist from whom he had learnt a great deal. The sandpaper tree, with its rough leaves, featured in local folklore, and Jordao showed me where it grew in the garden

"When a woman gives birth, her husband has to walk into the bush and gather a root of the sandpaper tree," said Jordao, picking a leaf for me to feel its raspy texture. "Once he has found the tree he must walk in a direct line back to his house, and, on the way, find a dead tree, from which he cuts a piece of root." He demonstrated a nearby stump with its roots sticking out of the sand.

"When the man gets back home, he makes a fire and burns the live sandpaper tree root together with the dead tree root, gathers the ashes, stirs them into a glass of water, and gives it to his wife to drink. This potion ensures that the afterbirth comes away and there is no infection."

The tree was well named as the leaf that Jordao gave me to hold was just like sandpaper.

೮೦೦೮

In the summer months we didn't walk around barefoot in the evenings – not even in the house – because this was scorpion time, and although the

Mozambican variety don't kill you, they cause terrible pain. Sometimes, though, we forgot to put on our shoes.

One sunset we were having a drink on the veranda when Tara came limping in, holding her right forepaw high in the air, close by her ear, and whimpering. Tara never complained, never made a sound, however much pain she was in, so this must have been really bad.

"What's wrong, Tara?" Robert asked our unhappy dog as she looked up at him mournfully, the foot waving by her head. "Come, let's see what you've got in your paw."

He tried to see if there were any bite marks, worrying about poisonous snakes, but there was nothing to see.

Tara lay down in her bed, panting heavily, and then became paralyzed and couldn't move.

"She's really ill, Robert," I said, a feeling of panic rising in my throat. "What can we do for her, she looks like she's dying."

Robert put his hand on my shoulder as I crouched by Tara. "There's nothing, really, we can do but stay beside her, talk to her and stroke her so she knows we're nearby. We'll take it in turns to watch her; after all, we're used to taking watches on passage in *Deusa*."

Tara lived through the night, and we carried her out on a blanket the next morning to pee, supporting her body as she squatted.

By now, we had guessed that it must be a scorpion sting that was afflicting her, and we waited to see if she could beat the poison in her little body; the locals often got stung by scorpions when working in their fields or walking home in the dark. Scorpions come out to hunt at night and are attracted to light, whether this be fire, torchlight, electric or gas light. Our night watchman, Sergio, would light a small fire in summer, but sit well away from it, enjoying the warm glow from a distance. His cure for a scorpion sting was to slice the wound with a razor, and pour gasoline into the cut. The pain must have been excruciating, but perhaps it finally deadened it.

It was a week before Tara could walk properly, and she never patted a scorpion with her paw again.

Robert was walking barefoot from the bedroom one evening when he gave a yelp of pain and swore at me for dropping a needle on the floor. Hobbling over to where I sat, he pointed to his foot, and asked me to pull it out. I couldn't see a thing, yet there he was, moaning and groaning with pain. It could only be a scorpion, so I picked up the mats, shook them out, and swept the floor, and there, amongst the bits of fluff and dust, was a tiny, baby scorpion, its tail arched defensively over its back. The cure, according to our medical books, was to bathe the affected part in water as hot as the body could stand. It was nearly ten days before the pain went away.

Our nephew, Kyle, stood on one in the dive centre, leapt in the air with a curse, and came down on the scorpion with the other foot. Now he didn't know which foot to put to the ground, and hopped from one leg to the other with cries of pain. The staff made sounds of sympathy but couldn't help laughing at his wild antics. The next morning he had to drive to Durban with throbbing feet. It was a long and painful journey.

TARA

The tumour on Tara's tummy was getting bigger and bigger, and was swollen, shiny and red. I bathed it with warm water to soothe the obvious pain it was causing her. Every now and then it would bleed, but I was able to staunch the flow of blood. She was getting weaker, slept a lot, and seldom went outside, only to relieve herself. I rang our vet friend, Stella, in Richards Bay, and she suggested a course of antibiotics. These seemed to help, and Tara became more animated: walking outside to take a little sunshine; barking at Tom Cat.

Tara was now fourteen years old, and we didn't know how much longer she would live with this terrible tumour draining away her energy. On the 22nd of May in 2009, she strolled onto the veranda, spotted Tom Cat in the grass below, stalking a bird, and rushed towards him with a happy bark. He was surprised, and for the first time, darted off into the thorn hedge circling the property. Tara was delighted: finally, Tom Cat had run away from her! With renewed energy, she bounded after him, pushing her way into the thorny Spinoza hedge. Tom Cat vanished into the next door property and Tara came back into the house, bleeding profusely from her swelling. Horrified, we tried to halt the flow, but the blood was pumping out in great gushes. Laying her on her bed, we held a cloth against her stomach, stroking her, and talking quietly to her as we watched her fade away. With a couple of heaving gasps, Tara shuddered and died.

nineteen

Epilogue

Desperately sad though her death was, Tara died doing what, towards the end of her life, she most enjoyed: annoying Tom Cat. He had finally given in to instinct and run from her, and she had chased him. Bleeding to death was so peaceful: she felt no pain as her life force slowly drained away, and she let go with a sigh. What better way to go ...?

We were devastated. We knew she wouldn't live for ever; even little dogs don't live much beyond fourteen years, and even if we had been in a more sophisticated country with veterinary help, would she have lived any longer? It's the 'what if' question that can never be answered.

Jordao dug a grave for Tara down by the hedge, overlooking the sea, and this is where we laid her to rest, with the sound of the ocean in her ears; the sound that she heard for so very many years of her adventurous life. A most appropriate resting place for such an amazing little dog.

Robert Louis Stevenson's own requiem - engraved on his tomb on Mt Vaea in Samoa - is a fitting epitaph for Tara, our constant companion and wonderful little seafarer, who we will never forget -

Under the wide and starry sky
Dig the grave and let me lie:
Glad did I live and gladly die,
And I laid me down with a will.

This be the verse you grave for me:
Here she lies where she longed to be;
Home is the sailor, home from the sea,
And the hunter home from the hill.

Index